The Constitutional Identity of The Netherlands

Gerhard van der Schyff
Editor

The Constitutional Identity of The Netherlands

Concepts, Arrangements and Themes

ASSER PRESS

Springer

Editor
Gerhard van der Schyff
Tilburg Law School
Department of Public Law
and Governance
Tilburg University
Tilburg, The Netherlands

ISBN 978-94-6265-778-6 ISBN 978-94-6265-779-3 (eBook)
https://doi.org/10.1007/978-94-6265-779-3

This book forms part of the editor's Tilburg Law School Incentive Grant for the project entitled: "Constitutional Identity Debates in The Netherlands and The European Union".

This T.M.C. ASSER PRESS imprint is published by the registered company Springer-Verlag GmbH, DE, part of Springer Nature.
The registered company address is: Heidelberger Platz 3, 14197 Berlin, Germany

Contents

Contributors

Maurice Adams Tilburg Law School, Tilburg University, Tilburg, the Netherlands

Hansko Broeksteeg Radboud University, Nijmegen, The Netherlands

Monica Claes Maastricht University, Maastricht, The Netherlands

Floor Fleurke Tilburg Law School, Tilburg University, Tilburg, The Netherlands

Jurgen Goossens Utrecht University School of Law, Utrecht University, Utrecht, The Netherlands

Ronald Janse Faculty of Law, Maastricht University, Maastricht, the Netherlands

G. Leenknegt Tilburg Law School, Tilburg University, Tilburg, The Netherlands

Ingrid Leijten Tilburg Law School, Tilburg University, Tilburg, The Netherlands

Adriaan Overbeeke Faculty of Law, VU University Amsterdam, Amsterdam, The Netherlands

Joost Sillen Maastricht University, Maastricht, The Netherlands

Han Somsen Tilburg Law School, Tilburg University, Tilburg, The Netherlands; Lund Law School, Lund University, Lund, Sweden

Gerhard van der Schyff Tilburg Law School, Tilburg University, Tilburg, The Netherlands

Hanneke van Eijken Utrecht University School of Law, Utrecht University, Utrecht, The Netherlands

B. P. Vermeulen Faculty of Law, Radboud University Nijmegen, Nijmegen, The Netherlands

Caia Vlieks Utrecht University School of Law, Utrecht University, Utrecht, The Netherlands

Sophie Vonk Tilburg Law School, Tilburg University, Tilburg, The Netherlands

E. Y. van Vugt Faculty of Law, Maastricht University, Maastricht, The Netherlands

Johan Wolswinkel Tilburg Law School, Tilburg University, Tilburg, The Netherlands

P. J. J. Zoontjens Tilburg Law School, Tilburg University, Tilburg, The Netherlands

Chapter 1
The Constitutional Identity of the Netherlands: An Introduction

Gerhard van der Schyff

Contents

Abstract Constitutional identity has become a commonly used instrument in the studying of legal orders. For present purposes, it is understood as the core or fundamental elements or values of a particular constitutional order as the expression of its individuality. The constitutional identity of the Netherlands is investigated. The Netherlands is not coterminous with the Kingdom, but a constituent country. This chapter contextualises the Netherlands in this regard, and based on the various chapters in the volume reflects on the possible features of the country's constitutional identity.

Keywords The Netherlands · Constitutional law · Constitutional identity · Democracy based on the rule of law · Fundamental rights · Political and legal constitutionalism

G. van der Schyff (✉)
Tilburg Law School, Tilburg University, Tilburg, The Netherlands
e-mail: G.vdrSchyff@tilburguniversity.edu

G. van der Schyff (ed.), *The Constitutional Identity of The Netherlands*,
https://doi.org/10.1007/978-94-6265-779-3_1

1.1 Delineating the Netherlands

"Constitutional identity" is an important topic in the study of legal orders. The observation made by Gary Jacobsohn a number of years ago that constitutional theorists have little to say about the identity of the constitutions they analyse seems less relevant today.[1] This is because the concept of identity is increasingly used to research constitutional orders. Although not limited to it, this has especially been the case in the European legal realm.[2] Scholarship and case law from various national highest and constitutional courts and the Court of Justice of the European Union (CJEU) proves the point.[3] Article 4(2) of the Treaty on European Union (TEU) also requires the EU to respect the "national identities" of the Member States.[4] The EU itself has not been left out of the equation either. Scholarship has investigated the notion of an EU constitutional identity, while the CJEU has referred to the values in article 2 Treaty on European Union (TEU) as part of "the very identity" of the EU as "a common legal order".[5] The European Court of Human Rights has also accepted the term "constitutional identity" in the context of the legitimate aim test for limiting rights.[6]

Although the mentioned examples have put Jacobsohn's observation into perspective, it can be said that there is something of a gap when it comes to studying the constitutional identity of the Netherlands.[7] While the term itself is not generally employed in Dutch constitutional law, unlike in some other orders, it could nevertheless be helpful for analytical and comparative purposes.[8] At this point it becomes necessary to delineate the topic of this study more precisely. The Netherlands, as the subject of this work, is not coterminous with the Kingdom of the Netherlands. The Kingdom is a composite state comprising four autonomous and equivalent countries, which, apart

---

1 Jacobsohn 2006, p. 361.

2 For examples beyond Europe, see Polzin 2021 on the "basic structure" doctrine in India; Polzin 2023 on the doctrine in Malaysia.

3 See Claes and Reestman 2015, pp. 941–967; Calliess and Van der Schyff 2020a; Saiz Arnaiz and Alcoberro Llivina 2013. To mention but three of the many rulings, see German Constitutional Court, 2 BvE 2/08, judgement of 30 June 2009 (*Lisbon*); Belgian Constitutional Court, Case No. 62/2016, judgement of 28 April 2016; Court of Justice of the European Union, Case C-208/09, judgement of 22 December 2010, ECLI:EU:C:2010:806 (*Sayn-Wittgenstein*).

4 This is often understood as synonymous with or open to "constitutional identity". For various views, see Cloots 2015; Von Bogdandy and Schill 2011; Van der Schyff 2012.

5 Court of Justice of the European Union, Case C-156/21, judgement of 16 February 2022, ECLI:EU:C:2022:97 (*Hungary v. Parliament and Council*), para. 232; Court of Justice of the European Union, Case C-157/21, judgement of 16 February 2022, ECLI:EU:C:2022:98 (*Poland v. Parliament and Council*), para. 145. See De Poorter et al. 2023.

6 European Court of Human Rights, App. No. 49270/11, judgement of 9 June 2022 (*Savickis and Others v. Latvia*), para 196–199. See also López Guerra 2013.

7 For various discussions of "constitutional identity" in the Dutch context, see Hirsch Ballin 2020; Oomen 2014, pp. 25–51; Van Bijsterveld 2005.

8 On its standard use in Germany, for instance, see Calliess 2020.

from the Netherlands, also includes Curaçao, Aruba and Sint Maarten.[9] The Charter for the Kingdom of the Netherlands (*Statuut voor het Koninkrijk der Nederlanden*) of 1954 is the highest domestic legal norm and regulates the relationship between the countries.[10]

The adoption of the Charter marked the end of a long colonial history by creating a new order in the Kingdom between the Netherlands and the participating former colonial territories.[11] The Charter provides for the regulation of a small number of joint matters, known as Kingdom affairs, leaving all others matters to the countries.[12] Each country belonging to the Kingdom has a unitary structure under its own constitution.[13] In the case of the Netherlands, this is the Constitution (*Grondwet*), the earliest version of which dates from 1814/1815 and was last comprehensively revised in 1983.[14] The Charter provides that the Constitution must have regard to it, thereby taking precedence over the Constitution.[15] Although this is the case, the Charter's scope of application is relatively limited, while in many areas it also refers to the Constitution for substantive and organisational governance if not provided for

[9] The Kingdom's population is approximately divided among the countries as follows: the Netherlands 17,400,000, Curaçao 158,000, Aruba 112,000 and Sint Maarten 41,000. The Netherlands includes the European territory and the Caribbean islands of Bonaire, Sint Eustatius and Saba (combined island population approximately 25,000). On the latter islands, see Borman 2012, pp. 63–71.

[10] The Kingdom is the subject of international law. Its form of state is sui generis, as it includes federal, confederal and unitary features, see Burkens et al. 2022, pp. 322–323. For an historical overview, see Borman 2012, pp. 1–20.

Amending the Charter involves a process of approval by each country's parliament (article 55 of the Charter), see Borman 2012, pp. 38–40.

[11] Since the reforms of 2010, the Kingdom consists of the mentioned Caribbean countries and the Netherlands (where the king resides as head of state; a governor represents the king in each of the other countries; see articles 1a-2 of the Charter). See Borman 2012, pp. 12–18.

[12] Article 41(1) of the Charter provides that the countries conduct their own affairs. Affairs belonging to the Kingdom (defence, foreign relations, nationality etc.) are listed or provided for mainly in article 3 of the Charter. The Charter has no bill of rights; the countries are the primary guardians of fundamental rights, legal certainty and sound governance (article 43 of the Charter). See Borman 2012, pp. 74–85. Kortmann and Bovend'Eert 1993, p. 21 explain that in general the countries "each with its own democratic system of law, function independently on the whole".

[13] See article 42(1) of the Charter. The Constitutions of the Caribbean countries are called *staatsregelingen*. See in general Rogier 2012; Borman 2012, pp. 52–57.

[14] In this chapter, the term "Constitution" refers to the *Grondwet*. The Dutch Constitution retained its original name after the Charter's adoption: Constitution for the Kingdom of the Netherlands (*Grondwet voor het Koninkrijk der Nederlanden*). See Borman 2012, p. 36 on this terminology.

[15] Article 5(2) of the Charter.

by the Charter.[16] This means that the Constitution applies not only to the Netherlands, but also in part to the Kingdom.[17] Rather than creating a completely new superstructure in the Kingdom from scratch in the 1950s, it was decided to draw on the longer established Constitution wherever feasible.[18] The institutional model under the Charter relies mainly on Dutch organs and procedures, sometimes adapted to allow the Caribbean countries' participation, instead of creating entirely new and separate Kingdom organs for joint matters.[19] Given its much larger population, economy and territory, the Netherlands dominates these arrangements, which explains why the Charter supposes the "equivalence" of the countries and not their "equality".[20] As there is no genuinely distinct federal level, the Kingdom is not a true federation, but in reality revolves largely around the Netherlands and its Constitution.[21] This means, in fact and law, a significant degree of overlap between the Netherlands and the Kingdom.[22] Should the Caribbean countries decide to exercise their right to independence, the Charter will become redundant, and the Kingdom will be fully aligned with the Netherlands under its Constitution.[23]

The Netherlands, it can be argued based on the outline above, is the constitutional mainstay of the Kingdom.[24] The purpose here, though, is not to study the structure of the Kingdom or the relationship between its parts, topics that deserve their own

---

[16] Article 5(1) of the Charter refers to the Constitution for important additional regulations on the monarchy, royal succession, royal and legislative power and the Kingdom's organs. Also, article 5(3) of the Charter implies that the Constitution contains provisions on Kingdom affairs. See Borman 2012, pp. 32–36.

[17] Kortmann et al. 2021, p. 108 explain that the Constitution is thus partly the constitution for relations within the Kingdom and wholly that of the Netherlands. See also Kortmann and Bovend'Eert 1993, p. 12.

[18] See Borman 2012, pp. 32–33.

[19] E.g., as to the Kingdom's organs, the Dutch government (king and ministers) also forms the Kingdom's government, while there is no Kingdom parliament as such. To pass Acts of Parliament for the Kingdom (*rijkswetten*), the Kingdom's council of ministers equals the Dutch council including a plenipotentiary minister from each of the Caribbean countries; while legislative bills are sent to the Caribbean countries' parliaments, they are only approved by the Dutch parliament. This creates a democratic deficit by excluding voters from the Caribbean countries (see Council of State 2024, p. 47). Given the considerable procedural overlap, Kingdom Acts arguably differ from Dutch Acts in their scope rather than their rank (compare Borman 2012, p. 47 and pp. 121–129 on the legislative procedure). There is also no separate court at the Kingdom level, the Dutch Supreme Court's authority extends to the Caribbean countries based on article 23 of the Charter. See also Borman 2012, pp. 87–113; Kraan 2004, p. 594; Kortmann and Bovend'Eert 1993, pp. 19–20.

[20] See also Borman 2012, pp. 23–24; Kortmann and Bovend'Eert 1993, p. 19.

[21] See Kortmann and Bovend'Eert 1993, 19 who explain that the Kingdom cannot be classified as "a normal federal State" because "no separate government organisation at federal level was created" when constituting its organs. See further the discussion by Croes 2006, pp. 30–33.

[22] See the discussion by Borman 2012, pp. 32–33; Kraan 2004, p. 594.

[23] Countries can leave the Kingdom, as Surinam did in 1975. However, the Netherlands' unilateral secession is limited by its international law obligations towards the other countries as its former colonial territories. See Borman 2012, pp. 28–32, 40–41.

[24] Compare Croes 2006, p. 33. He notes that, under the Charter, the Caribbean countries occupy a constitutionally subordinate position to the Netherlands in joint matters. Apart from this "clinical"

investigation.[25] Rather it is to study the country of the Netherlands in the light of the Constitution to address the mentioned gap.[26] Reference to the Kingdom, including the Charter, will be made when necessary to contextualise and understand the Netherlands in particular. Addressing the gap regarding the Netherlands is not only useful to understand the country's constitutional order, but can also function as a backdrop to study its relationship with and meaning for the Kingdom.[27]

1.2 Explaining Constitutional Identity

The concept of constitutional identity, as Michel Rosenfeld explained, is "essentially contested" as there is no general agreement on its meaning.[28] This makes it necessary to explain the concept for current purposes. As a point of departure, constitutional identity can be understood as the core or fundamental elements or values of a particular constitutional order as the expression of its individuality.[29] Identity does not refer to the order as such, in other words to its entire legal content.[30] Higher law is also not synonymous with constitutional identity.[31] Rather, identity refers to those defining aspects without which an order will no longer be recognisable as before.[32] The generation of identity is the prerogative of the order in question.[33] Approaches that equate constitutional identity solely with the existence or absence of eternity clauses are too narrow to portray what is at stake.[34] To capture constitutional identity an approach is required that covers not only codified constitutions, but also other constitutive norms whether they be written or unwritten.[35] It is within this field that

view of the Charter, he also points to the relevance of other factors, such as the political culture geared towards consensus and compromise.

25 See in particular Borman 2012; Croes 2006.

26 For a similar approach focussing on the Netherlands, see Kraan 2004, p. 594.

27 This study's general approach is to describe and comment on the law – be it local, national, Kingdom, international or EU law – as it effectively applies in the Netherlands as delineated here. Although (parts of) this study can serve as a reference work, it is not intended as a textbook as such.

28 Rosenfeld 2012, p. 756.

29 See Calliess and Van der Schyff 2020b, p. 7.

30 Van der Schyff 2012, p. 576.

31 Van der Schyff 2012, p. 578. Von Bogdandy and Schill 2011, pp. 1431–1432 point though to the "depth of the constitutional entrenchment" as an indicator for the protection of "national identity" in the context of article 4(2) TEU.

32 Grimm 2023, p. 14.

33 See Van der Schyff 2012, pp. 572–573. Compare Grimm 2023, p. 14 on "popular perception" and constitutional identity; Polzin 2017, p. 1602 on "self-identity" and constitutional identity; Jacobsohn 2010 p. 7 explains that "a constitution acquires an identity through experience".

34 On eternity clauses as a possible source of constitutional identity, see Van der Schyff 2020, pp. 308–309.

35 Van der Schyff 2022, p. 218.

the identity of an order manifests itself as an interplay between the relevant procedural and substantive constitutional norms.

1.3 Three Parts

In exploring the constitutional identity of the Netherlands, this volume is divided into three parts to provide a broad, although by no means exhaustive, representation of the constitutional field. The first part is devoted to "concepts", understood as general abstract terms of constitutional importance, such as "democracy based on the rule of law".[36] The second part is devoted to "arrangements", understood as constitutional relationships between various components or levels, such as that between national and international law.[37] The third part is devoted to "themes", understood as societal topics that deserve particular attention in relation to the constitutional order being studied, such as its relationship to religion, or education.[38]

1.3.1 Constitutional Concepts

The part on "concepts" opens with Chap. 2 by Maurice Adams and Ronald Janse on "democracy based on the rule of law" in the Netherlands. This chapter lays the foundation for understanding Dutch constitutional identity by emphasising the sober character of the Constitution, which is expressed in the absence of "grand rhetoric" in constitutional matters, such as debates about "sovereignty". However, the absence of such concepts and the sober text of the Constitution do not mean an absence of constitutional debate, as illustrated by the case law on climate change.[39] The authors also point to the need to understand constitutional *identity*, as the more formal features of the legal framework, against the background of constitutional *culture*, as the more or less stable patterns and practices of dealing with this framework.[40]

In Chap. 3, Sophie Vonk and Ingrid Leijten note that fundamental rights have always been part of the Constitution in one way or another. In revealing the identity of these rights, the 1983 general constitutional revision is used as the starting point for the analysis. The revision grouped fundamental rights together in the Constitution's first chapter and added social rights to this catalogue. The authors highlight the central role intended for the legislature in interpreting and shaping the protection afforded by fundamental rights in the light of the constitutional limitation system and the

[36] Chapters 2–5.

[37] Chapters 6–9.

[38] Chapters 10–13.

[39] See Chap. 2, Sect. 2.4.

[40] See Chap. 2, Sect. 2.6.

prohibition of constitutional review in article 120 of the Constitution.[41] They point out that the possible introduction of ex post judicial review of Acts of Parliaments' constitutionality should not diminish the continued importance of ex ante legislative review, as intended by the general revision.[42]

Although the concept of citizenship can be difficult to grasp, Hanneke van Eijken and Caia Vlieks argue in Chap. 4 that it forms the "hidden backbone of Dutch constitutional identity".[43] The authors explain that Dutch citizenship is to be understood in a composite sense, cutting across local, country, Kingdom, EU and international levels. When considering its functions, it becomes clear that citizenship (i) delineates the political community and organises political participation, (ii) is associated with various fundamental rights and obligations and (iii) regulates issues of inclusion and exclusion of groups in Dutch society. The chapter on citizenship also demonstrates the openness of such a domestic concept to international and EU law influences.

In Chap. 5, Eva van Vugt examines the Constitution in relation to change. Her analysis focuses on the relationship between the constitutional amendment procedure in article 137 and the absence of a constituent power. Van Vugt notes, similar to Adams and Janse, that concepts such as "constituent power" and "popular sovereignty" are absent not only from the Constitution but also from constitutional discourse.[44] Two theoretical consequences attach to this absence.[45] Firstly, the political power to amend the Constitution is practically unlimited, provided that the amendment procedure is followed. Adding the context of the Kingdom to this analysis, the remark and qualification can be made that the Constitution must have regard to the Charter.[46] And secondly, change is not based on the notion that constitutional amendments must be made by the people themselves. Instead, the power to amend the Constitution lies with the legislature.

[41] See Chap. 3, Sect. 3.4.

[42] See Chap. 3, Sects. 3.6–3.7.

[43] See Chap. 4, Sect. 4.6.

[44] See Chap. 5, Sects. 5.1 and 5.5. See also Besselink 2023, p. 427.

[45] See Chap. 5, Sect. 5.1.

[46] Article 5(2) of the Charter. In this regard, the constitutional amendment procedure can vary depending on the situation. Amendments to the Constitution that concern Kingdom affairs require a Kingdom Act of Parliament, instead of a simple Act (article 5(3) of the Charter juncto article 137 of the Constitution). Some constitutional amendments are deemed to affect the Caribbean countries and require discussion in the Kingdom's council of ministers (article 45 of the Charter). As to the Charter, it can be amended by a Kingdom Act of Parliament, following approval by the parliaments of the Caribbean countries (article 55(1)-(2) of the Charter). But amendments to the Charter that deviate from the Constitution also follow the constitutional amendment procedure, with the proviso that in the second reading an absolute majority suffices in the Dutch parliament without the need for a two-thirds majority (article 55(3) of the Charter juncto article 137 of the Constitution). Once the Charter has been amended, article 142 of the Constitution allows for it to brought in line with the Charter by an Act of Parliament.

1.3.2 Constitutional Arrangements

The part on "arrangements" opens with the Chap. 6 by Gert-Jan Leenknegt on the king, government and parliament. The chapter demonstrates that important elements regarding the role of the monarchy and the government, the process of cabinet formation and the functioning of the Dutch parliamentary system remained uncodified.[47] The Constitution, it is argued, creates an open and at times fragmented framework, which is supplemented with unwritten principles and rules, political practice and traditions. As a result, details and dynamics related to these issues, particularly at crucial moments or in cases of uncertainty, are ultimately left to parliament, which is elected based on proportional representation. This is characterised as political constitutionalism.

In Chap. 7, Hansko Broeksteeg discusses the vertical distribution of state power in the Netherlands against the background of constitutional identity. Although it is not mentioned in the Constitution as such, the country has been a decentralised unitary state since the nineteenth century. This type of division of state power captures an essential element of the legal order, as few aspects have been as characteristic for it as long. And insofar as the Constitution regulates decentralisation, such as the power to organise provinces and municipalities, it leaves the legislature a great deal of leeway.[48] This underscores the idea that the Constitution functions as a general legal framework without attempting to regulate the details of the legal order exhaustively.

The relationship between the courts and the Constitution is discussed in Chap. 8 by Gerhard van der Schyff. This chapter focuses on article 120 of the Constitution, which prohibits the courts from reviewing the constitutionality of Acts of Parliament and treaties.[49] This provision, which in its earliest form dates back to 1848, emphasises the primacy of the legislature on the basis of its democratic legitimacy. The effect is that political constitutionalism so prevails over legal constitutionalism. The argument is made that article 120 forms part of the constitutional identity of the Netherlands, as the self-understanding of the legal order would be very different without this provision. The chapter also notes that this provision is not uncontroversial, given past and current various proposals to amend it.

In Chap. 9, Monica Claes and Joost Sillen discuss the openness of Dutch constitutional law to international and EU law. The authors point out that since 1953, the Constitution has allowed treaties direct effect and primacy over national law,

[47] See Chap. 6, Sect. 6.7. The king is head of state of the Kingdom (articles 1a-2 of the Charter). Article 5(1) of the Charter refers to the Constitution for additional regulation of the monarchy. Article 5(1) of the Charter also refers to the Constitution for additional regulation of legislative power in Kingdom affairs.

[48] See Chap. 7, Sect. 7.3.2.

[49] See Chap. 8, Sect. 8.3. According to the Supreme Court (HR 14 April 1989, NJ 1989, 469 ECLI:NL:HR:1989:AD5725 (*Harmonisatiewet*, para. 4.5), the Kingdom's legal order is based on a "tradition of non-review", corresponding to that in the Netherlands. The Kingdom's other countries allow the judicial review of their Acts of Parliament against their respective constitutions (see Borman 2012, pp. 56–57; Goudappel and De Wit 2015). Accounts of their constitutional identities would therefore likely differ from that of the Netherlands.

including constitutional provisions.[50] On the one hand, this openness compensates for the prohibition of constitutional review in article 120 of the Constitution, as the courts review Acts of Parliament for compliance with fundamental rights in treaties. On the other hand, this shifts authority from national constitutional standards to international bodies, which do not possess the same democratic legitimacy as the Constitution and can only prescribe minimum standards. This openness can be unsettling when such sources do not satisfy constitutional standards or fail to protect fundamental rights.[51] Although a typical feature of Dutch constitutional law, such openness is therefore not necessarily essential, the authors conclude.

1.3.3 Constitutional Themes

Part III on "themes" opens with Chap. 10 by Adriaan Overbeeke on the relationship between the state and religion in the Netherlands. The historical development of this relationship is traced bearing in mind the religious developments in the Low Countries since the Reformation. The current relationship is a hybrid one. This is because there is a financial separation between the state and the religious communities on the one hand, while the state cooperates with and finances denominational education on the other. This constellation is potentially dynamic and the possible variations wide, as the Constitution neither prescribes nor excludes a specific model and therefore leaves the legislature a great deal of leeway.[52] On this basis, the conclusion is reached that there is no specific state and religion model that requires stronger constitutional protection or entrenchment as a matter of constitutional identity. However, the legislature's leeway is restricted by treaty law.

In Chap. 11, Ben Vermeulen and Paul Zoontjens delve into the relationship between law and education in the Netherlands. The basis of this relationship can be found in article 23 of the Constitution, which deals with education and is the longest provision of the Constitution's first chapter, the bill of rights. The provision creates a dual education system with public and public schools, both fully funded by the state. The chapter shows the far-reaching reinterpretation that the provision has undergone since its introduction in 1917, particularly due to secularisation and

---

[50] Chapter 9, Sect. 9.2.2. The relevant provisions, articles 93 and 94 of the Constitution, apply to the Kingdom by virtue of article 3(1)(b) of the Charter (see Borman 2012, p. 33). This means that international law takes precedence not only over Dutch regulations, but also over all other regulations in the Kingdom, including those of the other countries. EU law is generally accepted to apply by virtue of the CJEU's case law (see Chap. 9, Sect. 9.2.3). While the Kingdom belongs to the EU, the application of the EU Treaties is restricted to the European part of the Netherlands. The Netherlands' Caribbean parts and the Kingdom's other countries are Overseas Countries and Territories under articles 198–204 of the Treaty on the Functioning of the EU. See further Borman 2012, pp. 138, 146–157.

[51] Chapter 9, Sect. 9.5.

[52] Chapter 10, Sect. 10.4.2.

individualisation in the 1960s and 1970s. The authors conclude that the constitutional identity of Dutch education law today consists of four concepts, namely (i) quality education, (ii) pedagogical autonomy, (iii) administrative autonomy, and (iv) government restraint.[53]

A third theme, law and digitalisation, is explored by Jurgen Goossens and Johan Wolswinkel in Chap. 12. The authors remark that constitutional identity and digitalisation are sometimes seen as two different worlds. On the one hand, constitutional identity is seen as static and requires a look into the past to assess the development of the Dutch constitutional order, while digitalisation is seen as dynamic and requires a look into the future to determine the impact of technological developments on society, government and constitutional resilience. The authors, however, show that the topics are more entwined than might be expected at first glance. This is because digitalisation is shaped by constitutional identity, which they define as the core values and principles of democracy and the rule of law, while also impacting and challenging those core pillars.[54] Proposals for constitutional reform of fundamental rights are also mentioned to support and strengthen the supervision of the administrative algorithmic state.[55]

The fourth and final theme deals with law and the environment. In Chap. 13, Floor Fleurke and Han Somsen argue that Dutch constitutional identity is too anthropocentric in its approach. In addressing this human-centred emphasis, they point to the limited meaning of article 21 of the Constitution, which provides that the habitability of the country and the protection and improvement of the living environment will be the concern of the government. This limitation is attributed to the prohibition on constitutional review in article 120 of the Constitution. Conversely, the openness of the legal order to the application of international law, especially articles 2 and 8 ECHR, is shown to harbour a transformative potential in environmental matters. At the same time, the authors point to a number of factors that limit this potential, such as procedural requirements and the humanity/nature dichotomy perpetuated by rights frameworks. Unfettered by such constraints, the transformative force of legal scholarship is acknowledged in achieving a geo-centric constitutional identity endowing nature with legal personhood and rights.[56]

1.4 Reflections on the Constitutional Identity of the Netherlands

Recalling the first section of this chapter, it can be said that the Netherlands is the constitutional mainstay of the Kingdom. As explained, in fact and law, there is a significant degree of overlap between the Netherlands and the Kingdom. This is

[53] Chapter 11, Sect. 11.8.

[54] Chapter 12, Sect. 12.8.

[55] Chapter 12, Sect. 12.7.

[56] Chapter 13, Sect. 13.7.

because, although the Charter takes precedence over the Constitution, it relies extensively on the Constitution and Dutch organs and procedures. When characterising the constitutional order of the Netherlands in particular, the chapters of the three parts can not only be read separately, but also together. The chapters can be treated as fragments, the comparison of which allows for some speculation about a possible constitutional identity. This does not imply a complete or definitive view of such identity. However, raising the question of identity and attempting to address it may open up interesting avenues for wider comparison and more research on the topic. Taking this background into account, four general reflections can be offered to conclude this introductory chapter and stimulate further discussion of the contributions:

Firstly, the Constitution, including its amendments, must have regard to the Charter and is not subject to an eternity clause, an unamenable core or a constituent power. Apart from the fact that the Constitution does not indicate its ultimate source of authority, it also contains no lofty ideological statements.[57] Despite all their differences, the various chapters in this volume nonetheless reveal a common or overarching theme when it comes to characterising the constitutional order. This is best captured by the general provision, which was added to the Constitution in 2022 in lieu of a preamble, providing that: "The Constitution guarantees fundamental rights and democracy based on the rule of law."[58] The brevity of the provision and its simple wording are in themselves characteristic of the pragmatic and sober character of the Constitution.

Secondly, as to its constitutional arrangement, the legal order of the Netherlands operates as a parliamentary democracy within a constitutional monarchy, in a horizontal sense, and according to the principle of decentralisation, in a vertical sense. While the Constitution contains various provisions on the monarchy and system of government, the fundamental rule that the cabinet must retain the confidence of parliament in order to govern, remains unwritten.[59] In addition, the Constitution gives the legislature considerable leeway regarding decentralisation by restricting the scope of its own regulations in favour of Acts of Parliament.

Thirdly, the constitutional order is characterised by both political constitutionalism, as the primacy of the legislature in the context of article 120 of the Constitution, and legal constitutionalism, as the openness to and judicial enforcement of international and EU law. This amounts to a dichotomy or contradiction in the legal order. On the one hand, there is a strict separation of powers between the legislature and the courts, and on the other, there is a relative separation. The effect of political constitutionalism is reinforced by the fact that the Constitution does not and is not intended to be an exhaustive codification of the constitutional rules of the legal

[57] Chapter 2, Sect. 2.1 and Chap. 5, Sect. 5.1.

[58] Taken from the Constitution's 2023 translation by the Ministry of the Interior and Kingdom Relations. On this provision, see Oomen 2022; Zoethout 2022.

[59] Chapter 6, Sect. 6.4.

order.[60] This effect is constrained by the far-reaching importance of international and EU law in the domestic legal order.

Fourthly, the constitutional arrangement and tracks of political and legal constitutionalism are not ends in themselves, but serve to protect and uphold the standards of a democracy based on the rule of law. These standards are important for preserving the stability of the legal order and guiding its evolution across various areas, including its relationship with religion, education, digitalisation and the environment. In this regard, the general provision emphasises the importance of fundamental rights in particular. This is because rights are mentioned alongside and before the concept of a democracy based on the rule of law, rather than being incorporated into the concept as is customary in constitutional theory.[61] The concept of composite citizenship is important to locate and determine the rights and duties of individuals.

Acknowledgments Many thanks to Gert-Jan Leenknegt and Paul Zoontjens for their useful comments on this chapter. This volume is part of the editor's Tilburg Law School Incentive Grant project, entitled: "Constitutional Identity Debates in the Netherlands and the European Union".

References

Besselink L F M (2023) The Evolution and Gestalt of the Netherlands Constitution. In: Von Bogdandy A, Huber P M, Ragone S (eds) The Max Planck Handbooks in European Public Law: Constitutional Foundations. Oxford University Press, Oxford, pp. 381–430

Borman C (2012) Het Statuut voor het Koninkrijk. Kluwer, Deventer

Burkens M C, Kummeling H R B M, Uzman J, Vermeulen B P, Widdershoven R J G M (2022) Beginselen van de democratische rechtsstaat: inleiding tot de grondslagen van het Nederlandse staats- en bestuursrecht. Wolters Kluwer, Deventer

Calliess C (2020) Constitutional Identity in Germany: One for Three or Three in One? In: Calliess C, Van der Schyff G (eds) Constitutional Identity in a Europe of Multilevel Constitutionalism. Cambridge University Press, Cambridge, pp. 153–181

Calliess C, Van der Schyff G (eds) (2020a) Constitutional Identity in a Europe of Multilevel Constitutionalism. Cambridge University Press, Cambridge

Calliess C, Van der Schyff G (2020b) Constitutional Identity Introduced. In: Calliess C, Van der Schyff G (eds) Constitutional Identity in a Europe of Multilevel Constitutionalism. Cambridge University Press, Cambridge, pp. 3–8

Claes M, Reestman J-H (2015) The Protection of National Constitutional Identity and the Limits of European Integration at the Occasion of the Gauweiler Case. German Law Journal 16(4):917–970

Cloots E (2015) National Identity in EU Law. Oxford University Press, Oxford

Council of State (2024) 70 jaar Statuut voor het Koninkrijk. Council of State, The Hague

[60] Consider also Besselink 2023, p. 429 who writes that an "important feature of the Netherlands' Constitution is its very relative meaning in political and legal practice", while Voermans 2008, p. 12 writes that it "merely provides the bare skeleton" for the system to operate and that "less is more as it were".

[61] Democracy based on the rule of law (*democratische rechtsstaat*) can be understood as including the following five principles: democracy, legality, fundamental rights, separation of powers and judicial review. See the discussion by Burkens et al. 2022, pp. 16–31.

Croes A G (2006) De herdefiniëring van het Koninkrijk. Wolf Legal Publishers, Nijmegen
De Poorter J, Van der Schyff G, Stremler M, De Visser M, Leijten I, Van Oirsouw C (eds) (2023) European Yearbook of Constitutional Law 2022: A Constitutional Identity for the EU? T.M.C. Asser Press, The Hague
Goudappel F, De Wit J (2015) Constitutionele toetsing in het Koninkrijk in context. Caribisch Juristenblad 4(4):285–297
Grimm D (2023) Three Meanings of Constitutional Identity and Their Prospects in the European Union. In: De Poorter J, Van der Schyff G, Stremler M, De Visser M, Leijten I, Van Oirsouw C (eds) European Yearbook of Constitutional Law 2022: A Constitutional Identity for the EU? T.M.C. Asser Press, The Hague, pp. 13–24
Hirsch Ballin E (2020) Constitutional Identity in the Netherlands: Sailing with Others. In: Calliess C, Van der Schyff G (eds) Constitutional Identity in a Europe of Multilevel Constitutionalism. Cambridge University Press, Cambridge, pp. 222–242
Jacobsohn G J (2006) Constitutional Identity. Review of Politics 68:361–397
Jacobsohn G J (2010) Constitutional Identity. Harvard University Press, Cambridge/Massachusetts
Kortmann C A J M, Bovend'Eert P P T (1993) The Kingdom of the Netherlands: An Introduction to Dutch Constitutional Law. Kluwer Law and Taxation Publisher, Deventer/Boston
Kortmann C A J M, Bovend'Eert P P T, Broeksteeg J L W, Vermeulen B P, Kortmann C N J (2021) Constitutioneel recht. Kluwer, Deventer
Kraan K (2004) The Kingdom of the Netherlands. In: Prakke L, Kortmann C (eds) Constitutional Law of 15 EU Member States. Kluwer, Deventer, pp. 591–650
López Guerra L (2013) National Identity and the European Convention on Human Rights. In: Saiz Arnaiz A, Alcoberro Llivnia C (eds) National Identity and European Integration. Intersentia, Cambridge/Antwerp/Portland, pp. 305–321
Oomen B (2014) Rights for Others: The Slow Home-coming of Human Rights in the Netherlands. Cambridge University Press, Cambridge
Oomen B (2022) Algemene bepaling. In: Ellian A, Rijpkema B (eds) Een nieuw commentaar op de Grondwet. Boom, The Hague, pp. 81–90
Polzin M (2017) Constitutional Identity as a Constructed Reality and a Restless Soul. German Law Journal 18(7):1595–1615
Polzin M (2021) The Basic-structure Doctrine and its German and French Origins: A Tale of Migration, Integration, Invention and Forgetting. Indian Law Review 5:45–61
Polzin M (2023) The German Eternity Clause, Hans Kelsen and The Malaysian Basic Structure Doctrine. Comparative Constitutional Law and Administrative Law Journal 7(2):1–26
Rogier L J J (2012) Beginselen van Caribisch Staatsrecht. Boom Juridische uitgevers, The Hague
Rosenfeld M (2012) Constitutional Identity. In: Rosenfeld M, Sajó A (eds) The Oxford Handbook of Comparative Constitutional Law. Oxford University Press, Oxford, pp. 756–776
Saiz Arnaiz A, Alcoberro Llivina C (eds) (2013) National Constitutional Identity and European Integration. Intersentia, Cambridge/Antwerp/Portland
Van Bijsterveld S C (2005) Grondwet en constitutionele identiteit. Het constitutioneel verdrag voor de EU als spiegel voor de Nederlandse Grondwet. In: Zoontjens P, Peters H (eds) Getuigend staatsrecht: liber amicorum A.K. Koekkoek. Wolf Legal Publishers, Nijmegen, pp. 189–201
Van der Schyff G (2012) The Constitutional Relationship between the European Union and its Member States: The Role of National Identity in Article 4(2) TEU. European Law Review, 37(5):563–83
Van der Schyff G (2020) Member States of the European Union, Constitutions, and Identity: A Comparative Perspective. In: Calliess C, Van der Schyff G (eds) Constitutional Identity in a Europe of Multilevel Constitutionalism. Cambridge University Press, Cambridge, pp. 305–347
Van der Schyff G (2022) The Constitutional Identities of EU Member States: The Scope of Article 4(2) TEU Analysed. In: Jenart B, Bernaerts J, Peeters Y, Popelier P, Vanheule D, Verbelen V (eds) De Grondwet en Jan Velaers. Die Keure, Brugge, pp. 217–224

Voermans W (2018) A 200-Year-Old Constitution: Relic or Enigma? In: Ferrari G F, Passchier R, Voermans W (eds) The Dutch Constitution Beyond 200 Years: Tradition and Innovation in a Multilevel Legal Order. Eleven International Publishing, The Hague, pp. 11–28

Von Bogdandy A, Schill S (2011) Overcoming Absolute Primacy: Respect for National Identity under the Lisbon Treaty. Common Market Law Review 48(5):1417–1454

Zoethout C (2022) Algemene bepaling. In: Ellian A, Rijpkema B (eds) Een nieuw commentaar op de Grondwet. Boom, The Hague, pp. 91–98

Gerhard van der Schyff is an Associate Professor in the Department of Public Law and Governance at the Law School of Tilburg University, the Netherlands. His research interests cover European and comparative constitutional law, including fundamental rights.

Part I
Concepts

Chapter 2
Democracy Based on the Rule of Law: Dutch Constitutionalism Between Restraint and Pragmatism

Maurice Adams and Ronald Janse

Contents

Abstract The Dutch constitutional legislator has little appetite for grand rhetoric. Since 2022, after decades of debate, a general and unnumbered provision now precedes the Dutch Constitution, stating: "The Constitution guarantees fundamental rights and democracy based on the rule of law." Prior to this amendment, one would search in vain for the terms *democracy* and *rule of law* in the Dutch Constitution. Concepts such as *legality* and *sovereignty* are still absent. Terms like *Verfassungspatriotismus*, *Solange* jurisprudence and case law on constitutional identity, are virtually unknown in the Netherlands. *Restraint* and *pragmatism* are the adjectives most commonly used—not only by observers but also by the legislature itself—to characterise the Dutch constitutional tradition. Nevertheless, the Netherlands is no stranger to major constitutional questions, which frequently spark intense legal, political and public debate. In some areas—climate litigation being perhaps the most prominent example—Dutch jurisprudence has even become globally influential and groundbreaking. Can Dutch constitutional restraint be reconciled with the constitutional vibrancy that sometimes exists in practice? This chapter seeks to answer that question by offering a descriptive analysis of the Dutch democratic and rule-of-law system.

M. Adams
Tilburg Law School, Tilburg University, Tilburg, the Netherlands
e-mail: m.adams@tilburguniversity.edu

R. Janse (✉)
Faculty of Law, Maastricht University, Maastricht, the Netherlands
e-mail: ronald.janse@maastrichtuniversity.nl

G. van der Schyff (ed.), *The Constitutional Identity of The Netherlands*,
https://doi.org/10.1007/978-94-6265-779-3_2

The Constitution and its framework of checks and balances serve as the starting point, with the concepts of *constitutional identity* and *constitutional culture* providing frames of reference.

Keywords The Netherlands · Constitutional restraint · Constitutional pragmatism · Consociational democracy · Counter-democracy · Multiple politica

2.1 Constitutional Identity: The "Representative Standard" in the Basic Structure of Dutch Constitutional Law

Every democratic political system rests upon a dominant discourse.[1] In the Netherlands, this narrative has traditionally taken the following form: the population elects representatives to Parliament, who in turn ensure the formation of a government that enjoys the confidence of the parliamentary majority. Government and Parliament then jointly enact laws, thereby producing policy that, through the process of collective will-formation, can be regarded as an interpretation of the "public interest"—that is, what benefits the Dutch people as a whole and transcends mere sectional interests. In subsequent elections, voters assess the policies and legislation of the outgoing government, as well as the plans and policy proposals of those seeking office for the next term. The "contract" between Parliament and the government on the one hand, and the population on the other hand is thus renewed approximately every four years. From this perspective, democracy is a process in which political representation is closely linked to electoral cycles, and political decision-making is largely driven by the will of the parliamentary majority and the government. This is what we call the "representative standard" in Dutch constitutional law.

One of the central claims of this contribution is that the *constitutional identity* in the Netherlands—a concept here referring to the more or less formal features embedded in the constitutional structure and organisation of the state[2]—is, in its most general sense, aligned with the discourse outlined above.

Constitutionally, this is reflected in a constructive reading of several provisions of the Dutch Constitution: article 4 (active and passive suffrage), article 50 ("The States General shall represent the entire people of the Netherlands"), article 67 (freedom to parliamentary assemble and majority rule in parliamentary decision-making), article 71 (absolute immunity for members of Parliament) and article 81 ("Acts of Parliament

[1] This text partly builds on Adams and Janse 2022. See also Adams and Witteveen 2014, p. 37. References in this text to the English version of the Dutch Constitution are to the 2023 translation published by the Ministry of the Interior and Kingdom Relations. See https://open.overheid.nl/documenten/ronl-faa96875fef77af167a9133bd3625c0e9b45fa89/pdf.

[2] Whether that identity is also legally enforceable is not the subject of this chapter. Compare the definition by Kovács 2023, p 13: "[T]he notion of constitutional identity (...) refers to the fact that it is not the physical characteristics or the ethnocultural form of life of the community's members that matters, but the constitution itself."

shall be enacted jointly by the Government and the States General"), together with the unwritten rule of confidence. The latter entails that a member of Cabinet, or the cabinet as a whole, must resign if they no longer enjoy the confidence of the House of Representatives. Or to put it positively: a member of Cabinet or the cabinet as a whole can continue to exist as long as it has the support of the majority in the House of Representatives. Also particularly significant is article 120 of the Constitution, which prohibits constitutional review by the judiciary of Acts of Parliament and treaties. This provision can be interpreted as an affirmation of the trust placed in the legislature, as the legislature is supposed to ensure that Acts of Parliament and international treaties are in line with the Constitution—trust that lies at the heart of the aforementioned representative standard.

The dominance of this representative model is also reflected in the relatively sober design of the Dutch Constitution.[3] It is a rather austere document, focused primarily on identifying key state institutions and outlining procedures. For example, chapter 5 of the Constitution, which deals with the enactment of formal legislation, merely sets out the procedure that government and Parliament must follow to produce an Act of Parliament. While the idea remains that this is a procedure surrounded by many safeguards and typically leads to a balanced consideration of interests, the Constitution itself remains silent on such matters.[4]

And when it comes to the limitation of fundamental rights, Dutch constitutional law places particular emphasis on the *actor* authorised to impose such restrictions[5]—namely, the legislature. Article 7 of the Dutch Constitution, for instance, states that no one shall require prior permission to express thoughts or opinions through the press. However, it immediately adds: "subject to everyone's responsibility under the law". This seems logical enough. But it also implies that any legal restriction on freedom of expression must be enacted through legislation approved by Parliament—that is, by the legislature itself. The substantive grounds on which fundamental rights may

---

[3] A brief terminological note is in order. Dutch constitutionalism could be described as being a rich tapestry of customs and documents. Two national documents nevertheless stand out in this regard. On the one hand, there is the Charter of the Kingdom of the Netherlands (*Statuut voor het Koninkrijk der Nederlanden*) (1954) and, on the other hand, we find the Constitution of the Kingdom of the Netherlands (*Grondwet voor het Koninkrijk der Nederlanden*) (the first version dating back to 1814 but with its last major revision in 1983). Of the two, the Charter is the less known, although higher in terms of legal hierarchy. The Charter regulates the relationship between the countries forming the Kingdom, namely the Netherlands, Aruba, Curaçao and Sint Maarten (the latter three islands being situated in the Caribbean), stating them to be equal partners. The Dutch Constitution however, is only applicable to the Netherlands. When we refer to Dutch constitutionalism or the Dutch Constitution in this chapter, it is with this document in mind.

[4] As Witteveen also observed. See Witteveen (2014), p. 132. Admittedly, a general provision now precedes the Constitution, stating that the Netherlands guarantees fundamental rights and democracy based on the rule of law, but the legal significance of this is far from clear. The next section briefly addresses this.

[5] And not, for example, as is the case in South Africa, where the substantive grounds for such a limitation must be justified. Article 36(1) of the South African Constitution stipulates that a limitation may only be approved "to the extent that the limitation is reasonable and justifiable in an open and democratic society based on human dignity, equality and freedom". Similar phrasing is found in most of the fundamental rights described in the first 23 articles of the Dutch Constitution.

be restricted are therefore found primarily in a document external to the Constitution and of much later origin: the European Convention on Human Rights (ECHR), the role of which will be discussed further in the next section.

Another notable point is that while the principle of legality in criminal law is enshrined in the Constitution (article 16), the broader constitutional principle of legality—central to the rule of law—is not explicitly mentioned and is only minimally reflected (e.g., in articles 89(2) and 89(4) of the Constitution).

The sober design of the Constitution was for a long time reflected in the way both legal professionals and the general public relate to it—that is, in the Dutch *constitutional culture*. This concept refers to relatively stable patterns of practices, customs and assumptions that shape how constitutional law is interpreted and applied.[6] Until recently, relatively few people seemed to be concerned with the Constitution, even in arenas where one might expect it to carry significant weight—such as among professional politicians. As one colleague once wrote: "In The Hague, there are hardly any politicians who would attempt to win or lose a debate on the grounds of whether the contested decision is compatible with the Constitution."[7] All this gives the Dutch Constitution a flexible, open character, allowing it to adapt relatively easily to societal change. This also puts into perspective the significance of the fact that the Constitution is difficult to amend.[8]

From this perspective, the Dutch Constitution may be better understood as a general guideline for the exercise of political power rather than as a robust set of substantive legal guarantees.[9] It is more a codification of existing political practice than a normative blueprint for an ideal constitutional order. In the academic literature, this approach is often associated with *political constitutionalism*, a theory characterised by scepticism toward the idea that the judiciary should intervene in matters traditionally reserved for the legislature—let alone that courts should have the authority to nullify legislation.[10] According to this model, constitutional review should take place ex ante—by Parliament, government and possibly advisory bodies—rather than ex post by the judiciary.

Indeed, the Dutch Constitution has historically granted more latitude to political actors than is the case in some neighbouring countries, such as Germany or Belgium. Those countries, for example, have constitutional courts that actively review legislation for its compatibility with constitutional rules and principles, including fundamental rights. In the Netherlands, however, the rules of the constitutional game are mainly monitored by the political players themselves—namely, the government

---

[6] Cf. Nelken 2004, p. 1.

[7] Besselink 1998, p. 213.

[8] The amendment procedure is regulated in article 137 of the Constitution. See also Chap. 5 in this volume.

[9] As Van der Hoeven also observed in his groundbreaking PhD dissertation dating from 1958 (focusing on the rules regarding the functions of, and the relations between, the highest political institutions; state organisational law).

[10] Gee and Webber 2010, p. 273. Political constitutionalism comes in various forms, some of which are more descriptive, others more normative. Classic references for the normative position include: Waldron 2006, p. 1346; Waldron 1999; Bellamy 2007. See also Loughlin 2022.

and the States General. If we were to classify constitutional identities, the Dutch model more closely resembles that of the United Kingdom, where parliamentary sovereignty remains a central concept, than that of its continental neighbours. It is worth noting, incidentally, that the term *sovereignty* is entirely absent from the Dutch Constitution—consistent with the Dutch constitutional legislator's aversion of big concepts.

2.2 Need for Nuance

The analysis in the previous section is, of course, general in nature and requires nuance. A constitutional identity is never a cohesive or fully unified concept, nor is it static. The idea broadly referred to as the "rule of law"—which, according to Dutch constitutional and political doctrine, implies that government authority is constrained by law, fundamental rights are to be respected and power is distributed over various entities, which are often independent of one another and thus tempered[11]—does indeed also find expression in the Dutch Constitution. Thus, it is certainly not the case that political constitutionalism entirely dominates the Dutch constitutional landscape.

To begin with: while the Dutch Constitution may offer a restrained catalogue of fundamental rights, it nonetheless facilitates the incorporation of international law through articles 93 and 94. According to these provisions, international legal norms that are both binding on all persons and properly published possess direct effect and take precedence over conflicting national regulations, including legislation. All Dutch courts are authorised to assess whether domestic statutory provisions conform to directly applicable international law. This form of judicial review has become a routine feature of legal adjudication at all levels. In the realm of fundamental rights, the Constitution often plays only a marginal role in the judicial domain: discussions are predominantly shaped by the ECHR, other general and specialised human rights treaties such as the International Covenant on Civil and Political Rights (ICCPR) and the UN Convention on the Elimination of Discrimination Against Women (CEDAW), and the case law surrounding these instruments.

The basis for the direct effect and primacy of EU law in the Netherlands rests solely on the seminal rulings of the European Court of Justice in *Van Gend & Loos* and *Costa v. ENEL*.[12] Interestingly enough, the Dutch Constitution itself makes no mention of the European Union or of EU law, nor does it specify how this legal order should operate domestically. Furthermore, Dutch courts have never developed a *Solange*-style jurisprudence,[13] nor have they attempted to limit the effect or primacy

---

[11] Krygier 2016 and Krygier 2024.

[12] Court of Justice of the European Union, Case 26–62, judgement of 5 February 1963, ECLI:EU:C:1963:1 (*Van Gend & Loos*); Court of Justice of the European Union, Case 6–64, judgement of 15 July 1964, ECLI:EU:C:1964:66 (*Costa v. ENEL*).

[13] See a line of rulings by the German Federal Constitutional Court (*Bundesverfassungsgericht*) regarding the relationship between the EU and the national level: BVerfGE 37, 271, judgement of 29

of EU law by invoking a distinct Dutch constitutional identity. Dutch courts are as a matter of fact rather obedient towards European law.

The central role of European law and international human rights treaties in the Dutch legal order, combined with the fact that the interaction among state institutions is guided in part by principles and unwritten conventions, means that the Dutch constitution encompasses far more than just the sparse, written constitutional text. In this respect, the distinction often made in German constitutional theory between *Grundgesetz* (capital "C" constitution) and *Verfassung* (small "c" constitution) is also applicable to the Netherlands.

Moreover, in recent years, the Constitution itself has undergone several fundamental revisions. In 2022, after decades of debate, a general and unnumbered provision now precedes the Dutch Constitution, declaring the Netherlands to be a democratic state governed by the rule of law: "The Constitution guarantees fundamental rights and democracy based on the rule of law." Having said that, the legislator intentionally left the interpretation of this provision undefined, citing—unsurprisingly—the "sober character of the Constitution".[14] So far, this general provision has only had symbolic value; the judiciary has not yet assigned substantive meaning to it.

Additional constitutional revisions have included the codification of the right to a fair trial (article 17), the right to confidentiality of correspondence and telecommunications (article 13) and the expansion of the anti-discrimination clause in article 1 to align with international treaty obligations, such as the UN Convention on the Rights of Persons with Disabilities (2006). Furthermore, the Netherlands Institute for Human Rights—an independent monitoring human rights institute—is tasked with issuing *non-binding* opinions in individual cases involving discrimination.[15]

Finally, two important elements of the Dutch system of checks and balances deserve mention. First is the organisation of the national parliament—the *States General*—which is bicameral. The *House of Representatives* (*Tweede Kamer*), the lower house, is the more political of the two. It comprises 150 members which used to be elected approximately every four years—recently, elections have been more frequent (2021, 2023, 2025) due to the short lifespan of the past three governments. The fact that the Netherlands is a parliamentary democracy means that the government, which is formed after these elections, is generally dependent on a majority in the House of Representatives. In addition to its legislative function, the House also

May 1974 (*Solange I*); BVerfGE 73, 339, judgement of 22 October 1986 (*Solange II*); BVerfGE 89, 155, judgement of 12 October 1993 (*Maastricht*); BVerfGE 123, 267, judgement of 30 June 2009 (*Lisbon*); BVerfGE 126, 286, judgement of 6 July 2010 (*Honeywell*); BVerfGE 154, 17, judgement of 5 May 2020 (*PSPP/Weiss*). This line of case law has many dimensions. The core issue is that the German Constitutional Court holds that only insofar (*solange*) as EU law guarantees equivalent fundamental rights protection as the national German *Grundgesetz*, does it not object to the transfer of powers to the European level.

[14] Parliamentary Papers II 2015/16, 34 516, No. 3, para 3.4.

[15] One can observe here a form of political constitutionalism similar to that in the United Kingdom. Under sec. 4 of the Human Rights Act 1998, a court can only issue a "declaration of incompatibility" if a law is incompatible with the ECHR.

exercises oversight. Severe criticism of a minister or the entire cabinet can result in a motion of no confidence, compelling resignation if accepted. This *confidence rule* is based on constitutional convention and is now one of the foundational principles of Dutch parliamentary democracy.

The *Senate* (*Eerste Kamer*), the upper house—also informally referred to as the Dutch Senate—consists of 75 members elected every four years by the members of the twelve provincial legislatures. These elections are held approximately three months after the provincial elections and do not coincide with those of the House of Representatives. The senatorial position is a part-time role, officially amounting to one day per week. Although senators possess competences similar to those of the lower house, they do not have access to parliamentary staff. Notably, senators cannot propose or amend legislation themselves but must approve or reject bills as passed by the House of Representatives. The Senate thus has the power to veto legislation adopted by the lower house. According to constitutional convention, their review is however limited to the quality of proposed legislation and its compatibility with the Constitution.

A key institution in the constitutional review of legislation in the Netherlands is the *Council of State* (*Raad van State*). In addition to serving as the country's highest administrative court, the Council is the principal advisor to both government and Parliament on proposed legislation and policy. Its role is enshrined in articles 73 and 74 of the Dutch Constitution. Almost all legislative proposals, whether originating from the government or from members of Parliament, require a prior advisory opinion from the Council. Evaluating the constitutional validity of draft legislation is an explicit part of its mandate. In issuing such opinions, the Council considers the mainly legal (including constitutional) and technical quality of a proposal. It may also provide unsolicited advice—i.e., without a specific legislative proposal -, or can advise at the request of the government or either chamber of Parliament. It may issue general reports on legislation and governance.

2.3 Constitutional Culture and Political Practice: Pragmatism

The previous sections have outlined certain elements of the Dutch constitutional identity and its institutional expression. This identity is hybrid in nature, although, as we have argued, it is perhaps more structured than elsewhere by what we have referred to as *the representative standard*. Still, even this image requires qualification when viewed from the perspective of political and societal practice. Strikingly, this practical dimension has received relatively little attention in the constitutional literature.

In this section, we highlight one such aspect: the pragmatism with which the Constitution is handled in practice. We next discuss several recent shifts in attitudes toward the Constitution (Sect. 2.4). Another development - i.e., the development of a multiple politica - is addressed in the subsequent section (Sect. 2.5).

We already noted that the sober design of the Dutch Constitution is also reflected in the way both legal professionals and the broader public relate to it: few people—professional politicians included—seem to concern themselves deeply with it. From a normative perspective one might call this attitude problematic. But one could also say that the Dutch Constitution has an open character, which makes it capable of easily adapting to evolving societal contexts. In this way, the Constitution's design facilitates a pragmatic approach—*pragmatism*, then, seems just as fitting a characterisation of the constitutional order as *sobriety* or *soberness*. Constitutional law, in this model, does not exacerbate the tensions that arise from social transformation. This resulting flexibility also helps to mitigate the fact that the Constitution is formally difficult to amend—a process that requires two readings in Parliament, with general elections held in between, and the second reading must pass both chambers with a two-thirds majority.

But how did this pragmatism come into play? Well into the twentieth century, Dutch society was deeply divided along ideological and religious lines. The Dutch-American political scientist Arend Lijphart described how, despite this, political and societal elites managed to work together in the interest of the common good, coining the term *consociational democracy* to describe this political system.[16] In such a democracy, established political actors were compelled to find pragmatic ways to manage societal division. This led to the development of alternative mechanisms for political accommodation *beyond simple majority rule*, as well as an active effort by the various segments of society to cooperate, seek consensus and maintain stability. In practice, this meant political elites were seeking common ground and tried to avoid inflaming or politicising existing divisions. A substantial portion of political leadership collaborated in governance, thereby neutralising destabilising tendencies and encouraging compromise. This period of consociational democracy lasted up until deep into the 1960s.

What is important to note here is that although classic divisions have by now largely faded from public life (with traditional religious alliances weakened and large segments of society secularised), socio-economic compromise among political elites continues to be a key feature of political decision-making in the Netherlands. Political institutions—both formal and informal—still operate through channels other than those provided by constitutional law to manage social or political conflict and competing interests. This pragmatic tradition has acquired a well-known label: *polderen*.[17] Historically, a polder refers to a piece of land won from the water and enclosed by embankments such as dykes. Today, the term is used metaphorically to describe the Dutch approach to political decision-making. It refers to the historical situation, dating back to the Middle Ages, in which different communities living within the same polder were compelled to cooperate in order to prevent flooding and collective disaster, even when they were otherwise in conflict. So the potentially

[16] Lijphart defined "consociationalism" as "government by an elite cartel to turn a democracy with a fragmented political culture into a stable democracy". Lijphart 1969, p. 216. For an overview, see Lijphart 2004, pp. 96–109. See also Lijphart 1968; Lijphart 1977 and Lijphart 1984.

[17] On this, see also Woldendorp 2005.

destabilising effects of conflict paradoxically prompted the ruling actors to search for pragmatic ways to cooperate and to deal with the potentially disastrous effects of flooding.

In line with Lijphart's reasoning, it could then well be argued that the renowned late 20th-century Dutch political "polder model" is an offshoot of consociational democracy. The phrase "polder model", is thus shorthand for an institutionalised form of cooperation and consensus seeking between political actors, social partners and other societal organisations. In short, the Dutch system of political decision-making found new, distinctly non-judicial and non-legal ways to avoid potential bottlenecks in political decision-making processes. Today, not only Parliament but also pivotal organisations such as the Council of State and the Social and Economic Council (*Sociaal-Economische Raad*, or SER)—the latter brings together politically relevant actors such as representatives of employers and employees—play central roles in this process.

It is worth underlining the constitutional significance of both consociationalism and its successor, the aforementioned *polderen.* Because if we define the minimum threshold of any constitutional legal order as its capacity to facilitate diversity and pluralism and to avoid too much concentration of power, then the Dutch culture of political decision-making clearly plays a meaningful, substitute constitutional role.

2.4 Some Recent Changes

Secondly—and this immediately qualifies the previous section—it seems that Dutch constitutional culture, that is, the way the Constitution is dealt with in practice, has begun to shift somewhat in recent years. The Constitution has increasingly become a visible and explicit part of public and political debate.

Several key moments can be identified that have helped to spark and intensify this debate around the Constitution and constitutional matters. Certain court cases have been especially influential in this regard. Among the most prominent are the climate cases which attracted worldwide attention, first and foremost the so-called *Urgenda* and *Shell* cases.[18] Although these primarily take place in the field of private law (concerning civil liability), they are nonetheless deeply constitutional in nature: they frequently involve appeals to constitutional principles like proportionality, precaution and the rule of law, even if those norms are not always embedded in the Constitution itself. One could argue that, in the absence of formal constitutional review, the regular Dutch courts have begun to assume a constitutional role of their own.

Another example is the case concerning the Dutch supply of parts for F-35 fighter jets to Israel, where the question was whether this supply violated humanitarian law and the constitutional principle that a national legal norm must never be interpreted

[18] Dutch Supreme Court, Judgement of 20 December 2019, ECLI:NL:HR:2019:2006 (*Urgenda*); Court of Appeal of The Hague, Judgement of 12 November 2024, ECLI:NL:GHDHA:2024:2099 (*Shell*).

or applied in such a way that it leads the state to breach its constitutional obligations under international law. In this regard, article 90 of the Constitution states that the "Government shall promote the development of the international legal order."[19]

The COVID-19 crisis also led to numerous legal proceedings concerning the restrictions on individual freedoms imposed by the government: the curfew, QR codes, mandatory face masks. Suddenly, there was widespread discussion about personal freedoms, often explicitly framed in terms of the fundamental rights ("rights") as laid out in chapter 1 of the Dutch Constitution.[20]

Then there was the so-called Childcare Benefits Scandal (*toeslagenaffaire*), which seems to have awakened a degree of constitutional awareness among many politicians. A large group of citizens fell into financial ruin—with all the accompanying hardship—as a result of a combination of overly harsh childcare benefits laws, or excessively harsh interpretations and applications of those laws by the judiciary, and a failure of parliamentary oversight and legal protection. Partly as a result, the call for the introduction of formal judicial constitutional review has gained momentum, supported by, among others, the Venice Commission, which issued a report on the scandal.[21] In the same report, the Venice Commission also made broader recommendations concerning the Constitution, such as strengthening the government's duty to inform Parliament (article 68), and introducing hardship and proportionality clauses into legislation.[22]

Most striking of all, however, was the fact that the parties which formed the previous government,[23] before they were willing to begin government coalition negotiations in January 2024, agreed upon a so-called "common baseline" for safeguarding the Constitution, fundamental rights and the democratic rule of law.[24] This was, of course, a rather remarkable development: they felt the need to explicitly affirm something already explicitly guaranteed by the Constitution itself. The background was that the election manifesto of at least one party—the PVV—contained proposals that were incompatible with the rule of law and the Constitution, and that both the party leader and other members of Parliament had previously also made statements contrary to fundamental legal and democratic principles. Since the formation of the new government, the Constitution has continued to play a regular role in political debate—though rarely in relation to specific provisions.

Thus, a hybrid image emerges: the traditionally sober Dutch constitutional identity is increasingly being supplemented—if not corrected—by developments occurring

[19] The Court of Appeal of The Hague, 12 February 2024, ECLI:NL:GHDHA:2024:191, found that there was indeed a violation of the law of war. The Supreme Court confirmed this on 25 August 2025.

[20] See Adams et al. 2024.

[21] European Commission for Democracy through Law (Venice Commission), Opinion No. 1031/2021 of 18 October 2021.

[22] Ibid., para. 137.

[23] July 2024—June 2025.

[24] See Parliamentary Papers II 2023–2024, 36 471, No. 21. See also www.nederlandsegrondrechten.nl/nieuws/350-afspraken-informatie-over-rechtsstatelijkheid

in domains that sometimes ("poldering") often fall outside the direct professional gaze of constitutional lawyers.

2.5 The Netherlands as a *Multiple Politica* and *Counter-Democracy*

All the preceding qualifies the representative standard that characterises Dutch constitutional identity. Yet an additional qualification presents itself. We now live in a world in which a multitude of "assembly lines"[25] contribute to the production of political and regulatory decisions. Regulatory complexity—driven by decentralisation, privatisation, fragmentation, Europeanisation and internationalisation—has become the norm.[26] As a result, the direct steering influence of those presumed to represent the people—most prominently (members of) Parliament and government—has only diminished over the years. The ideal of collective will-formation through political-parliamentary representation has become nearly utopian.

In recent decades, this has been further compounded by a progressively fragmented political landscape—a reflection of an increasingly divided society—which can lead to government agreements that deviate sharply from the rhetoric and electoral programmes presented during election campaigns, even though those programmes served as guidance for voters at the ballot box. Yet, because the public discourse continues to regard representative democracy—and the manner in which the link between citizens and politics functions therein—as the benchmark for assessing democratic legitimacy, this situation faces substantial criticism: the experience of collective will-formation and political representation seems significantly undermined by these developments.

In this context, a more recent development merits independent attention. It is a development conceptualised by the French political theorist Pierre Rosanvallon as "counter-democracy" (*contre-démocratie*).[27] Rosanvallon seeks alternative understandings of political representation. He argues that, under the pressures of deep societal division and complexity, democracy is taking on a new form. He describes how the democratic order increasingly organises itself as a form of what he calls *organised distrust*: a constellation of movements, ideas and currents that exert pressure on official institutions. Rosanvallon conceptualises this as *counter-democracy*, not in opposition to or as a substitute for representative democracy, but as an essential element within a broader democratic framework that includes representative democracy. Counter-democracy consists of at least three dimensions.

The first dimension concerns more or less institutionalised oversight of parliamentary and executive bodies by organisations that monitor for abuses of power or ineffective policy. Rosanvallon notes that periodic elections, while important,

---

[25] The term originates from Huyse 2014, p. 21.

[26] Bovens 2005.

[27] On this, see Rosanvallon 2006 and Rosanvallon 2008.

are insufficient to ensure that legislation and governance align with citizens' values. Hence, mechanisms of oversight—*counterpowers*—have emerged, exerting pressure on representatives and government *in between* elections. These include mechanisms and institutions tasked with monitoring, investigating and evaluating. They exhibit three characteristics: they are permanent, they are usually exercised by more or less independent and impartial institutionalised organisations and they enhance society's ability to influence public policy. Think tanks, audits and evaluations, ombudspersons, Councils of State, audit chambers, socio-economic councils, Supreme Courts, scientific advisory bodies to the government and other public advisory, supervisory, or decision-making institutions—all of which are richly present in the Netherlands—serve such functions. Universities and media may also be functionally relevant here.

The second dimension of counter-democracy is marked by the *juridification* of societal conflicts and the political process. Citizens increasingly turn to the judiciary in their resistance against political and administrative authorities—and they are increasingly assisted by a judiciary that acts with growing creativity. In the Netherlands climate cases, as previously mentioned, are a clear example. Here too, independence and impartiality are vital. Citizens turn to the courts because they perceive the judiciary as a more effective venue for achieving tangible outcomes than the ballot box. Over the past two decades or so, the rise in the Netherlands of public interest litigation—lawsuits initiated by specific interest groups seeking societal change through the civil courts, in the name of the public interest (a competence made possible under article 3:305a of the Dutch Civil Code)—has in this regard been remarkable. From banning smoking in cafés, from exposing war crimes in the former Dutch East Indies to reconstructing state violence during the 1970s, from holding the government accountable for insufficient climate policy to addressing privacy violations through anti-fraud legislation—turning to the courts has proven an effective means of raising awareness for historical and contemporary (alleged) injustices. Often, the judiciary has ruled in favour of organisations litigating on behalf of the public interest.[28]

Strikingly, in the vast majority of such cases, the Dutch Constitution itself is not invoked. Rather, arguments are based on international (human rights) treaties. Given the aforementioned direct effect and priority of international law, this means that Parliament cannot overrule such outcomes, as international law prevails over domestic law (under certain conditions). Unsurprisingly, several political parties—especially those on the populist right of the spectrum—regularly propose in their election programmes to limit the ability of interest groups to pursue litigation in the public interest.

The third dimension concerns a situation in which *popular sovereignty increasingly manifests itself as a blocking power*; a form of mobilised distrust. This may be the most striking feature of counter-democracy. This blocking power often takes the form of citizens (or citizen organisations) acting as vigilant observers—or quasi-elected representatives—who draw attention to developments and render

[28] De Kramer 2025; Van den Broek and Enneking 2014.

them contestable, thereby enabling organised resistance. It is not so much a positive expression of the general will as it is a reaction against what the people *do not* want. Positively framed, this could be seen as *civil society*. It represents a dissenting voice, often partisan and issue-specific: *Occupy*, citizens' juries, *Wakker Dier*, NGOs, *GeenStijl/Peil.nl*, the Clara Wichmann Foundation, the Dutch Non-Smokers Association, etc. Some parliamentarians may even see themselves as part of this blocking power, generating internal resistance within parliament. The rise of opinion polling and referendums, such as the advisory referendum on the EU–Ukraine Association Agreement in 2015, also belong here: the latter functioned as a blocking mechanism, mainly used by initiators as a protest against the EU and against the supposed Dutch establishment's support for continued EU expansion. The fact that many competences concerning this Association Agreement resided with the EU rather than the Netherlands—and that therefore a national referendum could have no legal impact—was largely immaterial from this perspective.[29]

This dynamic and fragmented development can be interpreted in various ways. At the very least, it offers opportunities for a culturally attuned analysis: citizens are indeed politically represented in meaningful ways—just not exclusively through elections and parliamentary channels. According to Rosanvallon, elections remain a legitimate way to organise power democratically, but they are not sufficient. Viewed in this light, elections serve less as a method for articulating the common good or public interest and more as a means for selecting leaders.[30] When it comes to expressing societal plurality, elections can only do so by adhering to the majority principle (as a *supposed* externalisation of a collective will). But in doing so, two distinct legitimacy dimensions can be conflated: a realistic electoral principle versus a more demanding legitimacy principle. Elections, after all, exclude a substantial part of the population—namely, those not represented by the majority will. And in a society of increasing diversity, that group seems only to grow. Of course, one might ask whether such forms of "wild" democracy will, in the long run, not degenerate into mere interest-based lobbying, hollowing out the institutional, formal democracy.[31]

Still, viewed in this light, the citizen appears far from passive or politically indifferent, but rather engaged and willing to involve themselves in politics. Citizenship appears alive and well, even as enthusiasm for representative democracy and its accompanying standard (see Sect. 2.1) is waning. Citizens have found new ways to express their voice. While an electoral procedure every four years fits within a cyclical view of representative democracy, we are now witnessing the emergence of a different form of political representation: disconnected from elections, unpredictable yet persistent, territorially defined or transnational, and—like parliamentary bodies—capable of influencing political agenda-setting. They are reshaping the political and social configuration within which representative democracy and the Constitution must operate.

---

[29] Van Vugt 2018; Starink 2016.

[30] Rosanvallon 2008.

[31] Aerts 2022.

While the development outlined above certainly places pressure on the representative standard described in the introduction, it may also point toward a new democratic principle. The old maxim of representative democracy—*one person, one vote, one representative*—is giving way to, or being supplemented by, a new norm: *watchdog democracy*, or *multiple representation*: "*One person, many interests, many voices, multiple votes, multiple representatives.*"[32] One could also say that the traditional *trias politica* is evolving into a *multiple politica*. This acknowledges the dynamic between boundary-transcending and boundary-enforcing forces, between institutions of governance and lawmaking on the one hand, and blocking powers claiming to represent the interests of citizens on the other. It offers a new way to understand the contemporary control of power—even beyond formal institutional structures; a way in which elections no longer exclusively serve a legitimising function.

2.6 Conclusion: Dutch Constitutional Identity and Culture Between Continuity and Change

Can the Dutch constitutional sobriety and the vitality of democracy and the rule of law be reconciled? To address this question, we have in this chapter used the concepts of constitutional identity and constitutional culture and operationalised the tension between them. The term *constitutional identity* refers to the more or less formal characteristics embedded in the constitutional framework and structure of the state. In contrast, *constitutional culture* relates to the relatively stable patterns of practices, habits and assumptions that influence how we interact with and understand constitutional law—essentially, how we engage with that constitutional identity.

From the preceding discussion, a nuanced picture emerges of how democracy and the rule of law are organised in the Netherlands. Those who claim that the Netherlands is characterised by a sober or restrained constitutional identity and a form of political constitutionalism are, as demonstrated above, partially correct. The absence of a preamble and grand terminology (sovereignty, rule of law, separation of powers, etc.), the lack of substantive criteria for limiting fundamental rights and the absence of judicial constitutional review all contribute to the notion of a sober constitution. This is of course, in large part, a comparative observation: more so than in several other (particularly neighbouring) countries, the Dutch constitutional identity is sober or restrained.

However, there are several formal and informal structures that compensate for this sober identity. Formally, this includes the relatively unrestricted influence of international law and the impact of European law on the Dutch legal system. Moreover, the Dutch constitutional system is characterised by the presence of certain formal powers that can function as checks on the political sphere—particularly, we have

[32] See Keane 2009, p. 691.

discussed the role of the Senate (*Eerste Kamer*) and the Council of State (*Raad van State*, Advisory Division).

But there is also an informal aspect, deeply embedded in the political culture. This pertains to practices like consociationalism (Lijphart), the so-called *polderen* approach and the vibrant concept of counter-democracy, as defined by Rosanvallon. In this context, alternative strategies for dealing with the sober constitutional identity have been developed in a pragmatic way.

Naturally, both constitutional culture and identity are never static; they are always subject to change. This change is currently very visible in the Netherlands. Since the climate cases, the COVID-19 crisis, the Childcare Benefits Scandal (*toeslagenaffaire*) and the rise of the populist far right, terms like "constitution" and "rule of law" have become more prominent in political and societal discourse than they have been in recent times. However, due to the sober, somewhat vague nature of the Constitution, much of the discussion remains at the abstract level of grand terms; intensive debates over the concrete provisions of the Constitution remain rare. Therefore, we believe it is still too early to abandon the assertion that the Netherlands has a sober constitutional identity and culture.

References

Adams M, Janse R (2022) Tegendemocratie en het Nederlandse vertegenwoordigende bestel. In: Goossens J, De Poorter J, Van der Schyff G, Geldof T, Van Oirsouw C (eds) Rechtsvorming in een hypercomplexe samenleving. Wolf Legal Publishers, Oirschot, pp. 107–130

Adams M, Janse R, Daniels S, Herrenberg T, Van Schaik M (2024) Covid-19 country report: Netherlands. In: King J, Ferraz O (eds) Oxford Compendium of National Legal Responses to Covid-19. Oxford University Press, Oxford.

Adams M, Witteveen W (2014) Democratisch wetgeven en de rol van het parlement. Over de zoektocht naar het Algemeen Belang. In: De Poorter J C A (ed) De ordening van mechanismen van rechtsvorming in de democratische rechtsstaat: het primaat van wetgeving vanuit verschillende perspectieven belicht. Boom Juridische Uitgevers, The Hague, pp. 37–63

Aerts R (2022) Civil society of democratie. Een Nederlandse paradox. In: Aerts R (ed) Denkend aan Nederland. Over geschiedenis, nationaliteit en politiek. Prometheus, Amsterdam, pp. 151–173

Bellamy R (2007) Political Constitutionalism: A Republican Defence of the Constitutionality of Democracy. Cambridge University Press, Cambridge

Besselink L F M (1998) Entrapped by the Maximum Standard: On Fundamental Rights, Pluralism and Subsidiarity in the European Union. Common Market Law Review 35(3):629–680

Besselink L F M (2005) De invloed van Europeanisering op de constitutionele verhoudingen in Nederland. B en M: tijdschrift voor beleid, politiek en maatschappij 32(1):45–55

Bovens M A P (2005) De verspreiding van de democratie. B en M: tijdschrift voor beleid, politiek en maatschappij 32(3):119–127

Gee G, Webber G C (2010) What is a Political Constitution? Oxford Journal of Legal Studies 30(2):273–299

Huyse L (2014) De democratie voorbij. Van Halewyck, Leuven

Keane J (2009) The Life and Death of Democracy. Simon & Schuster/W W Norton & Company, New York

Kovács K (2023) Identities, the Jurisprudence of Particularism and Possible Constitutional Challenges. In: Kovács K (ed) The Jurisprudence of Particularism: National Identity Claims in Central Europe. Oxford, Hart Publishing, pp. 1–30
Kramer X (2025) Public Interest Litigation at the Intersection of Public Law and Private Enforcement. Netherlands International Law Review 71:391–402
Krygier M (2017) Tempering Power. In: Adams M, Meuwese A, Hirsch Ballin E (eds) Constitutionalism and the Rule of Law: Bridging Idealism and Realism. Cambridge University Press, Cambridge, pp. 34–59
Krygier M (2024) Well-Tempered Power: A Cultural Achievement of Universal Significance. Hague Journal on the Rule of Law 16(3):479–507
Lijphart A (1968) Typologies of democratic systems. Comparative political studies, 1(1):3–44
Lijphart A (1969) Consociational Democracy. World Politics 21(2):207–225
Lijphart A (1977) Democracy in Plural Societies: A Comparative Exploration. Yale University Press, New Haven
Lijphart A (1984) Measures of Cabinet Durability: A Conceptual and Empirical Evaluation. Comparative Political Studies 17(2):265–279
Lijphart A (2004) Constitutional Design for Divided Societies. Journal of Democracy 15(2):96–109
Loughlin M (2022) Against Constitutionalism. Harvard University Press, Cambridge/Massachusetts
Nelken D (2004) Comparing Legal Cultures. The Blackwell Companion to Law and Society, pp. 113–127
Rosanvallon P (2006) La Contre-démocratie, essai sur la société de défiance. Éditions du Seuil, Paris
Rosanvallon P (2008) Counter-democracy: Politics in an Age of Distrust. Cambridge University Press, Cambridge
Starink L (2016) Slag om Oekraine: referendum over een land in opstand. Atlas Contact, Amsterdam
Van den Broek B, Enneking L (2014) Public Interest Litigation in the Netherlands: A Multidimensional Take on the Promotion of Environmental Interests by Private Parties through the Courts. Utrecht Law Review, 10(3):77–90
Van der Hoeven J (1958) De plaats van de grondwet in het constitutionele recht (PhD dissertation University of Amsterdam). Tjeenk Willink, Zwolle
Van Vugt E (2018) Intrekking van de Wet raadgevend referendum: Over de nasleep van het Oekraïnereferendum. Nederlands Juristenblad 93(2):78–84
Waldron J (1999) Law and Disagreement. Oxford University Press, Oxford
Waldron J (2006) The Core of the Case Against Judicial Review. Yale Law Journal 115(6):1346–1406
Witteveen W (2008) De geordende wereld van het recht. Een inleiding, 4th edn. Amsterdam University Press, Amsterdam
Witteveen W (2014) De wet als kunstwerk. Boom, Amsterdam
Woldendorp J J (2005) The Polder Model: From Disease to Miracle? Dutch Neo-corporatism 1965–2000 (PhD dissertation, Vrije Universiteit Amsterdam). Thela Thesis, Amsterdam

Maurice Adams is Professor of Jurisprudence at Tilburg Law School in the Netherlands.

Ronald Janse is Professor of Law and Dean of the Faculty of Law at Maastricht University in the Netherlands. He is Editor-in-Chief of the Hague Journal on the Rule of Law.

Chapter 3
Fundamental Rights: Between Trust in Parliament and Judicial Review?

Sophie Vonk and Ingrid Leijten

Contents

Abstract Fundamental rights have always been a part of the Dutch Constitution. In 1983, during the general revision of the Constitution, they were grouped together in the first chapter. In this contribution, the 1983 revision is taken as a starting point for revealing the identity of the fundamental rights in the Constitution. Next to the addition of social rights, it was emphasised that fundamental rights form a crucial part of our parliamentary democracy, and that it is a central task of the democratic legislature to interpret and give shape to rights norms and their limitations. In times when judicial review is regarded as conditio sine qua non for fundamental rights protection and calls for constitutional review in line with ECHR review are growing louder, it is these democratic characteristics that should nevertheless be valued and preserved as well.

S. Vonk · I. Leijten (✉)
Tilburg Law School, Tilburg University, Tilburg, The Netherlands
e-mail: A.E.M.Leijten@tilburguniversity.edu

S. Vonk
e-mail: S.E.C.Vonk@tilburguniversity.edu

G. van der Schyff (ed.), *The Constitutional Identity of The Netherlands*,
https://doi.org/10.1007/978-94-6265-779-3_3

Keywords Constitution of the Netherlands · Constitutional identity · Fundamental rights · Parliamentary democracy · Judicial review and constitutional review · Constitutional reform

3.1 Introduction

The Dutch Constitution is often characterised as sober and lacking in normativity. It is relatively brief and devoid of symbolic language referring to "we the people" or a common history. The recently added "general provision" - preceding the articles of the Constitution as a preamble would - refers to the protection of democracy based on the rule of law and fundamental rights, at first glance adding a symbolic touch.[1] However, the way in which it highlights these values resembles the formal and often distant formulation of the other provisions of the Constitution. Its general nature has understandably prompted a discussion about the addressee(s) and added value of the provision and whether legal protection can be derived from it at all.[2]

Questions concerning the guardrails provided by the Constitution also arise in relation to its characteristic prohibition of constitutional review in article 120.[3] Traditionally, the Constitution emphasises the inviolability of Acts of Parliament that should therefore not be reviewed by unelected judges for their constitutionality. These Acts, often referred to as "formal laws" and made by the government together with the two chambers of parliament according to the procedure found in articles 81 to 88 of the Constitution, are thus presumed to be constitutional. This means that sufficient checks must be incorporated in the legislative process in order to ensure their constitutionality.

A chapter on constitutional identity focusing on fundamental rights cannot overlook the issue of the prohibition of constitutional review. First, because when thinking about such review, what primarily comes to mind is fundamental rights review. The lack of constitutional review therefore is crucial for how the Dutch "deal with" their constitutional fundamental rights. Secondly, the prohibition of review is closely linked to the way in which the rights in the Constitution and in particular their limitation clauses are formulated. Finally, another reason for addressing this topic is that there currently is a draft proposal to amend article 120 of the Constitution.[4]

---

[1] The general provision states that: "The constitution guarantees fundamental rights and democracy based on the rule of law."; Parliamentary Papers II, 34516.

[2] On this provision, see for example: Adams and Leenknegt 2015; Groen 2023; Oomen 2022; Stremler 2018; Zoethout 2022.

[3] Article 120 states that: "The constitutionality of Acts of Parliament and treaties shall not be reviewed by the courts." See also Chap. 8 in this volume. All English translations of the Dutch Constitution are taken from the 2023 translation by the Ministry for the Interior and Kingdom Relations. Translations of other texts are by the authors.

[4] See the proposal and the official explanation to it: https://internetconsultatie.nl/constitutioneletoetsing/b1. Accessed 23 October 2025.

According to this proposal, review should be made possible when it comes to the "classical" fundamental rights found in Chapter 1 of the Constitution.

On the one hand, this seems to entail not much of an actual change, since for decades already, courts may review Acts of Parliament against the rights enshrined in the European Convention on Human Rights (ECHR).[5] These rights are similar to the ones listed in the Constitution. It is therefore often said that the added value in legal terms of allowing constitutional review would be limited, and that the aim rather should be to enhance the importance and symbolic value of the Constitution as such.[6] On the other hand, however, by taking a closer look at the "identity" of the fundamental rights in the Dutch Constitution, this chapter will shed some light on how constitutional review would or could impact this identity, for example also when it comes to the status of classical, civil and political, versus the social and economic rights that can be found in the Constitution as well.

Indeed, if a closer look is taken at the historical development of the fundamental rights chapter of the Dutch Constitution, we can better understand their "identity" including the normativity that—despite their mostly "formal" wording—was anticipated. For this purpose, more specifically, the 1983 general revision of the Constitution will be discussed in some detail. Although this is sometimes overlooked due to the increasing attention paid to the ECHR, we argue that some of the distinctive features of the Dutch catalogue of fundamental rights are all the more relevant today, given the efforts being made to bring the Dutch Constitution into line with the judicial and balancing oriented protection embodied in the ECHR and other fundamental rights documents and practices. Starting from their particular (historical) features, what would this mean for the identity of the fundamental rights in the Constitution?

This chapter is set up as follows. We will begin with a short historical overview before focusing in particular on the 1983 general constitutional revision. We will discuss the (kinds of) rights enshrined in the Constitution and their accompanying doctrines. After a brief discussion of the role played by international and European fundamental rights norms, we will move to the current debate in the Netherlands on fundamental rights (review) and how it can be perceived.

3.2 Fundamental Rights in the Dutch Constitution: Brief Historical Remarks

With the constitutional amendment of 1983, the first chapter on fundamental rights was included in the Constitution. This does not mean that the Dutch Constitution did not recognise fundamental rights until then. However, there was a need to emphasise that fundamental rights "occupy a particularly important place in our legal system".[7]

[5] See further Sect. 3.5 of this chapter.

[6] Draft proposal, p. 2. https://internetconsultatie.nl/constitutioneletoetsing/b1. Accessed 23 October 2025.

[7] Parliamentary Papers II 1975/76, 13 872, No. 3.

But before we get to a detailed discussion of the general revision, it is helpful to first provide an overview of the fundamental rights that were already included prior to that.

Our Constitution dates back to 1814–1815,[8] and at that time already recognised a number of fundamental rights (mostly taken over from the Batavian-French period). These included (precursors to) rights such as the principle of equality (now article 1 of the Constitution), which had little practical significance,[9] the right of petition (article 5 of the Constitution), the right to freedom of religion (article 6 of the Constitution), freedom of the press (a distant precursor to the freedom of expression in article 7 of the Constitution), the right to privacy (article 12 of the Constitution), the right to property (article 14 of the Constitution) and the right to protection against arbitrary deprivation of liberty (article 15 of the Constitution). It is notable that even then, a precursor to the current fundamental social right now enshrined in article 20 could be found in the Constitution: the right to an adequate standard of living.

The constitutional revision of 1848 is known for introducing (the basis for) our parliamentary democracy, after the King—influenced by the revolutionary unrest in Europe—was prepared to limit his own power. This revision also introduced the right of association and assembly in the Constitution (currently articles 8 and 9 of the Constitution) after a period of absence.[10] However, given the turbulent European political context in 1848, a very broad limitation clause, for the sake of public order, was added to this fundamental right, so that its meaning was fairly non-existent.[11] The privacy of correspondence (article 13 of the current Constitution) was at that time also included in the Constitution.

During the constitutional revision of 1917, considerable attention was paid to freedom of education (now article 23 of the Constitution). Some parts of this fundamental right were already included in the Constitution of 1814, but this revision gave the fundamental right its typical and comprehensive form.[12] The remarkably long wording can be explained by the fact that this fundamental right consolidates the result of a political compromise between religious and liberal parties after half a century of political struggle. From 1917 onwards, this provision ensured financial equality between public-authority schools and private schools (i.e. mostly schools based on a religious foundation), at the time in exchange for political support from the religious parties for universal male suffrage.

The general constitutional revision of 1983 gave fundamental rights a prominent place in the Constitution by including them in the first chapter. Not only were fundamental rights now organised, but rights were also added and general principles of fundamental rights were developed. Additions included both additions to existing

---

[8] There is some debate about the exact year in which our Constitution came into being. We will not discuss this further in the context of our contribution.

[9] Loof 2022, p. 102 with reference to Buys 1883, p. 28.

[10] Koornstra 2022, pp. 157–158.

[11] Leenknegt 2021, p. 190 with reference to Buys 1883, p. 83ff; Koornstra 2022, p. 158.

[12] It includes eight paragraphs: the right to equal funding for public-authority and private schools is laid down in paragraphs six and seven. See also Chap. 11 in this volume.

fundamental rights and the introduction of entirely new rights. Noteworthy was the introduction of the principle of equality (in a new form) as the opening article, which has since become the "flagship" of the Constitution.[13] However, before discussing in more detail the content of the chapter on fundamental rights introduced in 1983, we first require some necessary context.

3.3 The 1983 General Revision of the Constitution

The general constitutional revision of 1983 was the last comprehensive constitutional revision.[14] The new fundamental rights chapter was meant to express the legal and normative objective of the constitutional revision by introducing general principles of fundamental rights and to ensure renewal through the introduction of social fundamental rights. Apart from the partly innovative chapter on fundamental rights, the updated Constitution would contain few of the far-reaching proposals for reform that had been put forward in the (long) run-up to the revision. This was the reason that despite high expectations, the revision was also considered a disappointment.[15]

3.3.1 A Crisis of Authority

The 1983 revision cannot be viewed separately from the democratisation movement of the 1960s. Until then, (political) authority had been characterised by a broadly accepted "benevolent paternalism". In the 1960s, social consensus began to decline and, for the first time since the Second World War, the political establishment was confronted with a crisis of authority. Politics was seen as too distant from the citizens, and the outdated political system had to be reformed to better reflect the new societal reality.

Until then, pacification politics had reigned supreme in the "pillarised" Dutch society. The pluralistic society was divided into different pillars (i.e., groups) based on ideology (mainly: the Catholic, Protestant-Christian, Socialist and Liberal groups). At the "top" of these pillars, the leaders were found who reached decisions by consensus. Within the pillars one could not really speak of democratic procedures; the centre of power lay in the consultations between their leaders. The strength of this system was that it brought order to the pluralistic society.

---

[13] Gerards 2016a; Gerards 2023; Hirsch Ballin 2003; Jägers and Loof 2021. This provision would deserve a chapter of its own. For reasons of space, we will not discuss it in more detail in this chapter.

[14] More recently, in 2022 and 2023, several (minor) changes were made, also to the fundamental rights catalogue, such as the addition of a general provision (at the beginning of the Constitution) and the right to a fair trial (article 17). For a comprehensive discussion of this constitutional revision, see: Gerards et al. 2023.

[15] Van Leeuwen 2013a; Van Leeuwen 2013b.

With the de-pillarisation of society and individualisation, however, authorities came under fire. The empowered citizen, no longer under the grip of the pillarised society, stood up against the paternalistic attitude of the (governmental) authorities. Various protest movements made the discontent among the population visible. Authorities were accused of having a regent mentality and of having little feeling for developments in society.[16] In politics, democratic reformers, including of the new and successful political party D'66, picked up on these sentiments. They tried to represent the discontent of the protest groups, especially young people, in politics. In line with this, they committed themselves to the further democratisation of society.[17] For them, the priority was to facilitate the liberated and emancipated individual by focusing on (adapting) democratic procedures and individual rights instead of maintaining order in a "modern" democracy.[18] Against this background, they proposed various constitutional reforms aimed at introducing competitive elements into the democratic system, in order to make it easier for citizens to understand and recognise what politicians stand for, and thus be able to more effectively influence political decision making.

By the mid-1960s, it was clear that there was a crisis of authority in society.[19] This was not only recognised by the democratic innovators. The feeling that politics had to do something about the unrest and developments in society was more widely endorsed. The political establishment also admitted the need for political renewal. Its commitment to maintaining the stability and order that the consensus-based political tradition brought about against the backdrop of an already pluralistic society, made the political establishment willing to make concessions.[20]

3.3.2 Two Paths to Revision

In this context of compromise, a general revision of the Constitution would ultimately be realised in which fundamental rights (for the individual) obtained a prominent role and where there would be more room for democracy. However, in a more traditional form than the reformers at the outset had envisaged.

The reformers advocated changing the electoral system in order to achieve clearer possibilities for political choice They argued that citizens had too little influence on the final political decision-making process. The polder democracy, with all its institutional safeguards aimed at reaching consensus, would be so focused on compromise in parliament that the final decision would be unrecognisable to voters. Instead, a more competition-oriented political system would have to be realised.[21] Critics

[16] Kennedy 1995, p. 147.

[17] Kennedy 1995, p. 148.

[18] Cf. Kennedy 1995, p. 160.

[19] Kennedy 1995, p. 154.

[20] Cf. Kennedy 1995, pp. 149–150.

[21] Cf. Van Leeuwen 2013a, pp. 108–110ff and p. 118.

however argued that reformers equated democracy too closely with the will of the people. This misjudged a fundamental characteristic of Dutch democracy, namely that it has always been focused on the participation of minorities. The "radical" innovators failed to recognise the important function of compromise when they criticised it as undesirable paternalism or shady politics.[22]

To the critics' relief, the proposed reforms of parliamentary democracy were ultimately not included in the Constitution in 1983. A compromise was found by giving parliamentary democracy more space, yet consistent with the framework of the established parliamentary democracy. A more direct translation of the will of the people in political decisions was not considered desirable. The debates concerning the revision of fundamental rights cannot be seen in isolation from those covering democracy and the electoral system. Due to the development of the latter—by the mid-1970s it had become clear that proposals to change the electoral system would not succeed[23]—the reformers' attention increasingly focused on the importance of (individual) legal protection.[24] Ultimately, fundamental rights would be given a prominent place in the Constitution from 1983 onwards. The introduction of a catalogue of fundamental rights at the beginning of the Constitution reflected the high expectations. This formed a break with the past; until 1983, fundamental rights had not been strongly developed and had been spread throughout the Constitution.[25]

The prominent place of fundamental rights protection in the "renewed" Constitution was thus able to bridge the gap between the wish to facilitate the assertive citizen and the desire for democratisation and the determination to uphold parliamentary democracy in its existing form.

3.3.3 Substantive Amendments

This facilitation of the empowered citizen is clearly recognisable in the substantive amendments to several fundamental rights made in 1983.[26] For example, the right to vote was included in the Constitution as a fundamental right. This provision recognises a right to participate in public affairs.[27] Prior to the revision, the right to vote did not have an independent place in the Constitution, but was addressed in the chapters on representative bodies. The emphasis was on the right as a derivative of the function of the state, or the function of parliament (composed of both chambers of the States General). The inclusion of suffrage as a fundamental right underlined the changing perception of suffrage as a self-standing right of the citizen rather than

[22] Cf. Van Leeuwen 2013a, pp. 118–119ff.

[23] Van Leeuwen 2013a, pp. 143–148.

[24] Van Leeuwen 2013a, p. 169.

[25] Kennedy 1995, p. 152.

[26] Van Leeuwen 2013a, p. 128ff.

[27] Parliamentary Papers II 1975–1976, 13 872, No. 3, p. 26; State Commission on the Constitution and the Electoral Act 1969 (Cals-Donner), p. 56.

a duty towards the state.[28] As such, it is in line with the broader emphasis that came to be placed on the empowered, autonomous citizen who occupies an independent position vis-à-vis the state.

This new view of the relationship between the citizen and the government can also be observed outside the established path of parliamentary democracy. The right to demonstrate is an example of a new right, included in article 9 of the Constitution, which facilitates the active participation of citizens in public debate. An important argument for including the right to demonstrate was the emancipatory effect it has on citizens who are less familiar (or unfamiliar) with other ways of expressing their views.[29]

The more autonomous citizens are in relation to the authorities, the greater the detachment from a paternalistic government that makes well-intentioned (but potentially also ill-intentioned) decisions in the interests (or potentially also against the interests) of its citizens. This is furthermore reflected in the inclusion of rights that protect the privacy of citizens. During the revision, a general, independent right to respect for the protection of privacy was included in the Constitution as article 10.[30] In line with this right, article 11 came to include a separate right to bodily integrity.

3.3.4 Socialisation of Fundamental Rights

It is also worth noting that the 1983 constitutional revision introduced a new category of fundamental rights: social rights. Their inclusion was in line with the broader desire to facilitate the empowered, autonomous citizen by guaranteeing active government intervention in certain areas and thus supporting self-development.

These social rights, listed at the end of the first chapter of the Constitution, require the government to take care of a certain area, promote a certain goal, take measures in a certain area or create the necessary conditions.[31] According to the Explanatory Memorandum, the fundamental social rights introduced were intended to protect social achievements that are "perceived as the government's duty with regard to human development".[32] More concretely: the protection of a subsistence minimum and social security, employment, habitability and the environment, public health, housing, cultural development and education (articles 18 to 23 of the Constitution).

With the incorporation of social rights in the Constitution, it was held that "social fundamental rights are no less important than the classic rights of freedom and

---

[28] Cf. Kortmann 1987, pp. 72–73.

[29] State Commission on the Constitution and the Electoral Act (Cals-Donner) 1969, p. 78. Donner 1969, pp. 33–34, together with others, resisted the recognition of the right to demonstrate in the Constitution. This right was said to be at odds with parliamentary democracy: the main objective would be to impress by a show of force, rather than to persuade others via consultation and the exchange of opinions.

[30] See Groothuis 2021, p. 220.

[31] Parliamentary Papers II 1975–1976, 13 873, No. 3, p. 6.

[32] Parliamentary Papers II 1975–1976, 13 873, No. 3, p. 3.

equality".[33] To give "full material meaning" to the ideal of freedom and equality, there had to be not only "mental and physical freedom and equality", as protected by the traditional fundamental rights, but also "security of livelihood for individuals and their individual and social development", as protected by the social fundamental rights.[34] From the outset, the two categories of fundamental rights were not seen as separate, but as rights that are clearly interrelated and complementary.[35] Although there was some debate about the legal-normative effect of social fundamental rights,[36] the government agreed in the memorandum that social fundamental rights "create a legal obligation to continue on the path that has been chosen".[37]

In addition to the inclusion of social fundamental rights, the renowned constitutional scholar Kortmann also interpreted the work of the framers of the 1983 Constitution as accepting a "socialising interpretation" of classic fundamental rights.[38] These rights would then not only entitle individuals to a government-free space, but could also entitle them to government services.[39] This observation is in line with the emphasis on the connection between classic and social fundamental rights and the fact that a fundamental right such as the right to legal aid in article 18 of the Constitution, which has a mixed character, was included. On the one hand, this fundamental right protects the right to legal aid, but on the other hand, it also imposes on the government the more "social" fundamental rights obligation to provide financial assistance in cases where such assistance is needed.[40]

3.4 Principles and Doctrines

A closer examination of the chapter on fundamental rights shows how strongly the fundamental rights catalogue is intertwined with democracy, and more specifically: the preservation of parliamentary democracy. The intertwining of fundamental rights and parliamentary democracy is also evident in the more general doctrines relating to fundamental rights. As we will return to later, this emphasis is of great value, but it also makes the construction vulnerable. The accusation of a certain naivety with regard to the functioning of democracy lurks in the background. In this context,

[33] Parliamentary Papers II 1973–1974, 12 944, No. 2, p. 12.

[34] Parliamentary Papers II 1973–1974, 12 944, No. 2, p. 12.

[35] Parliamentary Papers II, 1975–1976, 13 873, No. 3, p. 3; Parliamentary Papers II 1973–1974, 12 944, No. 2, p. 12.

[36] Burkens 1988, p. 99.

[37] Parliamentary Papers II 1973–1974, 12 944, No. 2, p. 11.

[38] Kortmann 1989, pp. 230, 238 and 239.

[39] Kortmann 1989, p. 238.

[40] Vlemminx and De Werd 2021, p. 379ff.

Hirsch Ballin refers to "an extremely optimistic view of Dutch democracy".[41] The design of the protection of fundamental rights seems to assume that the majority would not allow itself to be used to undermine fundamental rights.

3.4.1 The Ban on Constitutional Review

A much-discussed doctrine in the run-up to the 1983 constitutional revision was the prohibition on constitutional review by the judiciary, which was included in the Constitution in 1848. This prohibition, which applies to the entire Constitution, is of particular significance for fundamental rights. These rights—in an otherwise fairly modest document—most strongly address citizens.[42]

In the run-up to the 1983 constitutional revision, there was extensive discussion about lifting the ban on judicial review with regard to classical fundamental rights. The lifting of the ban was proposed several times, but ultimately did not make it into the 1983 constitutional revision.[43] The idea was that fundamental rights were too political in nature to be interpreted by the courts. This meant that citizens were formally dependent on the parliamentary legislature for the protection of their fundamental rights.

With the rejection of the abolition of the ban on judicial review, the normativity that was supposed to emanate from the possibility of this review would have to be expressed in other ways. To this end certain fundamental rights doctrines, such as stricter rules for restrictions on fundamental rights, were introduced.[44]

3.4.2 System of Limitations

Within the framework for fundamental rights limitations, the emphasis came to rest on the competence requirement as a condition for restricting fundamental rights. At its core, it requires that limitations of fundamental rights are laid down in Acts of Parliament that both parliamentary chambers need to agree upon. In addition to this competence requirement, there were also other conditions for restriction, such as those related to the aims of a limitation and the procedural requirements, but these were considered to be of relatively little significance. The "legitimate aims"[45] were

[41] Hirsch Ballin 2021, p. 33 on that design: "One might say that it reflects an extremely optimistic view of Dutch democracy: the idea that the majority in this model nation behind the dikes would ever allow a violation of fundamental rights seemed far-fetched."

[42] Cf. State Commission on the Constitution (Thomassen) 2010, p. 21.

[43] State Commission on the Constitution and the Electoral Act (Cals-Donner) 1969, pp. 34–41 following the "Proeve van een nieuwe Grondwet" 1966.

[44] Van Leeuwen 2013a, pp. 150–157.

[45] Such as "to combat or prevent disorders" and "in the interest of public order".

formulated in such broad terms that it was fairly easy to formulate a limitation in line with one or more of them. The procedural requirement is very rarely mentioned in the chapter on fundamental rights.[46] Taken literally, the chosen restriction requirements do not regulate the content of limitations. Against this background, it is not surprising that the system of limitation requirements has (recently) been criticised for its (perceived) lack of normative guidance.[47]

3.4.3 The Doctrine of Special Restrictions

The importance attached to the system of limitations in the Constitution is also reflected in the doctrine of special restrictions. This doctrine of special restrictions stipulates that any restriction of a fundamental right must be traceable to the applicable fundamental rights restriction clause. This doctrine contrasts with the doctrine of general restrictions, as advocated by various advisory bodies.[48] General restrictions are restrictions that unintentionally restrict a fundamental right as a side effect. These are regulations that lie entirely outside the sphere of a particular fundamental right.[49] The doctrine of general restrictions stipulates that these general restrictions are exempt from the restriction conditions laid down in the Constitution. An important reason for rejecting this doctrine is the risk of the "far-reaching erosion of the constitutional safeguard character of fundamental rights".[50]

The importance of the doctrine of special restrictions lies in its adherence to the restriction requirements included in the fundamental right. The emphasis in this system of limitations rests on following the formal legislative procedure. This implies high expectations of this procedure. According to the government, the doctrine of special restrictions (i.e., the formal legislative procedure) would allow the safeguard function for citizens and the normative effect for legislators and administrators to come into their own in the pluralistic Dutch society.[51]

The emphasis on following the formal legislative procedure in our parliamentary democracy assures the approval of both chambers of parliament. This approval guarantees that limitations have been subject to political debate in a parliament elected

---

46 The procedural requirement is only mentioned in articles 12 (inviolability of the home), 13 (privacy of correspondence) and 14 (expropriation, counterpart of the right to property). It requires following the procedure prescribed in the specific provision when limiting the particular fundamental right.

47 This is particularly understandable against the background of an increasingly rigid parliamentary democracy. As such strong emphasis has been placed on adherence to the parliamentary-democratic legislative procedure, the protection of fundamental rights has become highly dependent on the quality of that process. For criticism, see for example Leijten 2020; Barkhuysen 2025.

48 Vermeulen 2023, pp. 149–151. See for example: State Commission on the Constitution and the Electoral Act (Cals-Donner) 1969, pp. 45–46.

49 For example, fire regulations applicable to religious buildings.

50 Parliamentary Papers II 1976–1977, 13 872, No. 7, p. 12.

51 Parliamentary Papers II 1975–1976, 13 872, No. 4, pp. 78 and 79.

on the basis of proportional representation. The underlying idea(l) is that of an open debate by democratically elected parliamentarians, a debate in which different viewpoints and interests are proportionally represented, resulting in a well-considered appraisal of the issue at hand. Another safeguard is the compulsory consultation of the Council of State, which advises the government and parliament.

3.4.4 Significance of the Doctrines

Each of the doctrines introduced emphasises following the "formal" legislative procedure (the procedure for the enactment of an Act of Parliamentary). This legislative procedure has a normative effect and a safeguard function in the context of fundamental rights. In the parliamentary debate leading up to the general constitutional revision, an opponent of the introduction of judicial review made the connection between the empowered citizen and (the lack of) judicial review: "The empowerment of the citizen is reflected in his influence on the legislative power".[52] The protection of the empowered citizen, in other words, requires influence at the outset of the process. Correction by the judge ex post in this view resembles the paternalism that empowered citizens detest. If this argument is to remain valid regarding the meaningful protection of fundamental rights of individual citizens, then everyone's distinct interests must be taken into account in the democratic decision-making process. A democratic process that simply focuses on the will of the majority of the people would not be compatible with a democracy that must guarantee fundamental rights (including individual or personal rights). This approach is in line with the importance attached by the government to the institutional design of Dutch parliamentary democracy in the process leading up to the constitutional revision of 1983.

With the strong emphasis on the legislative procedure within parliamentary democracy, due to the framing of the limitation clause and the ban on constitutional review of Acts of Parliament by the judiciary, "the Constitution (...) express[es] great faith in parliament as the main protector of constitutional values".[53] This makes the Dutch Constitution "very much a textbook example of a politically enforced constitution".[54] However, as we will see in the next section, this observation needs to be viewed in a somewhat more nuanced way today.[55]

[52] Parliamentary Proceedings II 1974–1975, p. 2404.

[53] Uzman 2018, p. 259ff.

[54] Uzman 2018, p. 259.

[55] Uzman 2018 also provides this nuance, p. 263ff.

3.5 The "Irrelevance" of the Dutch Constitution

What can be concluded so far regarding the identity of the fundamental rights catalogue of the Dutch Constitution? Having had a closer look at the developments surrounding 1983, we can say that these rights are supposed to empower citizens in our parliamentary democracy, by enabling and allowing them to participate in various ways. Both classical (political) and social rights were considered important in this respect. This character moreover is mirrored in (the continuous choice for) the prohibition of constitutional review and doctrines concerning at their core formal limitation requirements that emphasise the democratic legislature's role in interpreting and protecting fundamental rights.

This identity, it can be said, has also made the fundamental rights enshrined in the Dutch Constitution more and more irrelevant.[56] Although expectations regarding the normativity of the constitutional rights were high, over time these have come to be increasingly overshadowed by in particular the rights in the ECHR and the tireless work of the European Court of Human Rights (ECtHR) in interpreting and applying them. Whereas our Constitution nowadays is said to resemble a "culture of authority"[57] that grants considerable power to the legislature, the international system for the protection of fundamental rights is increasingly characterised by judicialisation and substantive requirements such as proportionality tests to ensure the protection of rights in the context of individual circumstances.

To be fair, it must be said that openness to international standards as part of a strong focus on international developments can also be seen as part of the "identity" of the Dutch Constitution.[58] Since the reforms of 1953 and 1956, the Constitution has allowed for the development of the European legal order, and moreover contains a requirement for the government to promote the international legal order.[59] More specifically, in articles 93 and 94 it is stated that once provisions of treaties or resolutions of international organisations are "binding on all persons",[60] they will have direct effect. Laws that are in conflict with such provisions will not be considered applicable.[61] In other words, whereas Acts of Parliament cannot be judicially tested against the Constitution, they can be set aside in the event of conflict with treaty provisions concerning fundamental rights, provided a court rules such rights to be "binding on all persons" and that in the circumstances of the case such a conflict is present. This explains the increased prominence over the past decades of (in particular) the case law of the ECtHR in the Dutch legal order. While that body of case law grew

---

56 Gerards 2016b, pp. 217–218.

57 Cf. Uzman 2024, p. 31.

58 On international and EU law, see Chap. 9 in this volume.

59 Article 90: "The Government shall promote the development of the international legal order."

60 A provision is binding on all persons if it is unconditional and sufficiently clear (in the circumstances of a case) to be directly applied. It is the courts that determine whether this is the case.

61 It is the courts that decide this (both whether a provision is binding on all persons, and whether there is a conflict in the concrete instance).

and became more fine-grained over time, the opening chapter of the Constitution was eventually relegated to the reserve bench.

In fact, the emphasis that the protection of fundamental rights places on the primacy of the legislature means that the success of constitutional rights depends to a large extent on the attention that the formal legislature is prepared to devote to them. As the attention of the formal legislature has been focused on the ECHR for some time due to the presence of judicial review,[62] it has proved difficult to turn the tide on constitutional rights, which derive their normative power from dynamic interpretation. It is not their static nature that gives these rights their normativity, but their constant translation into the present tense by their protector. By neglecting to pay explicit attention to constitutional rights, they have been unable to develop in pace with the ECHR, our "alternative" fundamental rights catalogue. The legislature's failure to pay attention constitutional rights has a self-reinforcing effect. The less attention is paid to these rights, the less they develop and the more they lose their significance.

More fundamentally, the paradox is that whereas the prohibition of judicial review and the responsibility of the legislature is part of the fabric and identity of our constitutional rights, this identity is simultaneously undermined by the same Constitution, which allows for judicial interpretation and review on the basis of international rights norms.

3.6 The Future of Dutch Constitutional Fundamental Rights

Is there anything we could or should do about the lack of attention for constitutional fundamental rights? From a purely legal perspective, one could argue that rights protection can just as well be realised on the basis of the ECHR or other (European or international) fundamental rights norms. Several recent events, however, seem to have increased interest in the role the Constitution can or should play in protecting citizens and—more broadly speaking—the rule of law. This suggests that at least from a more symbolic point of view, there is a felt need for augmenting the visibility and usefulness of our own national rights catalogue.

Firstly, there was the Childcare Benefits Scandal that came to light near the end of the previous decade.[63] For a number of years, the government had insisted on a harsh treatment of benefit fraud, which meant that in the context of childcare benefits (that are granted to enable families to pay for childcare costs) even a minor mistake or misreporting of one's actual income or hours of daycare could have the consequence that the full amount of benefits had to be repaid. In identifying potential fraud, the Tax

[62] The presence of judicial review makes the legislature more inclined to pay attention to the ECHR. Yet it is the constitutional rights that require more attention due to the absence of such review. Groen and Verhey 2020, pp. 427–428 refer to this as the "paradoxical effect".

[63] European Commission for Democracy through Law (Venice Commission) 2021.

Authority made use of risk factors and algorithms that had discriminatory effects. Families affected fell into great debt, some lost their homes and children were placed out of their families.

If anything, the Childcare Benefits Scandal has led to the realisation that the rule of law and the protection of fundamental rights in the Netherlands is not a given. Secondly, also the Covid-19 crisis has made people realise that what seemed mostly unthinkable, can happen, and that everyone's fundamental rights can, from one day to the other, become subject to serious limitations. It is understandable that rather than the "international" ECHR, in these circumstances the general attention and public and political debate were (also) directed at our own Constitution.[64] What are Constitutions and the rights enshrined therein for, if these cannot guide us in times of crisis?

It is against this background that renewed interest for the topic of constitutional review has surfaced, and in a broader sense attention for the constitutional distribution of power.[65] As the legislature proved unable to guarantee adequate legal protection, the focus shifted more to the judiciary. Manifestations of this shift in focus are the inclusion of the right to a fair trial in article 17(1) of the Constitution during the revision of 2022–2023 and the renewed interest for the judicial review of the Constitution.[66]

As already indicated, the prohibition of constitutional review (against fundamental rights) never entirely was beyond criticism, and following the State Commission Cals-Donner in the 1970s, several other (State) Commissions have pleaded to amend it.[67] In 2002, a formal proposal to change the Constitution was launched, with the purpose of allowing constitutional review on the basis of classical rights norms.[68] The Dutch Constitution is a rigid one; it can only be changed when both chambers of parliament vote in favour of a proposed amendment, and after general elections—when parliament has a new composition—the proposal must again be adopted in both chambers, this time by a two thirds majority.[69] The 2002 proposal eventually was adopted in the first instance, but due to a changing political landscape never made it to an actual second round of voting.

In recent years, however, with the Childcare Benefits Scandal and the Covid-19 crisis fresh in people's minds, the pressure for constitutional reform seems to have intensified. Whereas the 2010s were characterised by caution (not least on the part of the ruling VVD party), the 2021 coalition programme contained a subtle

---

64 See for example: Julicher 2020; Leijten et al. 2022.

65 For further reading, see Van der Schyff 2020.

66 Widdershoven 2023 on the incorporation of the right to a fair trial into the Constitution; see also Leijten 2023.

67 Recent examples are State Commission on the Constitution 2010, pp. 43–49; State Commission on the Parliamentary System 2018, pp. 195–208; State Commission on the Rechtsstaat 2024, pp. 46–47.

68 Parliamentary Papers II, 2001/02, 28 331, No. 2.

69 Article 137 of the Constitution. On the constitutional amendment procedure, see Chap. 5 in this volume.

reference to "taking up" the introduction of constitutional review.[70] Steps in that direction in 2022 culminated in a policy letter from Ministers Bruins Slot (Interior and Kingdom Relations) and Weerwind (Legal Protection), in which a fairly detailed implementation plan was presented.[71] The discussion about the precise modalities of that review continued steadily, and the intention was to propose a constitutional amendment in the autumn of 2023—until the government fell prematurely in July of that year.

Our most recent government—including the right-wing PVV party of Geert Wilders—again took up plans for constitutional review, this time including adapting the system of limitations by adding a general clause requiring such limitations to be proportional. Due to the efforts of another coalition party, NSC, these plans were moreover accompanied by a proposal to also introduce a Constitutional Court.[72] At the time of writing, new general elections are in sight, and it remains to be seen whether constitutional review will again be part of the new coalition government's plans.[73] Looking at the respective party programmes, there is a possibility that this will be the case, although the proposal to create a Constitutional Court will most likely not be repeated.

What can be said about these developments in the light of the topic of the identity of the fundamental rights catalogue of the Dutch Constitution? It would be too simplistic to argue that allowing judicial review would save the relevance of the Dutch Constitution as well as the protection of fundamental rights. If anything, the historical outline of why and how the chapter on rights, which still occupies a prominent place at the beginning of the Dutch Constitution, came into being has shown that protecting rights involves more than just judicial review and that the democratic legislature can also play an important role in shaping fundamental rights and the protection they offer.

Have we been able to clearly define the identity of the Dutch fundamental rights catalogue? Probably not, but merely asking the question about identity has put us on an interesting path when it comes to the way in which we can perceive the current state of affairs.

Arguably, the emphasis placed on the ECHR and the case law of the ECtHR has not only relegated Dutch rights norms to the background, but also their particular ambition: to enable rights protection of minorities through laws that are created in accordance with procedures that entail various constitutional safeguards. And, in addition, to allow and enable citizens to have an active stake in political outcomes that not only affect them, but also touch upon fundamental rights. It is true though that the limitation clauses in the Dutch Constitution currently have a narrow focus on the formal requirement of ensuring that limitations are laid down in Acts of Parliament.

[70] Cabinet Rutte IV 2022, p. 2.

[71] Parliamentary Papers II 2021–2022, 35 925 VII, No. 169.

[72] Cabinet Schoof 2024; Minister of the Interior and Kingdom Relations and State Secretary for Legal Protection 2025.

[73] The proposal and the official explanation to it: https://internetconsultatie.nl/constitutioneletoetsing/b1. Accessed 23 October 2025.

At the same time, however, it can be said that this still requires a substantive check, albeit engrained in the legislative process. Shifting the focus to judicial review which includes proportionality requirements would not simply "solve" the existing lacunae in this sense, but may also result in us losing something that is important and particular to our Constitution.

It is therefore to be hoped that if plans for constitutional review are followed-up, that this will go hand in hand with the realisation that there is also still much value in "ex ante" constitutional review, i.e. a legislative process which gives sufficient weight to minority interests which takes seriously advice from the Council of State or the new Parliamentary Commission on Constitutional Review. In times of increasing autocratic tendencies, in which politicians emphasise a version of democracy that simply translates the (presumed) will of the majority into law, it is all the more important to highlight this point.

A final point can be made about the role of social rights. Due to their more open-ended formulation, it is no surprise that the fate of these rights has been that they are even less "visible" or "useful" than their classical counterparts. This is mirrored in the proposals for constitutional review, in which social rights norms are generally excluded. Despite (academic) criticism of this point of view,[74] it is argued that social rights merely involve political choices and that allowing courts to review laws on the basis of these rights would automatically lead to them overstepping the boundaries of their legitimate role.[75]

Having had a closer look at the coming into being of the Constitution's fundamental rights chapter, and the role of social rights in this respect, it can be argued that making a distinction between classical and social rights does not align with the importance attached to social rights as a means of supporting empowered and autonomous citizens that participate in democracy in various ways. Or at least that, when such a distinction is made for purposes of judicial review, the burden all the more falls on the legislature to breathe life into the fundamental social rights norms of the Constitution.

3.7 Conclusion

Fundamental rights have always been a part of the Dutch Constitution. As one of the oldest Constitutions in the world, the role of these fundamental rights has been impacted by its historical development. In particular, the fact that the Constitution places significant emphasis on and trust in the democratically elected legislature cannot be seen in isolation from the various fundamental rights norms and how

[74] Roundtable on Social Rights in Second Chamber, see the following link for notes and position papers: https://www.tweedekamer.nl/debat_en_vergadering/commissievergaderingen/details?id=2025A00233. Accessed 23 October 2025.

[75] Minister of the Interior and Kingdom Relations and State Secretary for Legal Protection 2025, p. 6.

they are phrased. Not only does the Constitution since 1848 contain a prohibition of judicial constitutional review of Acts of Parliament against the Constitution, but the limitation clauses also rely on the democratic legislature to interpret and shape fundamental rights in ways that protect the basic interests of majorities and minorities alike.

In tracing the identity of the fundamental rights in the Dutch Constitution, this chapter has devoted particular attention to the 1983 general revision of the Constitution. During that revision, fundamental rights were given a prominent place at the start of the Constitution, and social rights norms were added. At the same time, the constitutional revision confirmed the important role of parliamentary democracy, despite the desire to more fundamentally democratise the system in line with societal developments. It was shown in this chapter that this choice is also closely related to the way in which fundamental rights were understood. Namely as strengthening the autonomy of individual citizens that—by using their rights—can at the same time impact political decision-making and thus strengthen the parliamentary system.

Since 1983, however, the role of the ECHR and the case law of the ECtHR have increased significantly. Leaving fundamental rights at the disposal of the legislature in this context, has meant that their relevance and visibility have diminished over time. More recently, calls for allowing constitutional review—at least against the classical rights norms of the Constitution—have become louder. At the time of finishing this contribution, a draft proposal has been circulated to make this possible.

What the "identity" of the Dutch fundamental rights catalogue makes us aware of, however, is that judicial review is only one side of the coin when it comes to fundamental rights protection. Instead of focusing on judicial review ex post, the Dutch Constitution has traditionally emphasised the importance of a legislative process that strikes a proper balance between the interests of the various minority groups that have long characterised the Netherlands. If anything, it can be said that whereas judicial review might add to the visibility and guarantees offered by constitutional rights norms, it should not make us forget the ex-ante protection that the Dutch system of democratic constitutionalism also considers so important.

References

Adams M, Leenknegt G J (2015) "Artikel nul": een algemene bepaling over rechtsstaat, democratie en grondrechten in de Grondwet? Ars Aequi 2015:207–214

Barkhuysen T (2025) Contourennota constitutionele toetsing: het glas is halfvol. Nederlands Juristenblad 8:545

Burkens M C (1988) De harmoniserende functie van grondrechten in onze rechtsorde. In: Addink G H, Ten Berge J B J M, Burkens M C, Michiels F C M A, De Waard B W N (eds) Tussen eenheid en verscheidenheid: Opstellen over harmonisatie in staats- en bestuursrecht. W.E.J. Tjeenk Willink, Zwolle, pp. 83–108

Buys J T (1883) De Grondwet. Toelichting en kritiek, deel I. Gouda Quint, Arnhem

Cabinet Rutte IV (2022) Coalition Agreement: 'Omzien naar elkaar, vooruitkijken naar de toekomst'. https://www.rijksoverheid.nl/documenten/publicaties/2022/01/10/coalitieakkoord-omzien-naar-elkaar-vooruitkijken-naar-de-toekomst. Accessed 23 October 2025

Cabinet Schoof (2024) Government Programme: Uitwerking van het hoofdlijnenakkoord door het kabinet. https://www.rijksoverheid.nl/documenten/publicaties/2024/09/13/regeerprogramma-kabinet-schoof. Accessed 23 October 2025

Donner A M (1969) Dient de uitoefening van de grondrechten, welke meningsvorming, meningsuiting en informatie betreffen, grondwettelijk nader te worden geregeld? In: Handelingen der Nederlandse Juristen-Vereniging, I, tweede stuk. W.E.J. Tjeenk Willink, Zwolle, pp. 5–54

European Commission for Democracy through Law (Venice Commission) (2021) The Netherlands Opinion on the Legal Protection of Citizens: Adopted by the Venice Commission at its 128th Plenary Session. https://www.venice.coe.int/webforms/documents/default.aspx?pdffile=CDL-AD(2021)031-e. Accessed 29 October 2025

Gerards J H (2016a) Artikel 1 Grondwet - Goede gronden voor wijziging? Nederlands Tijdschrift voor de Mensenrechten 41:304–318

Gerards J H (2016b) The irrelevance of the Netherlands Constitution, and the Impossibility of Changing It. Revue interdisciplinaire d'études juridiques 2:207–233

Gerards J H (2023) De nieuwe discriminatiegronden van artikel 1 Grondwet - lijnen in het debat. In: Gerards J H, Goossens J, Van Vugt E Y (eds) Constitutionele verandering in Nederland? De grondwetswijzigingen van 2022-2023. Boom Juridisch, The Hague, pp. 273–307

Gerards J H, Goossens J, Van Vugt E Y (eds) (2023) Constitutionele verandering in Nederland? De grondwetswijzigingen van 2022–2023. Boom Juridisch, The Hague

Groen L C (2023) De Grondwet waarborgt de grondrechten en de democratische rechtsstaat. In: Heringa A W, Kroeze R, Yesilkagit K (eds) De Grondwet van 1848 tot nu: Ontwikkelingsgeschiedenis, cruciale leerstukken en toekomstperspectief. Boom Juridisch, The Hague, pp. 235–249

Groen L C, Verhey L F M (2020) De betekenis van grondwettelijke grondrechten voor de wetgever: dode letter of zelfstandig ijkpunt? RegelMaat 35:426–449

Groothuis M M (2021) Artikel 10 Eerbiediging en bescherming persoonlijke levenssfeer. In: Hirsch Ballin E M H, Janse de Jonge E J, Leenknegt G (eds) Uitleg van de Grondwet. Boom Juridisch, The Hague, pp. 219–249

Hirsch Ballin E M H (2003) Gelijk in waardigheid: Over de zin van artikel 1 van de Grondwet. RM Themis 4:196–206

Hirsch Ballin E M H (2021) Inleiding bij Hoofdstuk 1 Grondrechten. In: Hirsch Ballin E M H, Janse de Jonge E J, Leenknegt G (eds) Uitleg van de Grondwet. Boom Juridisch, The Hague, pp. 29–41

Jägers N M C P, Loof J P (2021) Artikel 1 Gelijke behandeling. In: Hirsch Ballin E M H, Janse de Jonge E J, Leenknegt G (eds) Uitleg van de Grondwet. Boom Juridisch, The Hague, pp. 43–65

Julicher M M (2020) Corona: de Crisis die de Grondwet doet wijzigen? Ars Aequi 2020: 1087–1091

Kennedy J C (1995) Nieuw Babylon in aanbouw: Nederland in de jaren zestig. Boom, Amsterdam

Koornstra J (2022) Artikel 8: Vrijheid van vereniging. In: Ellian A, Rijpkema B (eds) Een nieuw commentaar op de Grondwet. Boom, Amsterdam, pp. 156–170

Kortmann C A J M (1987) De Grondwetsherzieningen 1983 en 1987. Kluwer, Deventer

Kortmann C A J M (1989) Grondrechten in de nieuwe Grondwet: vijf jaren toepassing in wetgeving en rechtspraak. In: Heyde L, Leijten J, Mertens T, Vermeulen B P (eds) Begrensde vrijheid. Opstellen over mensenrechten aangeboden aan prof. dr. D.F. Scheltens bij zijn afscheid als hoogleraar aan de Katholieke Universiteit Nijmegen. W.E.J. Tjeenk Willink, Zwolle, pp. 230–241

Leenknegt G J (2021) Artikel 8: Recht tot vereniging. In: Hirsch Ballin E M H, Janse de Jonge E J, Leenknegt G (eds) Uitleg van de Grondwet. Boom Juridisch. The Hague, pp. 189–204

Leijten A E M (2020) Casus mondkapjesplicht: is onze beperkingssystematiek nog wel grondrechtenproof? https://www.nederlandrechtsstaat.nl/casus-mondkapjesplicht-is-onze-beperkingssystematiek-nog-wel-grondrechtenproof/. Accessed 23 October 2025

Leijten A E M (2023) De rol en plaats van de rechter in de Grondwet. In: Heringa A W, Kroeze D B R, Yesilkagit A K (eds) De Grondwet van 1848 tot nu: Ontwikkelingsgeschiedenis, cruciale leerstukken en toekomstperspectief. Boom Juridisch, The Hague, pp. 251–264

Leijten A E M, But J J, Burggraaf D, Brabander M, De Massier L, Ruitenbeek L, Van der Gaag H W, Van der Haeften F, Van Middelkoop T, Van Zee I (2022) Twitteren over grondrechten in tijden van de pandemie. Startpunt voor discussie of stok om mee te slaan. Nederlands Juristenblad 97:1372–1379

Loof J P (2022) Artikel 1: Gelijkheidsbeginsel. In: Ellian A, Rijpkema B (eds) Een nieuw commentaar op de Grondwet. Boom, Amsterdam, pp. 101–116

Minister of the Interior and Kingdom Relations and State Secretary for Legal Protection (2025) Parliamentary Letter: Constitutional Review Policy Outline. https://www.rijksoverheid.nl/documenten/kamerstukken/2025/02/21/kamerbrief-over-contourennota-constitutionele-toetsing. Accessed 23 October 2025

Oomen B (2022) Algemene bepaling. In: Ellian A, Rijpkema B (eds) Een nieuw commentaar op de Grondwet. Boom, Amsterdam, pp. 81–90

State Commission on the Constitution (2010) Rapport Staatscommissie Grondwet

State Commission on the Constitution and Electoral Law (1969) Tweede Rapport Staatscommissie Grondwet en Kieswet. Ministry of the Interior, The Hague

State Commission on the Parliamentary System (2018) Lage drempels, hoge dijken: democratie en rechtsstaat in balans. Boom, Amsterdam

State Commission on the Rechtsstaat (2024) De gebroken belofte van de rechtsstaat: Tien verbetervoorstellen met oog voor de burger. https://www.staatscommissierechtsstaat.nl/onderwerpen/rapport. Accessed 23 October 2025

Stremler M (2018) De voorgestelde algemene bepaling als fundamentele constitutionele norm. Tijdschrift voor constitutioneel recht 9:204–220

Uzman J (2018) Changing Tides: The Rise (and Fall?) of Judicial Constitutional Review in The Netherlands. In: Franco Ferrari G, Passchier R, Voermans W J M (eds) The Dutch Constitution Beyond 200 Years: Tradition and Innovation in a Multilevel Legal Order. Eleven Publishers, The Hague, pp. 257–271

Uzman J (2024) Onvoltooid Verleden Tijd. In: VAR-reeks 174 Toetsing door de bestuursrechter. Boom Juridisch, The Hague, pp. 7–105

Van der Schyff G (2020) The Prohibition on Constitutional Review by the Judiciary in the Netherlands in Critical Perspective: The Case and Roadmap for Reform. German Law Journal 5:884–903

Van Leeuwen C W (2013a) Uit het spoor van Thorbecke. Grondwetsherziening en staatsvernieuwing in Nederland, 1883–1983. PhD dissertation Radboud University, Nijmegen

Van Leeuwen C W (2013b) 30 jaar Grondwet 1983. Teleurstellingen ronde de oude dame. In: Haimé M L (ed) De grondwetsherziening van 1983: 30 jaar oud of 30 jaar jong? Ministry of the Interior and Kingdom Relations, The Hague, pp. 4–13

Vermeulen B P (2023) In memoriam: Prof. mr. M.C. (Marten) Burkens (1934–2022): Essay naar aanleiding van leven en werk van Marten Burkens. Tijdschrift voor Constitutioneel Recht 3:145–164

Vlemminx F M C, De Werd M F J M (2021) Artikel 18: Rechtsbijstand. In: Hirsch Ballin E M H, Janse de Jonge E J, Leenknegt G (eds) Uitleg van de Grondwet. Boom Juridisch. The Hague, pp. 379–389

Widdershoven R J G M (2023) Recht op een eerlijk proces: overbodige toevoeging of revolutionaire potentie? In: Gerards J H, Goossens J, Van Vugt E Y (eds) Constitutionele verandering in Nederland? De grondwetswijzigingen van 2022–2023. Boom Juridisch, The Hague, pp. 203–224

Zoethout C M (2022) Algemene bepaling. In: Ellian A, Rijpkema B (eds) Een nieuw commentaar op de Grondwet. Boom, Amsterdam, pp. 91–98

Sophie Vonk is a Ph.D. candidate in the Department of Public Law and Governance at the Law School of Tilburg University, the Netherlands. Her research interests cover constitutional law, including fundamental rights and parliamentary democracy.

Ingrid Leijten is Professor of Dutch and European Constitutional Law in the Department of Public Law and Governance at the Law School of Tilburg University, the Netherlands. Her research interests cover Dutch and European constitutional law, including fundamental rights.

Chapter 4
Citizenship: The Hidden Backbone of Constitutional Identity

Hanneke van Eijken and Caia Vlieks

Contents

Abstract This chapter examines Dutch constitutional identity through the lens of citizenship, situating citizenship within the broader constitutional framework and studying the impact of (changing) notions of citizenship in conceptualising the identity of Dutch constitutional law. The European dimension of citizenship is an integral part of the chapter, as we regard citizenship as composite citizenship: composed of different governmental layers from which citizens derive rights and possibilities to participate. We explore its relationship with Dutch constitutional identity using three important features: delineating the political community and organising political participation; fundamental rights and duties; and pluralism, in- and exclusion. Based on this exploration, we find that citizenship is the hidden backbone of Dutch constitutional identity. Citizenship remains a concept that is difficult to grasp yet has a key role in defining (political) belonging in the Netherlands while also functioning as a criterion for differentiation, determining entitlements and sometimes reinforcing inequalities. Its composite nature also creates ties between different layers of governmental structures as well as between different (groups or (legal) categories of) citizens.

Keywords Citizenship · Constitutional identity · EU citizenship · Fundamental rights · Nationality · Participation · Pluralism

H. van Eijken · C. Vlieks (✉)
Utrecht University School of Law, Utrecht University, Utrecht, The Netherlands
e-mail: c.vlieks@uu.nl

H. van Eijken
e-mail: h.vaneijken@uu.nl

G. van der Schyff (ed.), *The Constitutional Identity of The Netherlands*,
https://doi.org/10.1007/978-94-6265-779-3_4

4.1 Introduction

Citizenship is a key element of constitutional thinking. As a concept it is often, however, overlooked in studying the very identity of a constitutional order. This chapter explicitly places citizenship at the heart of constitutional identity, by studying the impact of (changing) notions of citizenship in conceptualising the identity of Dutch constitutional law.

Like many of the concepts in this volume, citizenship is hard to define and capture in words. The answer to the question what citizenship means, seems to be embedded in its many dimensions, *inter alia* a social, legal and political dimension. In scholarship, it is recognised that citizenship encompasses multiple perspectives: historical, empirical, theoretical, normative as well as citizenship as an aspiration.[1] The dimensions or conceptions of citizenship thereby distinguished include, for example, citizenship as legal status, citizenship as rights, citizenship as political activity and citizenship as collective identity.[2] It has been described as having a unique feature as it relates to "national belonging and its associated rights".[3] Citizenship can also be politically coloured and be based on ideals that are (neo)republican, (neo)liberal, communitarian, or a combination thereof.[4] Citizenship is furthermore seen as an inherited commodity, because of the way in which nationality is traditionally acquired.[5] However, it should not be forgotten that citizenship also contains both an element of inclusion and exclusion, as citizenship draws a distinction between those who are citizens—with a special status and therefore certain rights and duties—and those who are not.

Conceptions of citizenship are also analysed and elaborated at different levels. The European dimension of citizenship cannot be excluded from a comprehensive understanding of this concept in the Dutch context. This EU citizenship has been called a "cynical exercise in PR of the European Union".[6] However, it has become a motor for many citizenship rights based on EU law.[7] Since the Treaty of Maastricht entered into force in 1993, every national of one of the Member States of the EU is not only a national of their state, but also acquires supranational European citizenship.[8] While EU citizenship leans heavily on the structures of free movement (and therefore the economic market of the EU), the status has a constitutional core, consisting of political rights which are explored in more detail below. As Habermas puts it: "With the introduction of European citizenship, with the explicit reference to a European public interest and common weal, and with the recognition of the

[1] Irving 2016, p. 238.

[2] Bosniak 2000, p. 455.

[3] Bosniak 2010, p. 9.

[4] Honingh et al. 2025, pp. 18–22; Wetenschappelijke Raad voor het Regeringsbeleid 1992, p. 119.

[5] At birth, through descent or birth on the territory of a state, see also Shachar 2009, p. 21ff.

[6] Weiler 1998, p. 10.

[7] Van Eijken 2015.

[8] Treaty on European Union (TEU), OJ C 202, article 9; Treaty on the Functioning of the European Union (TFEU), OJ C 202, article 20.

Union as an autonomous legal personality, the treaties have become the foundation of a political community with a constitution of its own."[9] Besides national or European citizenship, local or urban citizenship is a notion that is also gaining relevance, stemming from (re)new(ed) forms of citizenship and identity that can be particularly expressed in cities.[10]

Citizenship furthermore relates to citizenship formation and education. What citizenship means in our society underpins how it can be formed and taught, but in a circular manner, education also shapes citizenship. In addition, citizenship promotes the participation of citizens and the contribution that citizenship can make to democratic society as a whole. "Active citizenship" plays an important role in this regard.[11] Insights about the meaning of citizenship in the Netherlands may be derived from the views on citizenship with regard to the law on citizen participation, but also the confidence of citizens in the government and the rule of law.

Given all the different dimensions that citizenship may have, it is perhaps not surprising that the concept of citizenship seems omnipresent in contemporary societal and political debates in the Netherlands. "Whether it is about climate, security, education, integration, the EU or (informal) care: more attention to citizenship is mentioned as part of the solution."[12] "The citizen"[13] and citizen's perspectives[14] are often used in (parliamentary) discussions about the relationship between citizen and government in the Netherlands, while it is also noted that "the citizen" can be a synonym for everyone in the country,[15] but at the same time does not really exist.[16] Precisely that point is interesting when trying to understand whether or how citizenship can be viewed as a core or fundamental element or value of the Netherlands' constitutional order as the expression of its "individuality".[17] This may mean we need to move beyond a strict legal interpretation of what citizenship is. This chapter therefore attempts to provide a first exploration of the impact of (changing) notions of European and national citizenship in conceptualising the identity of Dutch constitutional law.

---

[9] Habermas 2012, p. 342.

[10] Sassen 2006, p. 317. See also Adams et al. 2017, p. 2737ff.

[11] Cf. Brinkgreve 2015, p. 39ff.

[12] De Waal 2019, p. 5 (translation CV).

[13] E.g. in the context of the "capacity of citizens to act [doenvermogen van de burger]", see Tijdelijke commissie Uitvoeringsorganisaties 2021, p. 28; Wetenschappelijke Raad voor het Regeringsbeleid 2017.

[14] The State Commission on the Rule of Law made proposals from the perspective of the citizen, for instance, see Besluit [Decision] of 10 February 2023, No. 2023000264 houdende instelling van een staatscommissie rechtsstaat [concerning creation of a State Commission on the Rule of Law], Staatscourant. 2023, No. 7635 (Instellingsbesluit staatscommissie rechtsstaat); Staatscommissie rechtsstaat 2024.

[15] Staatscommissie rechtsstaat 2024, p. 8.

[16] E.g. Parlementaire enquêtecommissie Fraudebeleid en Dienstverlening 2024, p. 32.

[17] Van der Schyff 2012, p. 578.

4.2 Citizenship and Constitutional Identity: Analytical Framework

In this contribution we use the perspective of composite citizenship[18]: citizenship that is composed of various relationships with the different layers of the legal order: local, national, European and international. Different, yet complementary and intertwined key aspects in which the relationship between citizenship and the Dutch constitutional order emerges are considered below. These key aspects are based on the exploration of different dimensions of citizenship above. The first aspect we consider in Sect. 4.3 is that of *delineation of the political community and organisation of participation therein*. Citizenship has a function in (inter)national society by defining who is part of a certain political community or state. As such, it plays an important role in actualising other concepts relating to the Dutch constitutional identity, such as the democratic rule of law.

The second aspect in focus is *fundamental rights and duties* in Sect. 4.4. A range of rights are granted to individuals irrespective of their citizenship status by the Dutch Constitution and other laws. However, some rights are specifically tied to citizenship, such as voting rights in national elections and eligibility for public office—clearly connected to the political community that was mentioned above. Dutch citizens furthermore have certain obligations based on the Constitution and other laws, such as military service (though this is not currently enforced) and allegiance to the state.

Furthermore, citizenship as *pluralism, inclusion and exclusion* is examined in Sect. 4.5. The Dutch constitutional order supports the integration of diverse groups into Dutch society while promoting respect for democratic values and the rule of law. Both citizenship education and naturalisation processes reflect this, for instance by requiring new citizens to demonstrate an understanding of Dutch language and culture, with a view to building a political community. At the same time, the (legal) inclusion of some also leads to the (legal) exclusion of those without citizenship from this community.

In Sect. 4.6, we offer some concluding observations, demonstrating that citizenship can be considered the hidden backbone of Dutch constitutional identity.

4.3 Delineating the Political Community and Organising Political Participation

To fully understand the concept of citizenship as part of the Dutch constitutional identity, it should be remembered that the Kingdom of the Netherlands consists of four countries: Aruba, Curaçao, Sint Maarten and the Netherlands.[19] The relations

---

[18] Van Eijken 2015.

[19] In the Caribbean part of the Kingdom, we also find three islands (Bonaire, Saba and Sint Eustatius) that are included in the Netherlands as special municipalities.

between these countries are governed by the Charter for the Kingdom (*Statuut voor het Koninkrijk*).[20] The notion of Dutch citizenship (*Nederlanderschap*) is central to how the political community is delineated in the Kingdom. The Charter indicates that Dutch citizenship is a Kingdom affair in article 3(1)(c). This means that the Kingdom has one, undivided and equal citizenship—even if that was not always the case, and it has been argued that inequality continues to exist.[21]

Since the revision of the Dutch Constitution (*Grondwet*) in 1848, Dutch citizenship has been determined by an Act of Parliament and not by a government decree, implying the revocation of a royal prerogative, which has been considered to amount to a memorable (constitutional) moment.[22] Dutch citizenship, as defined by an Act of Parliament, has since undergone various changes and it should be noted that it started out clearly exclusionary—the indigenous colonial population was excluded from citizenship for instance.[23] The Dutch Constitution today affirms that Dutch citizenship is regulated by an Act of Parliament.[24] This act is the Netherlands Nationality Act (*Rijkswet op het Nederlanderschap*), which applies to the entire Kingdom and clarifies how one can become a Dutch citizen or can lose citizenship. The main rule for acquiring Dutch nationality is based on descent or the principle of *jus sanguinis*, meaning that children are Dutch citizens when their father or mother is a Dutch citizen at the time of birth.[25] It is, however, also possible to acquire Dutch citizenship through option—a number of specifically indicated situations in which some link with the territory is already present, e.g. where a child is born and has lived for a number of years on the territory and has been stateless since birth—or naturalisation.[26] Even though the Charter demonstrates that Dutch citizenship is granted on behalf of the Kingdom of the Netherlands, it is not the Kingdom, but the different countries of the Kingdom that decide on the (substance of) the rights and duties attached to this citizenship.[27] Dutch citizenship can also be lost when an adult voluntarily acquires another nationality.[28] The Minister of Justice and Security may also revoke citizenship, for example when someone is convicted of a particular crime or enters foreign military service.[29]

When examining the Charter, Constitution and Netherlands Nationality Act more closely, the terminology focuses on Dutch citizenship (*Nederlanderschap*) and not on "citizenship" ((*staats*)*burgerschap*) as such. At the same time, citizenship and nationality seem to be used as synonyms here, which requires more reflection. As noted in the introduction, citizenship is a concept with many dimensions, which can

---

[20] See also Chap. 1, Sect. 1.1.

[21] E.g. Karapetian 2024, pp. 155–169. More on this below.

[22] Hirsch Ballin 1998, p. 282.

[23] Jessurun d'Oliveira 2023; Karapetian 2024, pp. 157–161; Zweers 2025, pp. 172–174.

[24] Article 2(1) Dutch Constitution.

[25] Article 3(1) Netherlands Nationality Act.

[26] Cf. articles 6(1)b, 6(1)(q) Netherlands Nationality Act. See also Sect. 4.5 of this chapter.

[27] Karapetian 2024, p. 163.

[28] Article 15(1)(a) Netherlands Nationality Act.

[29] Article 14 Netherlands Nationality Act. See also Sect. 4.5 of this chapter.

also be non-legal. Nationality has been defined at international and European level in law as the legal bond between a person and a state, not indicating a person's ethnic origin[30] and "having as its basis a social fact of attachment, a genuine connection of existence, interests and sentiments, together with the existence of reciprocal rights and duties".[31] Nationality thus provides the legal qualification of a bond that exists between a person and a state. Citizenship has not been defined universally in law and may have a wider field of application as it is not directly tied to the state or nation as such.[32] In view of the focus of this chapter on citizenship as part of Dutch constitutional identity, this notion is considered in its broader dimensions, also moving beyond the law *stricto sensu.* As such, this piece primarily uses the concept of citizenship, while noting that in principle—and also in light of what has been laid down in the constitutional legal framework on Dutch citizenship (*Nederlanderschap*) (including its European dimension)—nationality and citizenship can be used as synonyms.

A Dutch citizen (*Nederlander*) has certain rights and privileges, as indicated by the Charter and the Constitution. These relate to participation in the political community or the democratic state under the rule of law in particular. Indeed, "the gradual extension of citizenship rights has been a major mechanism in the democratisation of European societies".[33] Citizenship plays a key role in citizens' participation in society, which is connected to (democratic) legitimacy of the rules applied to all and decisions made by the state. The legitimacy of government action and the state-citizen relationship are, however, currently under pressure.[34] Even if there are many conceptions of legitimacy, it is clear that for most (if not all) of these participation of citizens in society—whether it is by electing their representatives or otherwise meaningful participation and interaction during the process of exercising authority[35]—is linked to citizenship. As such, the role of citizenship in the legitimacy of state action and the reciprocal relationship between citizen and state, which is part of the "constitutional circle of life" and importantly includes trust,[36] should not be underestimated in understanding the relationship between citizenship and the Dutch constitutional identity.

When it comes to effectively delineating the political community, the Charter indicates that the representative bodies of the countries of the Kingdom are elected by residents who are also Dutch citizens, having reached an age specified by the countries (but not exceeding 25 years). Every Dutch citizen is furthermore eligible to stand for election, with the proviso that residency requirements and an age limit may be imposed by each of the Kingdom's constituent countries.[37] Moreover, the

---

[30] Article 2 European Convention on Nationality (ECN) 1997.

[31] ICJ, *Nottebohm Case (Liechtenstein v. Guatemala)*, Judgement of 6 April 1955, ICJ Rep 4.

[32] Cf. Hirsch Ballin 2014, p. 11; Weis 1979, pp. 4–5.

[33] Butenschøn 2003, p. 560.

[34] E.g. Goossens 2024a; Goossens et al. 2022. See also Sect. 4.4 of this chapter.

[35] Goossens 2024a, p. 35.

[36] Hirsch Ballin 2022, pp. 86, 196.

[37] Article 46(1) Charter.

Charter allows the countries to expand the right to vote and stand for election to Dutch citizens who are not residents and non-citizens who are residents, provided that at least the requirements for Dutch citizens who are also residents are observed.[38] The Dutch Constitution clearly frames participation of citizens through elections as a fundamental right that is—in principle—reserved for all Dutch citizens. That has not always been the case. Suffrage was not approached as a fundamental right until the 1983 revision of the Constitution and universal suffrage for men and women was not a reality until 1919 in the Netherlands.[39] Today, all Dutch citizens are equally appointable to public service and every Dutch citizen has the right to vote and stand for election, subject to restrictions and exceptions imposed by law, such as the condition of having reached the age of 18 on the day of voting.[40] Foreigners are not explicitly excluded from these rights.[41] However, with regard to the right to vote and stand for election, it is clear that residents without Dutch citizenship cannot participate in the elections for parliament or Provincial Councils based on the limits set by the Constitution.[42] Participation in municipal elections is possible for certain categories of non-Dutch residents, including citizens of other EU Member States (more below).[43] There thus appears to be a certain openness that is inherent in the conception of citizenship as delineation of the political community: non-Dutch residents are also allowed to participate (politically), albeit limited to their immediate surroundings, i.e. at the municipal level.

In the past, some politicians have raised concerns with regard to dual or multiple citizenship[44] in relation to the rights to vote and stand for election, or to be appointed to public service. They were concerned about the loyalty of Dutch citizens with dual or multiple citizenship, which justified questioning their appointment to public service or them standing for election. The Constitution is, however, clear that this cannot constitute an issue, as all Dutch citizens are equal in this regard.[45] Moreover, it is not possible to differentiate between votes cast by citizens, for instance by granting a citizen multiple votes. The right to vote is guaranteed equally, meaning that one person gets one vote.[46]

Equal Dutch citizenship exists within the Kingdom of the Netherlands, as we saw above. At the same time, it has been considered that this does not entail that there is a single peoplehood (*volkswezen*) within the Kingdom.[47] This relates, inter alia, to a difference that appears between Dutch citizens who are residents of the country

---

[38] Article 46(2) Charter.

[39] Van Vugt 2022, pp. 312–313.

[40] Articles 3 and 4 Dutch Constitution. See also the Electoral Act (*Kieswet*), e.g. article B1.

[41] Cf. Hirsch Ballin 2020, p. 68.

[42] Articles 54 and 130 Dutch Constitution. See also Leenknegt 2020.

[43] Article 130 Dutch Constitution jo. article B3 Electoral Act; article 10 Municipalities Act (*Gemeentewet*).

[44] On this topic, see also Vroonhof et al. 2024; De Hart 2012.

[45] See also Hirsch Ballin 2020, p. 71; Leenknegt 2020, p. 77.

[46] *Kamerstukken II* 1976/77, 13,872, No. 3, p. 27.

[47] Karapetian 2024, p. 168.

of the Netherlands and Caribbean Dutch citizens. Dutch citizens who reside in each of the countries of the Kingdom are in principle also able to vote for the parliament of their country. However, the parliament of the country of the Netherlands (*Staten-Generaal*) is *de facto* also the representative organ to decide on Kingdom Acts of Parliament (*rijkswetten*), i.e. the legal order of the Charter.[48] This exclusion of most Dutch Caribbean citizens (of Aruba, Curaçao and Sint Maarten) has been held to constitute (part of) a problematic democratic deficit, "because it is inconsistent with the principle that citizens are only bound by laws that they themselves agreed to, directly or indirectly".[49] Calls have been made to address this and include Dutch Caribbean citizens in voting rights for the parliament of the Netherlands (and the Kingdom) through a simple amendment to the Electoral Act.[50] This demonstrates that Dutch citizenship does not only include, but also excludes people from a political community who are Dutch citizens, which may lead to questions about who constitute the "people" (*volk*) of the Kingdom of the Netherlands or of the country of the Netherlands and whether that aligns with the group of people who has Dutch citizenship.

The European dimension of (Dutch) citizenship includes a promise to supranational political citizenship: EU citizenship has been introduced to bring Europe closer to its citizens.[51] The European dimension of citizenship is an important additional layer of rights for Dutch nationals, which creates a (political) bond between nationals of other Member States with hopes of creating a *demos* amongst EU citizens. To achieve this, the right to vote and stand for election were introduced in the Treaty of Maastricht. These electoral rights are preserved for the European and municipal elections (article 22 Treaty on the Functioning of the European Union (TFEU)). In 1976, the Decision and Act on European elections by direct universal election for the European Parliament (EP) were adopted, resulting in the first direct elections for the EP. Thereby, the EU created and enhanced the political dimension of European citizenship,[52] even before the formal introduction of EU citizenship. Granting electoral rights to non-nationals was a major step for building a constitutional identity in the sense of political citizenship.

The right to participate in elections has been described as a "hallmark of citizenship".[53] Two specific limitations of political citizenship in the EU should, however, be marked.[54] First of all, the rights are limited to municipal and European elections, being explicitly silent on national elections. There have been attempts to include also national elections in the scope of application of EU citizenship, including through a

[48] Cf. article 15ff Charter.

[49] Raad van State 2024, p. 43 (translation CV).

[50] Raad van State 2024, p. 47; Hirsch Ballin 2024.

[51] Tindemans 1976.

[52] Petrescu 2013.

[53] Gardner 1997, p. 39.

[54] Shaw 2007, p. 7.

citizens' initiative ("Let me vote"[55]). So far, these attempts have been unsuccessful. While EU citizenship creates more political rights for EU citizens, it may also result in the loss of electoral rights. If EU citizens exercise their free movement right and reside in a host Member State, the right to vote in national elections may be lost, while voting rights for national elections in the host Member State are not granted.[56] The second limitation is that EU voting rights are granted to EU nationals, i.e. to non-nationals, who are citizens of one of the Member States. The Member States may, however, give voting rights to additional specific groups as long as they regulate access to these rights in line with EU standards such as the principle of equal treatment.[57] The right to vote for the EP has furthermore been formulated as a fundamental right even in a purely internal situation within a single Member State,[58] and—building on this—the Court of Justice of the European Union (CJEU) has indicated that membership of a political party should not only be open to nationals but also to citizens of other Member States.[59] The Court recognises that the organisation of national political life, to which political parties contribute, is part of the national identity of a Member State.[60] At the same time, the EU's duty to respect national identity, as phrased in article 4(2) Treaty on European Union (TEU), cannot overrule the values of democracy and non-discrimination, as stated in articles 2 and 10 TEU.[61] In this way, the CJEU strengthens the idea of a democratic EU citizenship, which may come at the expense of national identity, thereby paving the way to further substantiate and enforce the value of democracy in the future.[62]

Another important source of the political dimension of EU citizenship is the creation of a direct democratic process, with the European citizens' initiative by the Treaty of Lisbon in article 11(4) TEU. While the EU citizens' initiative gained a lot of criticism, because it is hard to comply with the conditions and initiatives are rarely registered successfully, it does create an institutional form of direct democracy.[63] A

---

[55] European Citizens' Initiative "Let me vote", see https://citizens-initiative.europa.eu/initiatives/details/2012/000006_en. Accessed 3 February 2025.

[56] Poptcheva 2015.

[57] CJEU, *Spain v. UK*, Judgement of the Court (Grand Chamber), 12 September 2006, C-145/04, ECLI:EU:C:2006:543, para 79; CJEU, *M.G. Eman and O.B. Sevinger v. College van burgemeester en wethouders van Den Haag*, Judgement of the Court (Grand Chamber), 12 September 2006, C-300/04, ECLI:EU:C:2006:545.

[58] CJEU, *Thierry Delvigne v. Commune de Lesparre-Médoc and Préfet de la Gironde,* Judgement of the Court (Grand Chamber), 6 October 2015, C-650/13 ECLI:EU:C:2015:648; Van Eijken and Van Rossem 2016, pp. 114–132; Platon 2015.

[59] CJEU, *Commission v. Poland*, Judgement of the Court (Grand Chamber), 19 November 2024, C-814/21, ECLI:EU:C:2024:963, see also, CJEU, *Commission v. Czech Republic*, Judgement of the Court (Grand Chamber), 19 November 2024, C-808/21, ECLI:EU:C:2024:962.

[60] CJEU, *Commission v. Poland*, Judgement of the Court (Grand Chamber), 19 November 2024, C-814/21, ECLI:EU:C:2024:963, see also, CJEU, *Commission v. Czech Republic*, Judgement of the Court (Grand Chamber), 19 November 2024, C-808/21, ECLI:EU:C:2024:962.

[61] The national identity of Member States, provided for in Article 4(2) TEU, is also referred to as the constitutional identity of Member States. See on this point also Van der Schyff 2012.

[62] Schuler 2024.

[63] On the history and the issues regarding the EU citizens' initiative, see Van Eijken 2020.

new form of democratic life of citizenship in the EU was created by the Conference of the Future of the European Union, held in 2021. During that year, 800 citizens debated the future of the EU in citizens' assemblies.[64] These forms of direct democracy are also to be seen on the local level; in the Netherlands the National Citizens' Council on Climate (*Burgerberaad Klimaat*) started to debate with 175 citizens in 2025 measures to reduce climate change by humans.[65]

4.4 Fundamental Rights and Duties

The Dutch Constitution includes in Chapter 1 various fundamental rights that "belong to each individual person as such, without further qualification".[66] These rights protect people from government interference in their lives and guarantee active (political) participation in society, equality and pluralism.[67] In the light of the Netherlands' monist inclusion of international law in its legal order,[68] fundamental rights as enshrined in fundamental rights treaties of the United Nations (UN) and, in particular, the European Convention for the Protection of Human Rights and Fundamental Freedoms (ECHR) also have real significance for protecting people.[69] The European Court of Human Rights (ECtHR) has for instance held that citizenship can be part of a person's social identity, which is protected by the right to private life in article 8 ECHR.[70] Similar to some of the rights to political participation, certain fundamental rights are reserved for Dutch citizens only: the right to freely choose employment and the right to government assistance (*bijstand*).[71] That does not mean that in practice all non-Dutch citizens are excluded from these rights; further rules may be laid down by law. The Participation Act (*Participatiewet*), for example, also generally gives non-Dutch citizens who are lawfully resident on the territory entitlements to government assistance.[72] Furthermore, Dutch citizens have the right to be present on the territory of the state based on their status as such—for non-Dutch citizens (aliens) this is regulated by law and therefore subject to further rules and/or conditions (article 2 of the Constitution). The role of citizenship—considered here in the context of possessing the nationality of a state—in accessing citizens' rights has been

[64] Seubert 2024.

[65] On the National Citizens' Council on Climate, see https://www.burgerberaadklimaat.nl. Accessed 11 February 2025.

[66] Kortmann et al. 2021, p. 424.

[67] On fundamental rights, see also Chap. 3 in this volume.

[68] E.g. Belinfante et al. 2015, p. 200; HR [Dutch Supreme Court], *Grenstraktaat Aken,* Judgement, 3 March 1919, ECLI:NL:HR:1919:126; articles 93 and 94 Dutch Constitution.

[69] On international (and EU) law, see Chap. 9 in this volume.

[70] ECtHR, *Genovese v. Malta,* Judgement, 11 October 2011, App No 53124/09, ECLI:CE:ECHR:2011:1011JUD005312409, para 33.

[71] See articles 19(3) and 20(3) Dutch Constitution.

[72] Cf. article 11 Participation Act.

noted: some fundamental rights are only guaranteed to nationals and allow them "to take full and active part in the public life of their state".[73] Moreover, people without any nationality—the stateless—experience problems accessing fundamental rights as such (in addition to the rights reserved for citizens), as a person's nationality often acts as a guarantor for these rights too.[74] Fundamental rights not only give substance to Dutch citizenship, but Dutch citizenship is also relevant in accessing participatory rights—while leaving room for non-Dutch citizens to be included.

Dutch citizens not only have (specific) rights, but also duties. These duties, which the state can impose on its citizens, are decided by the democratically elected representatives of the citizens, thus guaranteeing their involvement through their participatory rights. Payment of taxes and military service (though currently suspended in the Netherlands[75]) often come to mind when considering citizens' duties. But these duties also include allegiance to the state, compliance with laws and the fulfilment of those duties that flow from those laws, which may include compulsory education, labour participation, participation in dyke monitoring, obeying traffic rules, respecting fundamental rights of others or social service. The Dutch Constitution barely speaks of duties, but international legal instruments such as the Universal Declaration of Human Rights (UDHR) and the ECHR note the duties and responsibilities that come with enjoying fundamental rights and free and full development of their personality.[76] Some of these duties are not (or no longer) included in law, yet often the concept of "citizens' duties" (*burgerplichten*) is used to describe them. A well-known example is keeping the pavement in front of your house free of ice and snow during winter, but it may also refer to abstract, unwritten citizens' duties or "all sorts of standards of decency [imposed] through various contractual forms or codes of conduct".[77] There is quite some discussion and concern about the legal implications of these duties in the light of the principles of legal certainty and legality, but it continues to be a topic of interest from a legal administrative point of view that provides further insight into the relationship between citizen and state,[78] which is based on the notion of citizenship.

It should be noted that the duties discussed above are not (necessarily) connected to Dutch citizenship, i.e. are exclusively imposed on those who possess Dutch nationality. Some of them, such as military service, are, but others are duties that can be applied to all people. These duties do, however, provide further content to the notion of citizenship as part of the Dutch constitutional identity with an emphasis on expectations of the citizen by the state. Similarly, in trying to understand the citizen-state relationship in which citizenship plays a foundational role, fundamental rights focus on regulating or curtailing government action towards citizens and provide content to the freedom of citizens and opportunity for personal development.

[73] Hirsch Ballin 2014, p. 11.

[74] E.g. Vlieks and Van Waas 2022, p. 328.

[75] Cf. article 98(1) Dutch Constitution; Framework Act on Military Service (*Kaderwet dienstplicht*).

[76] E.g. article 10(2) ECHR; article 29(1) UDHR. See also Oomen 2009, pp. 55, 65.

[77] Zijlstra 2009, para 3.2.

[78] Cf. Kortmann 2024.

The citizen-state relationship has been under pressure in the light of recent developments in the Netherlands, in particular in relation to the Childcare Allowance Scandal (*toeslagenaffaire*).[79] In general, citizens' trust in government has declined,[80] while there has also been a growing distrust by the government of its citizens for a long time.[81] This has raised the question of what role fundamental rights and duties—or responsibilities—on both sides can play in (re)building trust in this relationship based on citizenship.[82] Further research is needed, but ideas such as a fundamental right to access and meaningful contact with the administration have already been put forward.[83]

EU citizenship demonstrates rights and duties too (article 20(2) TFEU), which can also be found the Charter of Fundamental Rights of the EU. The TFEU includes several rights, such as the right to vote and stand as a candidate for European and municipal elections (as discussed in Sect. 4.3), and the key right to free movement (article 21 TFEU), but duties are not provided for. The closest to duties are the requirements for the right to reside in another Member State. These requirements can be found in Directive 2004/38/EC, in which conditions to reside in another Member State are laid down.[84] The right—very important in the EU context—to reside in another Member States is based upon the gradual integration in a host Member State; the longer EU citizens reside in another Member State, the more protection they are granted. The first three months of residency require identification,[85] after that, the EU citizens should have a comprehensive healthcare insurance and sufficient means. After a residency of five years, EU citizens acquire the right of permanent residency,[86] which means the conditions for residency will cease and that there will be stronger protection against expulsion.[87] The CJEU has expressed that the effective enjoyment of EU citizenship requires the right to reside, meaning that, in certain circumstances, a non-EU citizen may have a derived right to reside in the EU in order to facilitate the residency of the EU citizen, if that EU citizen and the non-EU

---

[79] Parlementaire ondervragingscommissie Kinderopvangtoeslag 2020. The Childcare Allowance Scandal concerns an administrative and political affair in the Netherlands, resulting from unjustified suspicions of childcare allowance fraud by the tax authorities. Violations of fundamental principles of the rule of law occurred within the government, with far-reaching consequences for the families involved.

[80] I&O Research/NRC 2021.

[81] E.g. Brenninkmeijer 2023.

[82] Van Eijken 2025.

[83] Goossens 2024b.

[84] Article 7 Directive 2004/38/EC of the European Parliament and of the Council of 29 April 2004 on the right of citizens of the Union and their family members to move and reside freely within the territory of the Member States [...]. OJ L 158, 30 April 2004, pp. 77–123.

[85] Article 6 Directive 2004/38/EC; CJEU, *Wijsenbeek*, Preliminary Judgement, 21 September 1999, C-378/97, ECLI:EU:C:1999:439.

[86] Article 16 Directive 2004/38/EC.

[87] See articles 27–28 of Directive 2004/38/EC.

citizen have "a relationship of dependency".[88] Hence, EU citizenship creates the right not to be forced to reside outside the territory of the EU, creating therewith a clear right to reside in the EU for its' citizens, expanding the scope of application of EU citizenship outside the scope of free movement, similar to the EU political rights discussed in Sect. 4.3.

4.5 Pluralism, Inclusion and Exclusion

The previous sections illustrate how citizenship may include and exclude various groups, depending on their nationality, (factual) connections or rights. At the same, citizenship as part of Dutch constitutional identity tries to indicate a "togetherness" and bond between people that is difficult to capture in words. This is sometimes expressed through citizen responsibilities or duties as discussed above. This togetherness is also reflected in pluralism, understood as the coexistence of different groups, religions, beliefs, cultures, opinions and so forth. And as discussed also, fundamental rights and political participation are instrumental to this pluralism in creating that "invisible bond" that citizenship seeks to capture. In this respect, social values are an important part of what (new) citizens are taught. As Oomen explains, "[a]ttempts to define Dutch citizenship in the early 2000s via civic integration tests and in the civic studies curriculum, for instance, strongly place[d] emphasis on (the acceptance of) social values instead of formal rights and the formal legal structures".[89] But what ultimately determines a person's inclusion or exclusion? What binds people together is relevant here, which may be translated into national identity[90] (which is notoriously hard to define), or shared (human) values, goals, past and future. Legal structures related to citizenship are often important in addressing the question of inclusion and exclusion.

Taking civic integration (*inburgering*) as an example, we can see that legislative developments have been fast-paced in recent decades, even though a clear definition of the concept of "integration" has been lacking.[91] Emphasis, however, has been placed on active participation in Dutch society by means of knowledge of the Dutch language and of society, including the labour market.[92] In addition, the previous exclusion of groups with clear connections to Dutch society has also been corrected. Take for instance the special residency arrangement that was enacted in 2025 for undocumented Surinamese former Dutch citizens with a clear (historical) link to the Netherlands, or the relaxation of the documents required for naturalisation for a large

---

[88] Iglesias Sánchez 2017; Van Eijken and Phoa 2018; CJEU, *Chavez-Vilchez and Others*, Judgement, 10 May 2017, C-133/15, ECLI:EU:C:2017:354.

[89] Oomen 2016, pp. 248–249.

[90] Tiemeijer 2021.

[91] Groenendijk et al. 2021, p. 2731.

[92] Cf. Civic Integration Act 2021 (*Wet inburgering 2021*).

group of so-called *pardonners* in 2021.[93] The latter group of people used the slogan *#wijhorenerookbij*[94] to indicate that they felt like Dutch citizens, even though they were not legally recognised as such.

Exclusion of citizens, including legally, can occur where individuals have behaved in a way that is prejudicial to the interests of the state or when a meaningful connection between the individual and state is deemed not to be present (any longer). Such situations may include a conviction for certain crimes or terrorist acts as well as prolonged residence outside of the territory of the Kingdom and the EU.[95] An important legal guarantee in this regard is that such a loss of citizenship should generally not result in someone becoming stateless.[96] This means that the deprivation of Dutch citizenship based on national security concerns may, for example, only occur when the person in question has more than one nationality. If a person only has Dutch nationality, they cannot be deprived of their citizenship. This has raised questions from a fundamental rights perspective regarding the principle of non-discrimination.[97] In this context, the Administrative Jurisdiction of the Dutch Council of State has ruled that the situation of the two groups, those with a single nationality and those with dual/multiple nationalities, is different and that their different treatment is therefore not discriminatory. According to the ruling, there are objective reasons that explain the difference in treatment of these two groups, agreeing with the Dutch government on the importance of protecting national security and that nationals who participate in terrorist organisations have disconnected themselves from the state.[98] However, another Dutch court ruled in March 2025 that revoking citizenship does amount to discriminatory treatment on the basis of descent, rendering the decision to revoke invalid and in violation of international treaties.[99] This shows that fundamental rights can place restrictions on government actions regarding the legal qualification of citizenship through (severing) the bond of nationality.

The EU dimension of citizenship also provides for additional guarantees in cases where states want to sever their legal ties to an individual. Even if nationality matters are generally within the exclusive powers of the Member States, the jurisprudence of the CJEU demonstrates an increased influence on this topic through the notion of EU citizenship. The case of *Tjebbes and Others v. the Netherlands* is exemplary.[100] In this case, the CJEU examined the legality of the loss of nationality under Dutch law,

---

[93] This term refers to the group of people who were allowed to stay in the Netherlands after the general pardon of 2007—a scheme whereby migrants who have been in the country for a significant period of time are granted a (previously refused) residence permit under certain conditions, such as continuous residence. See *Kamerstukken II* 2020/21, 19637/30573, No. 2757, pp. 5–7.

[94] "We belong too" (translation CV).

[95] Articles 14 and 15 Netherlands Nationality Act.

[96] Article 14(8) Netherlands Nationality Act.

[97] Jessurun d'Oliveira 2022; De Hart 2024.

[98] ABRvS [Administrative Jurisdiction Division of the Council of State], Judgement, 30 December 2020, ECLI:NL:RVS:2020:3045, para 6.1.

[99] Court of Amsterdam, Judgement, 24 March 2025, AMS 23/6089, ECLI:N:RBAMS:2025:1849.

[100] CJEU, *Tjebbes and Others v. Netherlands*, Judgement, 12 March 2019, C-221/17, ECLI:EU:C:2019:189.

as this led to the automatic loss of EU citizenship. The Court ruled that while states have the right to define their nationality laws, they must assess the proportionality of such decisions, considering their impact on individuals' rights under EU law. In this case, the Court emphasised that the loss of nationality and EU citizenship must be examined considering fundamental rights while ensuring that individuals are not disproportionately deprived of their EU rights. In addition, it has been held that EU citizenship jurisprudence may also affect the acquisition of citizenship and the inclusion of people as EU citizens, particularly in the light of developments around investor citizenship schemes or "golden passports".[101] The European Commission challenged the latter practice in *Commission v. Malta*,[102] arguing that it undermined the integrity of EU citizenship by allowing individuals to obtain nationality without a substantive connection to the state in question. The case underscores the EU's growing interest in ensuring that nationality acquisition processes reflect genuine ties to Member States and do not compromise EU values. The *Malta* case is seen as a significant milestone regarding EU citizenship, but also regarding the division of powers between the EU and its Member States. While the European Commission referred to *Nottebohm*[103] in the pleadings in the case, arguing that a genuine link should be required before granting citizenship, the Court seems to base its ruling directly on EU citizenship and loyal cooperation between the Member States. The reference to *Nottebohm* is, indeed, perhaps somewhat odd, since an international dispute about the recognition of nationality (not acquisition) differs significantly from granting Maltese nationality in the light of EU citizenship. The Court referred in the *Malta* case to EU citizenship as "one of the principal concrete expressions of the solidarity which forms the very basis of the process of integration" and "an integral part of the identity of the European Union".[104] There is a lot to say about this case,[105] but for the context of this chapter, we would like to highlight the way the Court defines EU citizenship as creating a political space and a European identity. The fact is that the Court of Justice used these arguments to cross the Rubicon on nationality acquisition and European citizenship, thereby creating a new aspect to the European constitutional identity.

---

[101] Vlieks 2022, pp. 207–209.

[102] CJEU, *European Commission v. Republic of Malta,* Opinion of Advocate General Collins, 4 October 2024, C-181/23, ECLI:EU:C:2024:849. See also Van Eijken 2024.

[103] ICJ, *Nottebohm Case (Liechtenstein v. Guatemala)*, Judgment, 6 April 1955, ICJ Rep 4.

[104] CJEU, *European Commission v. Republic of Malta,* Judgement, 29 April 2025, C-181/23, ECLI:EU:C:2025:283, para 93.

[105] See for instance Kochenov 2025; Van den Brink 2025.

4.6 Conclusion

Citizenship is the hidden backbone of Dutch constitutional identity. It is both its strongest and its weakest link. As a concept, it is difficult to grasp and therefore it is hard to determine its relationship and impact on Dutch constitutional identity. At the same time, it has a key role in defining (political) belonging in the Netherlands while also functioning as a criterion for differentiation, determining entitlements and sometimes reinforcing inequalities.[106] This dual nature is particularly evident in the Dutch context, where citizenship delineates the boundaries of political participation while also accommodating non-Dutch residents in specific ways (see Sect. 4.3). Within those boundaries, all citizens are equal, but not entirely when it comes to the question of including Dutch Caribbean citizens. Citizenship, as the foundation for the reciprocal relationship between citizen and state, is faced with challenges, while also contributing to the legitimacy of state action. The EU dimension of citizenship adds a layer of political participation and community, which influences the legal regulation of the political community and thereby Dutch constitutional identity. Fundamental rights and duties, also at EU level, furthermore provide content to the notion of citizenship as part of Dutch constitutional identity, including the (declining) trust between citizen and state (Sect. 4.4). The notion of citizenship in the Dutch context furthermore attempts to make explicit what binds citizens in a pluralistic manner, which proves difficult to characterise using law, as the fast-paced developments regarding integration show for instance. When considering the various ways in which people are included or excluded, it becomes clear that the basis for inclusion as a citizen is often a factual, genuine link, to the territory of the state or to other citizens—in the EU context as well. At the same time, the possibility to (legally) sever the link between the state and the (former) citizen demonstrates that conduct that goes against the values and norms that underlie the notion of citizenship—and perhaps of Dutch constitutional identity—will lead to exclusion, even where that may amount to differences in treatment between (former) citizens (Sect. 4.5).

Citizenship as part of Dutch constitutional identity thus has a specific way of translating what binds people (factually/socially) together into conceptions and law that regulate "peoples' access to public resources and institutions, creating legal distinctions […]".[107] It is composite in nature, as it creates ties between different layers of governmental structures as well as between different (groups or (legal) categories of) citizens. The concept as such is based on rights and entitlements. Dependent on their specific situation, a citizen derives rights and duties from the local, country, Kingdom or European level, which creates a dynamic or pluralistic concept of citizenship and thereby of the constitutional identity of the Netherlands. Differences can therefore exist between Dutch citizens or long-term residents in the Netherlands who hold the nationality of another EU Member State, or between Dutch citizens holding only Dutch nationality and Dutch citizens with dual nationality. These inequalities are justified using legal constructs that are based on genuine links or the protection of

[106] Isin and Turner 2007.

[107] Butenschøn 2003, p. 559.

the community as a whole, while limitations to them are also influenced by the EU dimension of citizenship. In some respects, however, a trend towards more inclusive and participatory citizenship seems to be discernible, for example when considering the (legal) developments on EU citizenship, the deprivation of nationality, as well as the central role of the citizen in addressing the reciprocal relationship between citizen and state.

The different aspects of citizenship discussed in this chapter make up, like vertebrae that communicate with each other, the hidden backbone of the body that is Dutch constitutional identity. Some of these aspects also concern other parts of the body, or constitutional identity, such as fundamental rights. The relationship between the (hidden) backbone and the body(parts), or between citizenship and Dutch constitutional identity (and its various aspects), is deeply intertwined and remains a dynamic and reciprocal nexus. Citizenship is both a constitutive element of constitutional identity and a product of it, shaping and being shaped by legal, political and societal norms. This dynamic highlights how citizenship and constitutional identity both are not static constructs, but evolving frameworks that respond to shifts in national and European governance.

Acknowledgments The authors thank Dennis Wegink for editing the references.

References

Adams M et al. (2017) Constitutionalisme in de eeuw van de stad. Over stadsrecht en rechtsstaat. Nederlands Juristenblad 37:2729–2739

Belinfante A D et al. (2015) Beginselen van het Nederlandse staatsrecht. Wolters Kluwer, Deventer

Bosniak L (2000) Citizenship Denationalized. Indiana Journal of Global Legal Studies 7:447–509

Bosniak L (2010) Persons and Citizens in Constitutional Thought. International Journal of Constitutional Law 8:9–29

Brenninkmeijer A (2023) Een vertrouwde overheid. In: Allewijn D et al. (eds) Vertrouwen in de rechtsstaat. Bloemlezing uit het werk van Alex Brenninkmeijer. Wolters Kluwer, Deventer, pp. 151–159

Brinkgreve C (2015) Ruimte voor actief burgerschap. In: Wetenschappelijke Raad voor het Regeringsbeleid (ed) Koninkrijk der Nederlanden. Contouren van de derde eeuw. Amsterdam University Press, Amsterdam, pp. 39–49

Butenschøn N A (2003) Citizenship and Human Rights. Some Thoughts on a Complex Relationship. In: Bergsmo M (ed) Human Rights and Criminal Justice for the Downtrodden. Essays in Honor of Asbjørn Eide. Martinus Nijhoff Publishers, Leiden/Boston, pp. 555–571

De Hart B (2012) Een tweede paspoort. Dubbele nationaliteit in de Verenigde Staten, Duitsland en Nederland. Amsterdam University Press, Amsterdam

De Hart B (2024) Het intrekken van het Nederlanderschap van mensen met meervoudige nationaliteit: juridische, morele en praktische bezwaren. Montesquieu Instituut, https://www.montesquieu-instituut.nl/id/vmj4ja4ctcn7/nieuws/het_intrekken_van_het_nederlanderschap. Accessed 13 April 2025

De Waal T (2019) Tussen kwetsbaarheid en weerbaarheid. Over het belang van burgerschap. Nationaal Comité 4 en 5 mei, Amsterdam

Gardner J P (1997) Citizenship: The White Paper. Institute for Citizenship Studies/The British Institute of International Comparative Law, London

Goossens J (2024a) De terugkeer van het staatsrecht. Inaugural lecture Utrecht University. Boom, The Hague

Goossens J (2024b) Het opvullen van een lacune in de Grondwet. Naar een grondrecht op toegang en zinvol contact met het bestuur. In: Twaalf pleidooien voor modernisering van de Grondwet. Essaybundel op uitnodiging van het Ministerie van Binnenlandse Zaken en Koninkrijksrelaties. Ministerie van Binnenlandse Zaken en Koninkrijksrelaties, The Hague, pp. 85–119

Goossens J et al. (eds) (2022) Rechtsvorming in een hypercomplexe samenleving: Bundel n.a.v. de Staatsrechtconferentie 2022 (Tilburg University). Wolf Legal Publishers, Oisterwijk

Groenendijk C A et al. (2021) Lessen van 25 jaar inburgering in Nederland. Nederlands Juristenblad 33, pp. 2722–2732

Habermas J (2012) The Crisis of the European Union in the Light of a Constitutionalization of International Law. European Journal of International Law 23(2):335–348

Hirsch Ballin E M H (1998) The European Constitution of the Netherlands: Reflections on Interdependent Statehood. Acta Politica 33:281–299

Hirsch Ballin E M H (2014) Citizens' Rights and the Right to be a Citizen. Developments in International Law vol 66. Brill Nijhoff, Leiden/Boston

Hirsch Ballin E M H (2020) Artikel 3 Gelijke benoembaarheid. In: Hirsch Ballin E M H, Janse de Jonge E J, Leenknegt G (eds) Uitleg van de Grondwet (student edition). Boom Juridisch, The Hague, pp. 67–72

Hirsch Ballin E M H (2022) Waakzaam burgerschap: vertrouwen in democratie en rechtsstaat herwinnen. Querido Facto, Amsterdam

Hirsch Ballin E M H (2024) Zeventig jaar Statuut voor het Koninkrijk der Nederlanden (part I): de kracht van het Statuut. Blog nederlandrechtsstaat.nl, 11 December 2024 https://www.nederlandrechtsstaat.nl/zeventig-jaar-statuut-voor-het-koninkrijk-der-nederlanden-deel-i/. Accessed 8 January 2025

Honingh M et al. (2025) De mensen in het land. Wat burgerschap eigenlijk (nog) is. Nederlandse School voor Openbaar Bestuur, The Hague

I&O Research/NRC (2021) Vertrouwen in de overheid na drie grote kwesties. I&O Research, Amsterdam, https://www.ioresearch.nl/wp-content/uploads/2021/03/bwebpr21_mrt_nrc_betrouwbare-overheid_def.pdf. Accessed 13 April 2025

Iglesias Sánchez S (2017) A Citizenship Right to Stay? The Right Not to Move in a Union Based on Free Movement. In: Kochenov D (ed) EU Citizenship and Federalism. Cambridge University Press, Cambridge, pp. 371–393

Irving H (2016) Citizenship, Alienage and the Modern Constitutional State: A Gendered History. Cambridge University Press, Cambridge

Isin E F, Turner B S (2007) Investigating Citizenship: An Agenda for Citizenship Studies. Citizenship Studies 11(1):5–17

Jessurun d'Oliveira H U (2022) Intrekking van de Nederlandse nationaliteit. Ook de wetgever maakt zich schuldig aan institutioneel racisme. Blog NJB, https://www.njb.nl/blogs/intrekking-van-de-nederlandse-nationaliteit-ook-de-wetgever-maakt-zich-schuldig-aan-institutioneel-racisme/. Accessed 13 April 2025

Jessurun d'Oliveira H U (2023) Natiestaat en kolonialisme: een ongemakkelijk verbond. Ras en nationaliteit in de negentiende eeuw. Boom Juridisch, The Hague

Karapetian G (2024) Thorbecke en het hedendaagse staatsburgerschap. In: Fatah-Black K, Lauret L (eds) Koloniaal burgerschap: Geschiedenis en erfenis. Boom, Amsterdam, pp. 155–169

Kochenov D (2025) Op-Ed: Never Mind the Law, Again: Commission v. Malta (C-181/23), EU Law Live, April 2025, https://eulawlive.com/op-ed-never-mind-the-law-again-commission-v-malta-c-181-23/. Accessed: 18 May 2025

Kortmann C A J M et al. (2021) Constitutioneel recht, 8th edn. Wolters Kluwer, Deventer

Kortmann C N J (2024) Burgerplichten, voorzichtigheid geboden. Nederlands Tijdschrift voor Bestuursrecht 2024/92

Leenknegt G-J (2020) Artikel 4 Kiesrecht. In: Hirsch Ballin E M H, Janse de Jonge E J, Leenknegt G (eds) Uitleg van de Grondwet (student edition). Boom Juridisch, The Hague, pp. 73–84

Oomen B (2009) Constitutioneel bewustzijn in Nederland: Van burgerzin, burgerschap en de onzichtbare Grondwet. Recht der Werkelijkheid 30:55–79

Oomen B (2016) Strengthening Constitutional Identity Where There Is None: The Case of the Netherlands. Revue interdisciplinaire d'études juridiques 77:235–263

Parlementaire enquêtecommissie Fraudebeleid en Dienstverlening (2024) Blind voor mens en recht. Tweede Kamer der Staten-Generaal, The Hague

Parlementaire ondervragingscommissie Kinderopvangtoeslag (2020) Ongekend onrecht. Tweede Kamer der Staten-Generaal, The Hague

Petrescu O M (2013) The Political Citizenship in the Context of the Lisbon Treaty. Romanian Journal of European Affairs 13:44–56

Platon S (2015) The Delvigne Judgment and the European Franchise: Going Boldly… But Perhaps not Boldly Enough. Verfassungsblog.de, https://verfassungsblog.de/the-delvigne-judgment-of-the-cjeu-going-boldly-but-perhaps-not-boldly-enough/. Accessed 13 April 2025

Poptcheva E (2015) Disenfranchisement of EU Citizens Resident Abroad. Situation in National and European Elections in EU Member States. European Parliamentary Research Service. https://www.europarl.europa.eu/RegData/etudes/IDAN/2015/564379/EPRS_IDA(2015)564379_EN.pdf. Accessed 13 April 2025

Raad van State (2024) 70 jaar Statuut voor het Koninkrijk. Samenwerking op basis van wederzijds begrip. Raad van State, The Hague

Sassen S (2006) Territory, Authority, Rights: From Medieval to Global Assemblages. Princeton University Press, Princeton

Schuler M (2024) Paving the Way for an Enforcement of Democracy under Article 10 TEU? The Court's Judgments in Cases C-808/21 Commission v Czechia and C-814/21 Commission v Poland. European Law Blog, https://www.europeanlawblog.eu/pub/fsca541k/release/2. Accessed 7 March 2025

Seubert S (2024) The Conference on the Future of Europe as a Chance for Democratic Catching Up? Towards a Citizen-centred Perspective on Constitutional Renewal in the European Union. Global Constitutionalism 13:429–447

Shachar A (2009) The Birthright Lottery. Citizenship and Global Inequality. Harvard University Press, Cambridge MA

Shaw J (2007) The Transformation of Citizenship in the European Union. Cambridge University Press, Cambridge

Staatscommissie rechtsstaat (2024) De gebroken belofte van de rechtsstaat. Tien verbetervoorstellen met oog voor de burger. Staatscommissie rechtsstaat, The Hague

Tiemeijer W (2021) Verkenning: Project Nederland. Van feitelijke naar gewenste nationale identiteit. Wetenschappelijke Raad voor het Regeringsbeleid, The Hague

Tijdelijke commissie Uitvoeringsorganisaties (2021) Klem tussen balie en beleid. Tweede Kamer der Staten-Generaal, The Hague

Tindemans L (1976) Report by Mr Leo Tindemans to the European Council, Bulletin of the European Communities, Supplement 1/76. Publications Office of the European Union

Van den Brink M (2025) Why Bother with Legal Reasoning? The CJEU Judgment in Commission v Malta (Citizenship by Investment). Robert Schuman Centre, https://globalcit.eu/why-bother-with-legal-reasoning-the-cjeu-judgment-in-commission-v-malta-citizenship-by-investment/. Accessed: 18 May 2025

Van der Schyff G (2012) The Constitutional Relationship between the European Union and its Member States: The Role of National Identity in Article 4(2) TEU. European Law Review 37:563–584

Van Eijken H (2015) EU Citizenship and the Constitutionalisation of the European Union. Europa Law Publishing, Groningen

Van Eijken H (2020) Direct Democracy and the EU Citizens' Initiative: A Paper Tiger that Never Bites? In: Marguery T, Platon S, Van Eijken H (eds) Les élections européennes 40 ans après -

The European Elections, 40 Years After: Bilans, Enjeux et Perspectives - Assessment, Issues and Prospects. Larcier, Brussels, pp. 359–373
Van Eijken H (2024) Nationality for Sale: Different Fruits in One Basket? EU Law Live, https://eulawlive.com/op-ed-nationality-for-sale-different-fruits-in-one-basket/. Accessed 13 April 2025
Van Eijken (2025) We zijn een menigte: Duurzaam en samengesteld burgerschap in het huis van de gelaagde democratische rechtsstaat. Inaugural lecture Utrecht University, 3 April 2025 (forthcoming)
Van Eijken H, Phoa P S (2018) The Scope of Article 20 TFEU Clarified in Chavez-Vilchez: Are the Fundamental Rights of Minor EU Citizens Coming of Age? European Law Review 43:949–970
Van Eijken H, Van Rossem J W C (2016) Prisoner Disenfranchisement and the Right to Vote in Elections to the European Parliament: Universal Suffrage Key to Unlocking Political Citizenship? Court of Justice of the European Union Case C-650/13, Request for a Preliminary Ruling from the Tribunal d'instance de Bordeaux, Made by Decision of 7 November 2013, in the Proceedings in Thierry Delvigne v. Commune de Lesparre-Médoc and Préfet de la Gironde, 6 October 2015, ECLI:EU:C:2015:648. European Constitutional Law Review 12:114–132
Van Vugt E Y (2021) De Staten-Generaal vertegenwoordigen het geheele Nederlandsche volk. Een onderzoek naar de veranderingen in de betekenis van artikel 50 Grondwet tussen 1814 en 1983. Boom Juridisch, The Hague
Vlieks C (2022) Nationality and Statelessness in Europe. European Law on Preventing and Solving Statelessness. Dissertation Tilburg University. Intersentia, Cambridge/Antwerp
Vlieks C, Van Waas L (2022) Stateless Persons. In: Binder C et al. (eds) Elgar Encyclopedia of Human Rights. Edward Elgar, Cheltenham, pp. 327–332
Vroonhof P et al. (2024) Onderzoek juridische dilemma's meervoudige nationaliteiten: Eindrapportage. Panteia, Zoetermeer, https://panteia.nl/bestanden/rapport-onderzoek-juridische-dilemmas-bij-meervoudige-nationaliteiten-3-pdf. Accessed 9 February 2025
Weiler J H H (1998) European Citizenship, Identity and Differentiation. In: La Torre M (eds) European Citizenship: An Institutional Challenge. Kluwer Law International, The Hague, pp. 1–26.
Weis P (1979) Nationality and Statelessness in International Law, 2nd edn. Sijthoff & Noordhoff International Publishers, Alphen aan den Rijn/Germantown MD
Wetenschappelijke Raad voor het Regeringsbeleid (1992) Eigentijds burgerschap. WRR-publikatie vervaardigd onder leiding van H.R. van Gunsteren. Sdu uitgeverij, The Hague
Wetenschappelijke Raad voor het Regeringsbeleid (2017) Weten is nog geen doen: Een realistisch perspectief op redzaamheid. Wetenschappelijke Raad voor het Regeringsbeleid, The Hague
Zijlstra S E (2009) Burgerplichten en burgerlasten in het bestuursrecht. Nederlands Tijdschrift voor Bestuursrecht 2009/1, pp. 1–9
Zweers M (2025) Disrupting the Silent Legacy. Slavery and Criticality in the UU Law School. In: Milo J M et al. (eds) Sol Iustitiae Setting. The Utrecht Law School and its Relation to Slavery. Boom, The Hague, pp. 147–192

Hanneke van Eijken LL.M. Ph.D., is Professor Rule of Law and Democracy, affiliated to the Montaigne Centre for Rule of Law and Administration of Justice at Utrecht University, the Netherlands.

Caia Vlieks LL.M. Ph.D., is Associate Professor of Fundamental Rights, affiliated to the Montaigne Centre for Rule of Law and Administration of Justice at Utrecht University, the Netherlands.

Chapter 5
Constitutional Change: Constitutional Amendment Without a Constituent Power

E. Y. van Vugt

Contents

Abstract Many constitutions in the world derive their status as a fundamental law from the idea that they form the expression of the unfettered will of the sovereign people. Typical for the Dutch Constitution is that it does not. One of the defining aspects of the constitutional identity of the Netherlands is that notions of constituent power and popular sovereignty are not mentioned in the Constitution itself, nor do they form part of the constitutional discourse. This chapter argues that the absence of a constituent power has two major implications for understanding constitutional change in the Netherlands. Firstly, without a notion of a sovereign people that is exclusively capable of "making the concrete, comprehensive decision over the type and form of its own political existence", the power to amend the Dutch Constitution is ultimately unlimited. Secondly, constitutional amendment in the Netherlands is not predicated upon the conviction that fundamental changes to the Constitution should be made by the people themselves.

E. Y. van Vugt (✉)
Faculty of Law, Maastricht University, Maastricht, The Netherlands
e-mail: eva.vanvugt@maastrichtuniversity.nl

G. van der Schyff (ed.), *The Constitutional Identity of The Netherlands*,
https://doi.org/10.1007/978-94-6265-779-3_5

Keywords Constitutional amendment · Dutch Constitution · Constituent power · Constitutional identity · The Netherlands · Constitutional change

5.1 Constitutional Identity and Constituent Power

In his chapter on "Types of Constitutions" for the Oxford Handbook on Comparative Constitutional Law, Dieter Grimm states that there are various criteria according to which constitutions can be typified. The relevance of these criteria depends on the research interest of the constitutional scholar. For a scholar wishing to study constitutional identity, Grimm suggests to "distinguish constitutions according to the source of constituent power".[1] Constituent power refers to the power to create a constitution and is therefore to be distinguished from the constituted powers that are created and simultaneously constrained by the constitution.[2] Constituted powers derive their validity from the constitution, whilst the constitution derives its authority from the constituent power.[3] In contemporary constitutional theory, constituent power is attributed to the people,[4] giving it a clear democratic connotation.[5] According to this approach, a constitution derives its status as a fundamental law from the idea that a constitution is an expression of the unfettered will of the sovereign people.[6] This idea has become a basic tenet of modern constitutionalism and is reflected in numerous constitutional preambles across the globe.

One of the defining aspects of the constitutional identity of the Netherlands is that there is no articulation of a constituent power. The authority of the Constitution of the Netherlands has been presupposed from the very beginning. In 1814 it was deemed obvious that a new state could not be maintained without a basic law that would comprise the main rules for that state's organisation.[7] However, the idea that such a basic law would derive its authority from an unfettered sovereign—regardless of whether that sovereign was the monarch or the people—was considered dangerous and therefore dismissed.[8] Consequently, the Constitution has never mentioned anything about a constituent power or sovereign people from which this document derives its authority.[9] Therefore, it is the general consensus among

[1] Grimm 2012, pp. 98–99.

[2] Verdugo 2023, p. 15.

[3] Böckenförde 2017.

[4] Verdugo 2023, p. 23; Doyle 2019, p. 162ff; Kumm 2016, p. 697; Loughlin 2014, p. 218.

[5] Negri 1999, p. 1. See also Kalyvas 2005, p. 237 and Colón Ríos 2012, p. 102.

[6] Corrias, interestingly, characterises this attribution of constituent power to the people as "populist". See Corrias 2016, p. 10. See also Roznai 2017, p. 106.

[7] Van der Tang 1998, p. 194ff.

[8] Van Rossem 2014, p. 108ff.

[9] Te Velde 2019, pp. 164–165.

constitutional scholars in the Netherlands that constituent power is a redundant concept.[10]

In this chapter, it will be argued that the absence of a constituent power has two major implications for understanding constitutional change in the Netherlands. Firstly, without a notion of a sovereign people that is exclusively capable of "making the concrete, comprehensive decision over the type and form of its own political existence",[11] the power to amend the Dutch Constitution is ultimately unlimited. Secondly, constitutional amendment in the Netherlands is not predicated upon the idea that fundamental changes to the Constitution should be made by the people themselves and not by their representatives.[12] Even though the Constitution requires intervening elections for the Lower House between the first and the second reading of the amendment procedure, these elections cannot be conceived of as an extraordinary moment that facilitates the re-emergence of the sovereign people to decide on constitutional change. Ultimately, it is the legislature that decides on the content of the Constitution.

5.2 Constituent Power in the Netherlands

5.2.1 The Revolutionary Roots of Constituent Power

The "predominant account" of constituent power that ascribes this power to a sovereign people originates from the French Revolution.[13] When the absolute monarchy was overturned and sovereignty transferred to the people, Emmanuel-Joseph Sieyès justified this transfer of sovereignty by claiming that "all the parts of a government are answerable to" and ultimately "dependent upon the nation". Since the will of the nation exists prior to any constitution, the nation cannot be "bound by the formalities of the constitution to which it had subjected those it had mandated".[14]

The Batavian Revolution in the Netherlands (1794–1799) was heavily influenced by the French Revolution. In the Republic of the United Netherlands (1581–1795), sovereignty had resided with the administrative assemblies of each of the provinces. The Republic, however, retained a monarchical element in the office of the stadtholder, whose office was only filled in by members of the House of Orange.[15]

---

[10] Kortmann 2003; Hoogers 2007; Van Rossem 2014, p. 111. Loughlin calls this the "normativist" perspective on constituent power, see Loughlin 2014, pp. 219, 221–223.

[11] Schmitt 2008, p. 125.

[12] Van der Tang 1998, pp. 162–168.

[13] See Verdugo 2023, p. 23 for this predominant account. Cf. Rubinelli 2020, pp. 33–74, who argues that Sieyès conceptualised constituent power as an alternative for popular and national sovereignty, because both notions of sovereignty attributed an unfettered and absolute will to the people or representatives of the nation in Parliament.

[14] Sièyes 2014, pp. 136–137.

[15] Lesaffer 2009, pp. 336–337.

The growing discontent with the authoritarian regime of stadtholder William V of Orange led to a democratic revolt.[16] This resulted in the proclamation of the Batavian Republic and the adoption of the first ever master-text constitution in the Netherlands: the *Bataafsche Staatsregeling* of 1798.[17] The *Staatsregeling* was a typical revolutionary constitution. A sovereign people had created it and the government was subjected to it: the Batavian people, holders of the "Supreme power",[18] commanded "the faithful maintenance" of the Constitution by the constituted powers ("the representative body, the executive government, the judiciary, as well as other administrative bodies").[19]

The democratic experiment of the Batavian people was short-lived. Already in 1801, the Batavian Republic was replaced by a more authoritarian form of government. In 1806, Napoleon installed his brother on the throne in the "Kingdom of Holland", which was incorporated in the French Empire in 1810.[20] When Napoleon suffered a defeat in the Battle of Leipzig in 1813 against the allied powers, he withdrew his troops.[21] The Netherlands regained its independence and adopted a new Constitution in 1814, which is still in force today.[22]

5.2.2 The Counterrevolutionary Constitution of 1814

Unlike previous constitutions in the Netherlands,[23] which all came into effect upon the approval by either the sovereign people in a plebiscite or an organ representing that sovereign people,[24] the Dutch Constitution is not based on the doctrine of popular sovereignty at all. The Constitution did not refer to the people as the sovereign at the time and has never done so.[25] The Constitution was drafted by a committee that

---

[16] Leeb 1973.

[17] Palmer 2014, pp. 505–529.

[18] Article 6: "The Supreme power resides in the collective members of society, called citizens." All translations in this chapter are my own, unless indicated otherwise.

[19] Proclamation to the *Staatsregeling*.

[20] Lesaffer 2009, p. 414.

[21] Joor 2015, pp. 53–66.

[22] Disagreement exists on whether the 1814 Constitution is actually the original version of the present Constitution. In 1815, the 1814 Constitution needed to be amended in order to reflect the unification with Belgium. This amendment could, however, not be legitimately passed in accordance with the formal amendment rules at the time, as that would only involve the institutions of the Netherlands without any representation of the Belgians. The changes to the 1814 Constitution therefore did not take place in accordance with the formal amendment procedure, meaning that the 1815 Constitution was formally a "new" Constitution. See e.g. Eftymiou 2019. Others, however, argue that the 1815 Constitution was, materially speaking, a continuation of the 1814 Constitution, which in that sense was the original one. See Besselink 2023.

[23] That is to say the master-text constitutions of 1798, 1801, 1805, 1806 and 1810.

[24] The plebiscites took place on respectively 23 April 1798, 1 October 1801 and 16 April 1805; Hoogers 2007, pp. 100–101.

[25] Te Velde 2019, pp. 164–165.

associated democracy and popular sovereignty with revolution, violence, instability and foreign occupation. In the committee's view, the Netherlands was in dire need of unity, stability and autonomy. Therefore, the idea of popular sovereignty was to be completely set aside.[26] The members of Parliament would not be elected by the people but appointed by administrative assemblies of the provinces. These assemblies were in turn composed of representatives of the nobility, the urban bourgeoisie and land-owning farmers. William-Frederik ("Prince") of Orange, son of former stadtholder William V, became the head of state: article 1 of the 1814 Constitution attributed the sovereignty over the Netherlands to him and his descendants.

The "reinstalment"[27] of the Prince of Orange in the Netherlands had been encouraged by Britain, Russia, Austria and Prussia. When these allied powers had defeated Napoleon, they convened at Vienna to debate a new European order. The Congress of Vienna resulted, inter alia, in the drawing of a new territorial map of Europe and a restoration of monarchical power structures. In France, the Bourbon monarchs were restored to the throne.[28] King Louis XVIII granted the people of France a new master-text constitution by royal prerogative. The preamble to this constitution reads that:

> We [i.e. King Louis XVIII] have voluntarily, and by the free exercise of our royal authority, accorded and do accord, grant and concede to our subjects, as well for us as for our successors forever, the constitutional charter which follows: (…).[29]

A constitution conceded by a monarch to his subjects is a so-called chartered constitution (or *constitution octroyée*).[30] This type of constitution reckoned with the revolutionary principle of the constituent power of the sovereign people. Since the monarch was the constituent power, that had granted his subjects a constitution from the fullness of his power, he could also unilaterally decide to revoke the constitution or replace it with another. For the same reason, the chartered constitution lacked any rules for amendment: as the constituent power the monarch would be completely free to unilaterally change the legal relationships that he had established with his subjects by granting them a constitution.[31]

Like the French Charter of 1814, the 1814 Constitution of the Netherlands was counterrevolutionary in nature.[32] It was, however, not chartered. The Prince of Orange did not unilaterally accord, grant and concede a Constitution to the people of the

---

[26] According to Van Hogendorp, chair of the constitutional committee, see Colenbrander 1908, p. 81.

[27] See also De Haan 2020.

[28] Lesaffer 2009, pp. 415–417.

[29] The French text is: "NOUS AVONS volontairement, et par le libre exercice de notre autorité royale, ACCORDÉ ET ACCORDONS. FAIT CONCESSION ET OCTROI à nos sujets, tant pour nous que pour nos successeurs, et à toujours, de la Charte constitutionnelle qui suit: (…)", see https://www.conseil-constitutionnel.fr/les-constitutions-dans-l-histoire/charte-constitutionnelle-du-4-juin-1814. Translations are my own.

[30] Prusch 2013.

[31] Tang 1998, p. 176.

[32] Ibid., pp. 176, 181.

Netherlands. Instead, the 1814 Constitution was adopted by a Grand Assembly of 600 notable members of society representing the Netherlands. Consistent with the counterrevolutionary spirit of the 1814 Constitution, the Grand Assembly was not a constituent assembly in the democratic sense. It did not adopt the Constitution "in name and by power of the nation",[33] could not propose any changes to the Constitution, and its members were not elected by the people. In fact, the Prince of Orange had compiled the list of members of the Grand Assembly in close consultation with the committee that had drafted the Constitution.[34]

The Constitution of the Netherlands was thus not unilaterally imposed by the monarch on the nation. It rather qualifies as a pact between the two.[35] Consequently, the constituent power resides with neither of them. In fact, the Grand Assembly adopted the Constitution the day before William of Orange was officially proclaimed the Sovereign Prince of the Netherlands. At the ceremony that preceded his inauguration, William had to take an oath to respect and uphold the Constitution. The Sovereign Prince thus derived his power from the 1814 Constitution, and not the other way around. This again confirms that he was not the constituent power but one of the constituted powers.[36] As a constituted power, the Sovereign Prince was bound by the Constitution. This was also evidenced by the fact that the "Sovereign" was not free to change the 1814 Constitution at will. Instead, the Constitution stipulated the formal rules for its own amendment.[37]

5.3 Formal Constitutional Change in the Netherlands

5.3.1 The Formal Amendment Rules in the 1814 Constitution

Since the very beginning, the formal amendment procedure has comprised two stages ("readings"). According to article 142 of the 1814 Constitution, an Act of Parliament had to declare the necessity for a change to the Constitution and specify the nature of the proposed change. After Parliament and the Sovereign Prince approved of this Act of Parliament, it was sent to the provinces. Article 143 stipulated that the provinces then had to appoint an equal number of extraordinary members to Parliament in the same manner as they had appointed the ordinary members. According to article 144, Parliament (now composed of double the number of members) had to reconsider the proposed amendment in the same manner as in the first round, "with the sole exception that a majority of votes amounting to at least two-thirds of the present members was

[33] The constitutional committee voted against the proposition of one of its members to do so. See Hoogers 2007, p. 102; Colenbrander 1927, pp. 82–88; Hoogers 2004, p. 69ff.

[34] Van Rossem 2014, pp. 109–110.

[35] Cf. Van der Tang 1998, pp. 180–182.

[36] A couple of years later he would argue the opposite as a justification for his expansion of powers. About this notion of "prealable sovereignty", see Van Velzen 2005, pp. 151–173, 213, 248–250.

[37] Van Rossem 2014, pp. 109–110.

required". If this qualified majority was obtained, and the Sovereign Prince approved the proposed change to the Constitution, the Constitution was successfully amended.

The formal amendment rules aimed at making constitutional change "neither too easy nor too difficult".[38] Again, this is best understood against the historical background of 1814. To prevent future revolutions, the idea was that change ought to be possible without having to completely overturn the existing constitutional framework. Now that a new state was established, continuity was important. Change was therefore possible, but the amendment procedure contained hurdles to make constitutional change more onerous than changes to other laws and regulations. After all, the idea was that the Constitution should guarantee a unified, stable and enduring constitutional order.

5.3.2 The Current Procedure for Amending the Dutch Constitution

The current rules for amending the Dutch Constitution are found in article 137. The procedure still comprises two readings, a change to the composition of Parliament in between these readings, and the requirement of a qualified majority in second reading. Paragraph 1 concerns the first reading of the constitutional amendment procedure and reads as follows:

> An Act of Parliament shall be passed stating that an amendment to the Constitution in the form proposed shall be considered.[39]

The first reading of a proposed amendment to the Constitution essentially takes place in the same way as a normal legislative procedure, in the sense that Government and Parliament have to adopt an Act of Parliament that proposes a certain change to the Constitution. In doing so, the legislature basically instructs itself to consider an amendment to the Constitution.[40] As with all Acts of Parliament, the Act shall be approved by a simple majority in both Houses of Parliament and then ratified by Government.[41] Once this "Consideration Act" is published, the first reading is completed and the second reading can start. Paragraph 3 sets out the rules for the second reading:

> The Lower House elected after the Act of Parliament referred to in the first paragraph has been published shall consider, at second reading, the proposed amendment of the Constitution

[38] Minutes of the meeting of the Constitutional Committee on 27 December 1813, No. 47, p. 76: "Achtste Hoofdstuk. *Van bijvoegselen en veranderingen. Dezelve noch te gemakkelijk, noch te moeijelijk te maken.*" [Eight Chapter. Of amendments and changes. To render these neither too easy nor too difficult.]

[39] Taken from the Ministry of the Interior and Kingdom Relations' 2023 translation of the Constitution.

[40] Oud 1970, pp. 34–35.

[41] Arts. 81–88 of the Dutch Constitution.

> as referred to in the first paragraph. If this Lower House does not decide on the proposed amendment, it will fall by operation of law. As soon as this Lower House has passed the proposed amendment, the Upper House shall consider it at second reading. The proposed amendment shall be passed by both Houses only if at least two-thirds of the votes cast are in favour.[42]

After completion of the first reading, both Houses of Parliament have to consider the actual change to the Constitution, again proposed in the form of an Act of Parliament. The second reading may only commence after elections have been held for the Lower House. The newly elected Lower House has to put the amendment proposal up for a vote. If it fails to decide on the proposal before the end of its term, it ceases to exist *ipso iure*. In that case, the proposed amendment cannot be considered at second reading by a subsequently elected Lower House. If the Lower House passes the amendment proposal by two-thirds of the votes cast, the Bill is submitted to the Upper House for consideration. If the Upper House passes the Bill with two-thirds of the votes cast as well, the amendment is adopted. Articles 139 of the Constitution stipulates that the amendment will enter into force upon ratification by the Government.

5.3.3 Amendments to the Constitutional Amendment Procedure

Although the contours have remained roughly the same, there have also been some significant changes to the formal amendment procedure. Already in 1815, the unicameral system of Parliament was replaced with a bicameral system. The fact that not one but two Houses of Parliament had to consider an amendment proposal heightened the barrier for constitutional change.

Another change to the composition of Parliament that has had significant implications for the formal amendment procedure took place in 1848. The comprehensive constitutional reform of that year resulted, *inter alia*, in direct elections for the Lower House and indirect elections for the Upper House. According to the 1848 Constitution, the members of the Lower House were elected for four years, but not all at the same time. Elections would take place every two years, for half of the seats. The members of the Upper House, in turn, were elected for nine years and elections would take place every three years for one-third of the seats. In this rotation system, general elections would never result in the renewal of the mandate of the full Lower and Upper House.

This change had important consequences for the constitutional amendment procedure.[43] In order to guarantee that a completely new Parliament would consider an

[42] Based on the Ministry of the Interior and Kingdom Relations' 2023 translation of the Constitution, although that translation uses the term "Bill" instead of "proposed amendment", which term I believe reflects the original wording better.

[43] Van Gennip 2021, pp. 21–32.

amendment proposal in second reading, the 1848 Constitution prescribed the dissolution of both Houses after the adoption of an amendment proposal in first reading. In 1884 and 1887, both Houses were dissolved immediately after the publication of an Act of Parliament that instructed the legislature to consider an amendment to the Constitution.[44]

In 1887, the Constitution was amended so that all the members of the Lower House would be simultaneously elected.[45] Since general elections would now result in the renewal of the mandate of its members all at once, a separate dissolution of the entire Lower House immediately after completion of the first reading was no longer necessary.[46] From that moment on, the dissolution of the Lower House in between the first and second reading of the formal amendment procedure was delayed, so it would coincide with the dissolution that had to take place after general elections anyway. As a specific prerequisite for constitutional amendment, dissolution had become a mere formality. Therefore, it was erased from the formal amendment procedure in 2022. Article 137, paragraph 3, of the Dutch Constitution no longer requires the dissolution of the Lower House. It merely states that an amendment proposal can only be considered at second reading by the Lower House that is elected after the publication of the Act of Parliament that instructs the legislature to consider an amendment to the Constitution.

The constitutional reform in 2022 also introduced a discontinuity mechanism (*valbijl*) for the second reading. If the Lower House that assembles after elections does not vote on an amendment proposal at second reading, the proposal lapses by operation of law meaning that it is not carried over to the next Lower House. This amendment to the formal amendment procedure was prompted by an incident that occurred in practice. In 2009, a proposal to amend Article 120 of the Dutch Constitution was adopted at first reading. The elections that took place in 2010, however, did not result in the qualified majority that was needed to pass the amendment proposal in the Lower House at second reading. Instead of putting the amendment up to a vote, the initiator wanted to wait until after the next elections. However, the elections in 2012 did not result in a qualified majority either. When the Lower House was re-elected in 2017, i.e. the third time since the completion of the first reading, it wondered whether it could still consider the amendment proposal. The text of the Constitution was unclear on whether the Lower House that was elected directly after completion of the first reading was exclusively competent to consider an amendment proposal at second reading. In the end, the Lower House declared that the amendment proposal had lapsed. The change of procedure in 2022 was motivated by the desire to avoid this situation in the future.[47]

---

[44] Ibid., pp. 56–57.

[45] Ibid., p. 54.

[46] Van Vugt and Van Gennip 2023, p. 257.

[47] Van Gennip 2019, pp. 1404–1406; Breunese 2019, p. 1675; Van Vugt and Van Gennip 2023, pp. 249–253.

5.4 Consequences of the Absence of a Constituent Power for Constitutional Amendment

5.4.1 Limits to the Amendment Power

As mentioned earlier, the first person to invoke the distinction between constituent power and constituted power was Sieyès. Through the creation of a constitution, the nation entrusts state institutions with power. According to Sieyès, it is not up to these state institutions to "alter the limits of the power with which it has been entrusted" by the constituent power.[48] When exercising power, state institutions are bound by the conditions laid down by the nation in the constitution, which state institutions consequently cannot change to their own accord.[49] By this logic, the bodies empowered by the sovereign people to amend the constitution would exceed their constituted amendment power if they were to abolish or extend the limits imposed on this power by the constituent power. The argument even goes that these bodies would be completely released from their obligations under the constitution, if their power to amend that constitution would extend to all parts of the constitution, including those provisions that regulate the amendment power.[50]

Carl Schmitt—"the famous professor of constitutional and international law who later became a Nazi"[51]—also invoked the distinction between the constituent and constituted powers in order to claim that constitutional amendment has inherent limits. As the basis of all other powers, only the constituent power itself was able to decide on fundamental questions relating to the "type and form of its own political existence".[52] According to Schmitt, these fundamental questions (e.g. the form of government, the separation of powers, fundamental rights) formed the essential norms of a state's constitution. These essential norms had to be distinguished from other provisions in the written constitution. As not all of these provisions regulate fundamental political matters, the written constitution should not be conflated with the fundamental decisions made by the exercise of constituent power.[53] Schmitt argued that the power to amend the constitution was a power to change these written provisions, "but only on the condition that the identity and continuity of the constitution as a whole are preserved".[54] In other words, the amendment power did not extend to the essential norms of the constitution, since these could only be altered by the constituent power.[55]

---

[48] Sieyès 2014, p. 136.

[49] Grimm 2016, p. 12.

[50] Hoogers 2007, referring to the dissertation by Möller 2004.

[51] Arendt 1955, p. 34.

[52] Schmitt 2008, pp. 125–126. See also Polzin 2016, p. 419ff.

[53] Loughlin 2014, pp. 224–225.

[54] Schmitt 2008, p. 150.

[55] Polzin 2021, p. 47.

Schmitt's account of constituent power has received considerable criticism.[56] The notion of inherent limits to constitutional amendment has nevertheless gained much traction among constitutional scholars. Böckenförde stated, for example, that the distinction between the constituted powers, "including the law-giving and constitution-altering power", and "the constituent power and the sovereignty of the people embodied by it" denies the former "access to the core and the totality of the constitution".[57] As such, the question of constituent power helps to separate:

> the normal change of the constitution by the constitution-altering legislator provided for in the constitution itself from a fundamental reshaping that touches on the core substance of the constitution, or eliminates the constitution, something that is no longer reserved to the constitution-changing legislator, but only to the creator of the constitution himself.[58]

This reasoning forms the core of the "unconstitutional constitutional amendment" doctrine.[59] This doctrine entails that if "every constitution is based upon a set of core principles which cannot be changed and that can be regarded as intrinsic to its specific identity",[60] amendments to the constitution that violate these principles should be deemed unconstitutional. The doctrine of unconstitutional constitutional amendment is not merely theoretical. Many jurisdictions acknowledge that there are substantive limits to constitutional amendment. These substantive limits may exist explicitly or implicitly. For example, article 79(3) of Germany's Basic Law stipulates that "amendments to this Basic Law affecting the division of the Federation into *Länder*, their participation in principle in the legislative process, or the principles laid down in Articles 1 and 20 shall be inadmissible".[61] Moreover, article 89 of the French Constitution states that "the republican form of government shall not be the object of any amendment". Another example is article 121 of the Norwegian Constitution, which stipulates that an amendment must never "contradict the principles embodied in this Constitution, but solely relate to modifications of particular provisions which do not alter the spirit of the Constitution". According to Grimm, these clauses clearly reflect the distinction between the constituent power of the sovereign people to make the fundamental decisions on their state's constitution and the constituted power of state institutions to amend the written constitution.[62]

In addition to these so-called eternity clauses, courts have accepted implicit substantive limits. The Indian Supreme Court, for instance, developed the so-called "basic structure doctrine", entailing that "the power to amend the constitution does not include the power to alter the basic structure, or framework of the constitution

[56] Verdugo 2023, pp. 25–26; Rubinelli 2020; Polzin 2016, p. 421; Dyzenhaus 2008; Doyle 2017, pp. 73, 77–80.

[57] Böckenförde 2017, pp. 176–177.

[58] Böckenförde 2017, p. 170.

[59] Roznai 2017.

[60] Fusaro and Oliver 2011, pp. 405, 428.

[61] Arts. 1 and 20 of the Basic Law give expression to fundamental constitutional principles, such as human dignity, the rule of law, the democratic and social nature of the state and popular sovereignty.

[62] Grimm 2015, p. 73.

so as to change its identity".[63] The basic structure doctrine clearly reflects French and German political thought on constituent power and has been adopted by courts in other countries as well.[64]

The unconstitutional constitutional amendment doctrine is alien to the Dutch constitutional tradition. The Constitution of the Netherlands grants the legislature full discretion to amend the Constitution. It does not declare any constitutional provision unamendable, nor does it state that amendments may not affect certain principles or the basic structure of the Constitution. Courts have never declared a constitutional amendment unconstitutional either. Article 120 of the Constitution namely states that the constitutionality of Acts of Parliament shall not be reviewed by courts. This ban on the constitutional review of Acts of Parliament by courts expresses that it is not up to the judiciary to assess whether or not an Act of Parliament is compatible with the provisions in the Constitution, and therefore as to how these provisions ought to be interpreted and applied, but up to the legislature itself. This implies that the legislature has the primary responsibility in ensuring that constitutional amendments are in line with the Constitution's overall objective of safeguarding democracy, the rule of law and fundamental rights, as expressed in a recently adopted general provision ("Article Zero") that precedes article 1 onwards.[65]

The Dutch legislature can thus change the Constitution as it pleases, as long as it follows the rules for formal amendment in article 137 of the Constitution. The legislature can even change these formal amendment rules, which has also happened several times. As demonstrated above, these changes were either necessitated by other amendments to the Constitution or intended to clarify the procedure. If the legislature would want to revise the formal amendment procedure more drastically, however, the Dutch Constitution would allow it to do so. Take the hypothetical example of a proposal to remove the hurdles that make the constitutional amendment procedure more difficult than the ordinary legislative procedure. If this proposal were to be i) adopted in first reading with a simple majority of votes in both Houses of Parliament; ii) adopted with a qualified majority of votes in a newly elected Lower House and in the Upper House; and iii) ratified by Government, that proposal would simply become law. The legislature could not be stopped on the ground that it cannot alter the limits of the power with which it has been entrusted by the constituent power,[66] despite the manifest undesirability of this change, which would affect the supremacy of the Constitution over ordinary Acts of Parliament.

The fact that the legislature would still have to follow the onerous amendment procedure of article 137 of the Constitution could be regarded as an adequate safeguard against radical or harmful changes. After all, the procedure facilitates debate over a longer period of time on the desirability of a constitutional amendment and requires that a proposal to amend the Constitution enjoys broad and sustained support.

---

[63] *Kesavananda Bharati v. State of Kerala* AIR 1973 SC 1461, 1480, Indian Kanoon—<http://indiankanoon.org/doc/257876/>.

[64] Polzin 2021, pp. 45–61; Roznai 2013; Yap 2015.

[65] See more elaborately Van Vugt 2024, p. 33.

[66] Hoogers 2007.

Constitutional amendment is thus a cumbersome process, especially considering the political context.[67] Ever since the electoral system changed into a system of proportional representation in 1917, not one political party has managed to single-handedly obtain a majority of the seats in the House. Instead, majorities have to be formed by at least two (and more recently even four) parties. Since different parties have diverging and often even clashing ideals and interests, the threshold of a two-third majority is seldom achieved.[68]

The onerous amendment procedure does not change the fact, however, that it is primarily upon the legislature to ensure that constitutional amendments are adopted in conformity with the Constitution. In fact, the Supreme Court of the Netherlands has ruled that article 120 of the Dutch Constitution not only prohibits courts from reviewing whether an Act of Parliament is consistent with the Constitution in terms of substance, but also from reviewing whether an Act of Parliament has been adopted in accordance with the procedure as prescribed by the Constitution.[69] This implies that in the hypothetical case that both Houses adopt an Act of Parliament that proposes an amendment to the Constitution in second reading by a *simple* instead of a *qualified* majority of votes, and Government subsequently ratifies that same Act of Parliament, the court could not declare the amendment to be incompatible with article 137 Constitution, but would have to respect this decision from the legislature.

5.4.2 Intervening Elections: The Return of the Sovereign?

The idea of constituent power is that it manifests itself in the act of constitution-making. Once the constitution is enacted, only the constituted powers can act. Meanwhile, the constituent power remains “latent”,[70] according to Grimm. In his view, the creation of the constitutional state has made the sovereign invisible. A constitutional state is characterised by the lack of a supreme power *within* the state: the powers within the state are all constituted and therefore bound by the constitution. Consequently, the bearer of the constituent power—the sovereign people—is located outside the constitutional order, only to re-emerge in the act of constitution-making. Grimm rejects the idea that the people would express themselves as sovereign when voting in elections and referendums. Since these procedures are regulated by the constitution, the people exercise constituted powers in this capacity and not constituent power.[71]

Sieyès on the contrary, stated that once the sovereign people has exercised its power to create a constitution, it does not lose “the right to change it as soon as

[67] Adams and Van der Schyff 2017, p. 369.

[68] Van Vugt 2024, p. 40.

[69] Supreme Court, 27 January 1961, NJ 1963/248, (*Prof. Van den Bergh/Staat der Nederlanden*).

[70] Grimm 2015, p. 71.

[71] Ibid., pp. 72–74.

its interest requires".[72] Schmitt similarly stated that constituent power cannot be "expended and eliminated, because it is exercised once". Instead, constituent power continues to exist "alongside and above the constitution".[73] In other words, since constituent power cannot be contained by a constitution, it can be exercised at any time after a constitution entered into force.[74] Böckenförde argued as well that if the constitution derives its claim to validity from the constituent power of the people, the people "cannot be juristically dismissed into nothingness once it has done so; it is and continues to exist as this factor and power".[75] Therefore, the constituent power of the will of people must be kept "connected as much as possible to its manifestation and decision [i.e. the constitution], but without eliminating it as a political factor and power".[76] This could be achieved through establishing democratic procedures that could capture and channel the sovereign will of the people into political decision-making, especially when that will is manifested "in connection with a fundamental revision of the constitution".[77] In this regard, the constituent power would also comprise the power to "fundamentally amend" or "remake" the constitution.[78]

Several scholars indeed believe that popular sovereignty requires the participation of the people in processes of constitutional change. Schwartzberg stated that "the ability to engage in constitutional change is a fundamental act of popular sovereignty".[79] Colón-Rios moreover argued that democracy requires that constitutions "provide an opening" or "an outlet for constituent power to manifest when important constitutional transformations are needed".[80] Seen from this perspective, formal amendment procedures that include democratic mechanisms such as intervening elections or a referendum could allow the sovereign people to "re-emerge"[81] in order to authorise the changes put forward by their representatives, thereby ensuring that the constitution remains to be an expression of the will of the people.

Intervening elections form part of the formal amendment procedure in the Netherlands. Article 137 stipulates that the Lower House can only consider an amendment proposal at second reading after elections. However, these elections cannot be regarded as a moment in which the sovereign people reassert themselves to decide on the proposed amendment. As explained above, the Constitution of the Netherlands is not drafted by or in the name of the sovereign people of the Netherlands. The notion of popular sovereignty was, in fact, utterly dismissed in 1814. At the time, democracy was deemed a threat to the stability of the state. Drafting, adopting and amending a

---

[72] Sieyès 2014, p. 127.
[73] Schmitt 2008, p. 125.
[74] Colón-Rios 2010, pp. 208–209.
[75] Böckenförde 2017, p. 175.
[76] Ibid., p. 176.
[77] Böckenförde 2017, pp. 176–178.
[78] Duke 2023; Loughlin 2014, p. 219.
[79] Schwarz 2009, p. 6.
[80] Colón-Rios 2010, pp. 201, 214.
[81] Roznai 2018, p. 310.

constitution was a matter for "the wealthy and propertied few".[82] According to the 1814 Constitution, the provincial elites appointed the members of Parliament and, in case of a formal amendment procedure, a same number of extraordinary members of Parliament that were needed to consider an amendment proposal in second reading.

The constitutional reform of 1848 resulted in the introduction of direct elections for the Lower House and indirect elections for the Upper House. Although this change constituted an important first step in the democratisation of the parliamentary system, the introduction of elections was not motivated by the "revolutionary" desire to give power back to the people. If anything, the politicians that had pushed for the constitutional reform were still very wary of democracy.[83] Suffrage was therefore only granted to the small portion of men that could pay a certain amount of taxes. The idea was that since the majority of the population were struggling for a living, they were too fixated on their own interests. The wealthy few, on the other hand, would understand and value the general importance of peace, stability and prosperity. Therefore, they could be entrusted with the weighty responsibility to choose the men they deemed capable of rising above particular interests and promoting the common good.[84]

The compulsory dissolution of both Houses of Parliament after the adoption of a proposal to amend the Constitution in first reading was, in other words, not introduced in 1848 with the purpose of consulting the sovereign people on the matter. According to the explanatory memorandum, "an amendment to the Constitution should be regarded of such importance, that such an amendment is examined and considered by men who are not as much attached to [decisions made in] the past, but who by casting a new light will only take part in the promotion of the good".[85] The objective of dissolution after the first reading was thus to ensure that a change to the Constitution would not result from the transient whims of a contingent majority, but would be endorsed by a Parliament that did not have any stakes in the amendment proposal itself. As such, intervening elections aimed to guarantee that changes to the Constitution were only adopted if an independent Parliament regarded them as sensible and necessary.

Despite the democratisation of the system of representative government resulting from the gradual expansion of general suffrage and the introduction of proportional representation, intervening elections still do not serve as a plebiscite on pending constitutional amendments. They are first and foremost general elections for the Lower House, which over the course of four years must make all kinds of decisions for the common good of society. In theory, citizens might base their vote during these general elections on the specific stance that a party has taken on a constitutional amendment proposal.[86] However, that mere possibility is insufficient to characterise

[82] Van der Tang 1998, p. 193.

[83] Te Velde 2019, p. 165.

[84] Van Vugt 2021, pp. 86, 116, 165, 310.

[85] *Kamerstukken* II, 1847–1848, XLIX, No. 23, p. 356.

[86] Amendment proposals do not usually play a role in electoral campaigns in the Netherlands, though. See Broeksteeg 2008, p. 330.

the intervening elections for the Lower House as a plebiscite on a pending constitutional amendment, let alone to conceive of these elections as an opportunity for the sovereign people to re-emerge as the constituent power that has the final say on changes to the constitution. After all, once elected the members of the Lower House are not bound by any instructions from their voters but have a free mandate to make their own considerations and decisions regarding all kinds of proposals,[87] including those to amend the Constitution. The fact that the Constitution requires that these elections take place before the Lower House can consider an amendment proposal at second reading is merely to ensure that the support for an amendment is sustained and does not vanish the moment the political composition of the Lower House changes.[88]

5.5 The Dutch Constitution: A Political Affair

Many constitutions in the world derive their status as a fundamental law from the idea that they form the expression of the unfettered will of the sovereign people. Typical for the Dutch Constitution is that it does not. The notions of constituent power and popular sovereignty are not mentioned in the Constitution itself, nor do they form part of the constitutional discourse. What does that tell us about the constitutional identity of the Netherlands?

The Dutch Constitution derives its authority from the pragmatic conviction that any state needs a basic law that comprises the main rules for its organisation. The idea that such a law would have to derive its authority from an unfettered sovereign was considered dangerous in 1814 and therefore dismissed. The pragmatic attitude of the Constitutional Committee resulted in the adoption of a procedural constitution: it mainly sketches the institutional and legal framework for government but barely articulates any substantive values or foundational principles. Instead, it leaves it up to the state powers to give meaning and further effect to constitutional norms. The primary responsibility for the interpretation, implementation and development of the Dutch Constitution lies with the legislature. This is not only reflected in article 120 of the Constitution, which prohibits courts from reviewing the constitutionality of Acts of Parliament, but also in the rules for constitutional amendment.

This chapter has shown that constitutional amendment is an institutional matter. Not the sovereign people but the legislature, formed by Government and both Houses of Parliament, decides on the content of the Constitution. Because the legislature does not derive its amendment power from the sovereign people, the amendment power is not bound to any restrictions. The Constitution does not declare any part of the Constitution unamendable, meaning that the legislature can change practically anything in the Constitution, as long as it follows the procedure that is stipulated in article 137. This procedure comprises hurdles such as intervening elections and

[87] Article 67(3) of the Dutch Constitution.

[88] *Kamerstukken* II 2017/18, 32 334 No. 11, p. 5; Van Vugt and Van Gennip 2023, pp. 252, 258–261.

a qualified majority to ensure that the Constitution is not changed unless it enjoys broad and sustained support within the legislature. The legislature, however, can also amend article 137. Moreover, article 120 prohibits courts from reviewing whether an Act of Parliament that seeks to amend the Constitution is adopted in accordance with the procedure that is set out in article 137. The Constitution thus reflects a great deal of trust in the wisdom and constitutional ethos of the legislature to bring about constitutional change.

References

Adams M, Van der Schyff G (2017) Constitutional Culture in the Netherlands: A Sober Affair. In: Adams M, Meuwese A, Hirsch Ballin E M H (eds) Constitutionalism and the Rule of Law: Bridging Idealism and Realism. Cambridge University Press, Cambridge, pp. 358–385

Arendt H (1955) The Personality of Waldemar Gurian. The Review of Politics 17(1):33–42

Besselink L F M (2023) The Evolution and *Gestalt* of the Dutch Constitution. In: Von Bogdandy A, Huber P M, Ragone S (eds) Constitutional Foundations. Oxford University Press, Oxford, pp. 381–430

Böckenförde E-W (2017) The Constituent Power of the People: A Liminal Concept of Constitutional Law [1986]. In: Künkler M, Stein T (eds) Constitutional and Political Theory: Selected Writings. Oxford University Press, Oxford, pp. 169–185

Breunese H-M (2019) Over een *dead parrot* en een valbijl. Nederlands Juristenblad 23:1675

Broeksteeg J L W (2008) Het plebiscitaire element in de procedure van grondwetsherziening. In: Noorlander C W et al. (eds) Het volk regeert. Wolf Legal Publishers, Oisterwijk, pp. 315–330

Colenbrander H T (1908) Ontstaan der grondwet, Eerste Deel 1814. Martinus Nijhoff, The Hague

Colenbrander H T (1927) Vestiging van het Koninkrijk. Meulenhoff, Amsterdam

Colón-Rios J (2010) The Legitimacy of the Juridical: Constituent Power, Democracy, and the Limits of Constitutional Reform. Osgoode Hall Journal 48(2):199–245

Colon-Ríos J (2012) Weak Constitutionalism: Democratic Legitimacy and the Question of Constituent Power. Routledge, London/New York

Corrias L D A (2016) Populism in a Constitutional Key: Constituent Power, Popular Sovereignty and Constitutional Identity. European Constitutional Law Review 12(6):6–26

De Haan I (2020) A Monarchical Regime based on Republican Antecedents: The Constitution of the United Kingdom of the Netherlands. In: Broers M, Caiani A (eds) A History of European Restorations: Governments, States and Monarchy. Bloomsbury Academic, London pp. 159–170

Doyle O (2017) Constraints on Constitutional Amendment Powers. In: Albert R, Contiades X, Fotiadou A (eds) The Foundations and Traditions of Constitutional Amendments. Hart Publishing, Oxford, pp. 73–96

Doyle O (2019) Populist Constitutionalism and Constituent Power. German Law Journal 20:161–180

Duke G (2023) Can the People Exercise Constituent Power? International Journal of Constitutional Law 21(3):798–825

Dyzenhaus D (2008) The Politics of the Question of Constituent Power. In: Loughlin M, Walker N (eds) The Paradox of Constitutionalism: Constituent Power and Constitutional Form. Oxford University Press, Oxford, pp. 129–146

Eftymiou N (2019) De Grondwet van 1814 en de Grondwet van 1815. Tijdschrift voor Constitutioneel Recht 10(1):24–50

Fusaro C, Oliver D (2011) How Constitutions Change—A Comparative Study. Hart Publishing, Oxford

Grimm D (2012) Types of Constitutions. In: Rosenfeld M, Sajó A (eds) The Oxford Handbook on Comparative Constitutional Law. Oxford University Press, Oxford, pp. 98–132
Grimm D (2015) Sovereignty: The Origin and Future of a Legal and Political Concept. Columbia University Press, New York
Grimm D (2016) Constitutionalism: Past, Present, and Future. Oxford University Press, Oxford
Hoogers H G (2004) De verbeelding van de rede en de Europese Unie. Over politieke representatie in Nederland en haar toekomst. In: Engels J W M, Nap M (eds) De ontwikkeling en toekomst van de vertegenwoordigende democratie. Kluwer, Deventer, pp. 61–89.
Hoogers H G (2007) De herziening herzien: over de (on)vanzelfsprekendheid van het wijzigen van hoofdstuk 8 van de Grondwet. RegelMaat 3:99–114
Joor J (2015) The Napoleonic Period in Holland from a Dutch Historical Perspective. In: Planert U (ed) Napoleon's Empire: European Politics in Global Perspective. Palgrave Macmillan, London, pp. 53–66
Kalyvas A (2005) Popular Sovereignty, Democracy, and the Constituent Power. Constellations 12(2):223–244
Kortmann C A J M (2003) Souvereiniteit: on s'amuse. In: De Reede J L, Reestman J H (eds) Op het snijvlak van recht en politiek: Opstellen aangeboden aan Prof. Mr. L. Prakke. Kluwer, Deventer, pp. 155–168
Kumm M (2016) Constituent Power, Cosmopolitan Constitutionalism, and Post-positivist Law. International Journal of Constitutional Law 14(3):697–711
Leeb I L (1973) The Ideological Origins of the Batavian Revolution: History and Politics in the Dutch Republic 1747–1800. Martinus Nijhoff, The Hague
Lesaffer R (2009) European Legal History: A Cultural and Political Perspective. Cambridge University Press, Cambridge
Loughlin M (2014) The Concept of Constituent Power. European Journal of Political Theory 13(2):218–237
Möller H (2004) Die verfassungsgebende Gewalt des Volkes und die Schranken der Verfassungsrevision: Eine Untersuchung zu Art. 79 Abs. 3 GG und zur verfassungsgebenden Gewalt nach dem Grundgesetz. Verlag im Internet GmbH, Hamburg
Negri A (1999) Insurgencies: Constituent Power and the Modern State. University of Minnesota Press, Minneapolis/London
Oud P J (1970) Het constitutioneel recht van het Koninkrijk der Nederlanden deel II. W.E.J. Tjeenk Willink, Zwolle
Palmer R R (2014) The Age of the Democratic Revolution: A Political History of Europe and America, 1760–1800. Princeton University Press, Princeton
Polzin M (2016) Constitutional Identity, Unconstitutional Amendments and the Idea of Constituent Power: The Development of the Doctrine of Constitutional Identity in German Constitutional Law. International Journal of Constitutional Law 14(2):411–438
Polzin M (2021) The Basic-structure Doctrine and its German and French Origins: A Tale of Migration, Integration, Invention and Forgetting. Indian Law Review 5(1):45–61
Prusch M J (2013) Making Sense of Constitutional Monarchism in Post-Napoleonic France and Germany. Palgrave MacMillan, Basingstoke, pp. 10–35
Rossem J W C (2014) Soevereiniteit en pluralisme. Kluwer, Deventer
Roznai Y (2013) Unconstitutional Constitutional Amendments: The Migration and Success of a Constitutional Idea. American Journal of Comparative Law 61(3):657–720
Roznai Y (2017) Unconstitutional Constitutional Amendments: The Limits of Amendment Powers. Oxford University Press, Oxford
Roznai Y (2018) "We the People", "Qui, the People" and the Collective Body: Perceptions of Constituent Power. In: Jacobsohn G J, Schor M (eds) Comparative Constitutional Theory. Edward Elgar, Cheltenham, pp. 295–315
Rubinelli L (2020) Constituent Power: A History. Cambridge University Press, Cambridge
Schmitt C (2008) Constitutional Theory. Duke University Press, Durham
Schwarz M (2009) Democracy and Legal Change. Cambridge University Press, Cambridge

Sièyes E J (2014) What is the Third State. In: Sonenscher M (eds) The Essential Political Writings. Hackett Publishing Company, Inc, Indianapolis/Cambridge, pp. 92–162

Te Velde H (2019) The Emergence of the Netherlands as a "Democratic" Country. Journal Of Modern European History 17(2):161–170

Van der Tang G F M (1998) Grondwetsbegrip en grondwetsidee. Sanders Instituut/Gouda Quint, Rotterdam

Van Gennip T E J H (2019) Kanttekeningen bij de brief van Ollongren inzake de grondwetsherzieningsprocedure. Nederlands Juristenblad 19:1404–1406

Van Gennip T E J H (2021) De grondwetsherzieningsprocedure. Kluwer, Deventer

Van Hogendorp G K (1866) Brieven en Gedenkschriften van Gijsbert Karel van Hogendorp. Martinus Nijhoff, The Hague

Van Velzen P (2005) De ongekende ministeriële verantwoordelijkheid: theorie en praktijk 1813–1840. Wolf Legal Publishers, Oisterwijk

Van Vugt E Y (2021) De Staten-Generaal vertegenwoordigen het geheele Nederlandsche volk: een onderzoek naar de veranderingen in de betekenis van artikel 50 Grondwet tussen 1814–1983. Boom Juridisch, The Hague

Van Vugt (2024) Constitutional Idolatry or Irrelevance in Times of Crisis? The Case of the Netherlands. Constitutional Studies 10(1):29–62

Van Vugt E Y, Van Gennip T E J H (2023) Herijking van de grondwetsherzieningsprocedure. In: Gerards J H, Goossens J, Van Vugt E Y (eds) Constitutionele verandering in Nederland? De grondwetswijzigingen van 2022–2023. Boom Juridisch, The Hague, pp. 245–269

Verdugo S (2023) Is it Time to Abandon the Theory of Constituent Power? International Journal of Constitutional Law 21:14–79

Yap P J (2015) The Conundrum of Unconstitutional Constitutional Amendments. Global Constitutionalism 4:114–136

E. Y. (Eva) van Vugt LL.M., Ph.D., Assistant Professor of Constitutional Law in the Public Law Department at the Faculty of Law, Maastricht University, the Netherlands. Member of the affiliated Maastricht Research Centre for Society and Law (MOSaR).

Part II
Arrangements

Chapter 6
King, Government and Parliament: A Constitutional Jigsaw Puzzle

G. Leenknegt

Contents

Abstract Although a large part of the Dutch Constitution is dedicated to the functioning of its parliamentary system of government, crucial elements in relation to the role of the monarchy and the government, as well as the process of cabinet formation remain uncodified. The Constitution creates an open—and in some respects fragmented—framework, supplemented with unwritten principles and rules, and political practice or traditions. The details and dynamics are left to politics, which in the end means: a majority in parliament. This allows for the flexibility that is needed to build consensus and compromise, and to move along with changing ideas on the exact role of political institutions, and the balance between them.

Keywords Constitutional monarchy · Parliamentary democracy · Ministerial responsibility · Rule of confidence · Cabinet formation · Political practice and constitutional convention

6.1 Half the Constitution

Of the 142 articles of the Dutch Constitution, about 22 (depending on how one counts) deal with the King or the monarchy. Most of these provisions are about the succession to the Throne; they are meant to guarantee the continuity of the hereditary monarchy

G. Leenknegt (✉)
Tilburg Law School, Tilburg University, Tilburg, The Netherlands
e-mail: G.Leenknegt@tilburguniversity.edu

G. van der Schyff (ed.), *The Constitutional Identity of The Netherlands*,
https://doi.org/10.1007/978-94-6265-779-3_6

of the House of Orange-Nassau. This would seem to imply that the monarchy is of crucial importance to the functioning of Dutch constitutional democracy. But in fact, the King is a largely symbolic figure that has a limited role in the Dutch political system. Political power rests with the ministers, together with parliament: the bicameral States General.

The organisation of government and parliament, and the functioning of the Dutch parliamentary democracy are laid down in Chapters 2, 3 and 4 of the Constitution—roughly articles 42 to 80. Taken together, almost half the Constitution is about the King, the government, and parliament. Still, some crucial constitutional rules in this regard remain unwritten. Essential elements of the Dutch parliamentary democracy, such as the relation of confidence between government and parliament, or the process of cabinet formation, have no basis in the Constitution, or even in an Act of Parliament. They are based on constitutional convention and long-standing political practice. To some extent, the exact meaning of these principles and their application are left to political debate.

In relation to the monarchy and the functioning of the parliamentary system of government, the Constitution therefore only codifies part of Dutch constitutional law and practice. In this contribution, I will argue that this demonstrates the constitutional identity of the Netherlands in relation to its parliamentary democracy. It has its roots in Dutch politics, and in a continuous constitutional development that goes back more than 500 years.

6.2 King and Cabinet

The Dutch King[1] has multiple capacities. Firstly, the King is head of state[2]; secondly, together with the cabinet ministers[3] the King forms the government; and thirdly, the King is a private person. The Constitution addresses the King in all three capacities.

Article 24 of the Constitution states that the title to the Throne shall be hereditary and shall vest in the legitimate descendants of King William I, Prince of Orange-Nassau. The provision implies that the King is Head of State, although it does not state this explicitly. Articles 25 to 38 deal with the details of the succession to the Throne, and some other issues that aim to secure the continuity of the monarchy. The private sphere of the King is addressed briefly in article 41, which states that the King shall organise his Household, taking due account of the public interest.

[1] If the monarch is a woman, she is called “Queen” in everyday language; constitutionally though, her function is that of “King”.

[2] To be precise, the King is the monarch of the Kingdom of the Netherlands, which consists of four countries: the Netherlands, Aruba, Curaçao and Sint Maarten (articles 1a-2 of the Charter for the Kingdom of the Netherlands).

[3] And state secretaries: art. 46 Const. State secretaries are responsible for part of a ministerial department. Within the confinements of their task, they bear full ministerial responsibility, like “real” ministers. See: Janse de Jonge 2021b; Groeneveld 1989.

The King and the cabinet ministers together form the government[4]; within the government, the ministers, and not the King, are politically responsible (article 42 of the Constitution). Another element of ministerial responsibility is expressed in article 47: the King signs all bills and royal decrees, but his signature needs the counter signature of one or more ministers or state secretaries.

Perhaps surprisingly, the Dutch Constitution does not list the tasks and privileges of the King.[5] Apart from the signing of bills and royal decrees, only some specific tasks are mentioned in provisions scattered throughout the text of the Constitution. According to article 65, the King opens the parliamentary year on the third Tuesday in September by reading the *Troonrede*, the Royal Address to the joint members of both Houses of Parliament on behalf of the government. The King formally presides over the Council of State, the highest advisory body of the Government (article 74(1)). In reality though, this is a purely ceremonial function: the vice-president chairs the meetings of the Council, while the King is hardly ever present. Apart from these provisions, and a few more in relation to the installation of new ministers or state secretaries, the Constitution contains very little regarding the formal or more symbolic powers of the King.

The Constitution leaves many questions open in relation to the functioning of the King and the cabinet ministers. What are the ceremonial tasks of a King? Can the King refuse to sign a bill? Can a King publicly utter personal opinions—perhaps contrary to the opinions of the ministers? What would be the consequences if the King did so? Where and when does the private sphere of a King end? What is the role of the King in the process of cabinet formation? The Constitution and other laws are silent on these issues. The pivotal provision in relation to the functioning of King and cabinet is article 42(2), on ministerial responsibility. But its text is short and provides little guidance: "The Ministers, and not the King, shall be responsible for acts of government." What does that mean exactly?

6.3 Ministerial Responsibility

Firstly, article 42(2) means that within the government, the opinion of the ministers is decisive. This also implies the principle of the "Unity of the Crown": publicly, the King and the cabinet speak with a single voice. There is no room for differing opinions; if the ministers and the King disagree on government policy, this is kept behind closed doors.[6]

---

[4] The term "cabinet" refers to the collective of ministers and state secretaries; the "government" consists of the King and one or more ministers or state secretaries. A third institution worth mentioning is the Council of Ministers, which consists of the ministers only.

[5] The Spanish Constitution, for example, contains a list of tasks and powers of the King in articles 62 and 63. See https://www.constituteproject.org/constitution/Spain_2011 (last accessed 17 November 2025).

[6] Vermeulen et al. 2005, pp. 66–68.

Secondly, the ministers are responsible for all actions of the King that have a public impact. This may even include rather private decisions of the King, such as the choice of country to go on holiday, depending on the political situation in that particular country.[7] The scope of that responsibility is not even limited to the King: it can extend to the actions of other persons closely associated with the functioning of the monarchy, such as the spouse, and the probable heir to the Throne.[8] In order to limit the potential scope of the ministerial responsibility for other royalty somewhat, an Act of Parliament defines the number of family members who belong to "the Royal House." It consists of the King, the probable heir to the Throne, the King's relatives to the second degree in the line of succession to the Throne, the previous King in case of abdication, and the spouses of these persons.[9] In principle, ministers bear no political responsibility for other members of the family of Orange.[10] Nevertheless, it is not entirely unthinkable that the actions of other members of the Royal family do have direct implications for the monarchy. In those cases, ministers will be responsible to parliament for how they deal with this.[11]

Thirdly, and most importantly, ministers are responsible to parliament individually for their own actions and actions of civil servants in their ministries, and collectively for the general government policy.[12] This element of ministerial responsibility is a crucial principle in the cooperation between the government and parliament. Ultimately, the political ministerial responsibility is sanctioned by the rule of confidence.

6.4 Government and Parliament: The Rule of Confidence

The Netherlands has a parliamentary system of government. After each general election for the Lower House, the political factions negotiate a governing coalition which relies on the confidence of a majority in the Lower House. There is no constitutional or legal requirement to form a majority coalition, but any government needs the support of a majority in both Houses of Parliament to pass legislation. For this reason, governing coalitions usually represent a political majority in the Lower House, and preferably also in the Senate—although this is not always possible. The formation

[7] In February 2000, Queen Beatrix went on her annual skiing holiday in Lech, Austria, immediately after the extreme right-wing party FPÖ had formed a new government in that country. This led to some discussions in the media; see: Ophef over Oostenrijkse skivakantie van Beatrix, in: Volkskrant, 7 February 2000.

[8] This is called the "derived" ministerial responsibility; Vermeulen et al. 2005, p. 71; Kortmann 2016, pp. 318–320.

[9] Articles 1–2 of the Act on Membership of the Royal House (*Wet lidmaatschap koninklijk huis*).

[10] *Kamerstukken II* 2001/02, 28 223, No. 3, p. 3; Bovend'Eert 2004, p. 2.

[11] Kortmann 2016, pp. 318–320.

[12] Janse de Jonge 2021a.

process habitually results in a detailed written agreement (*regeerakkoord*) between the coalition partners in the Lower House.[13]

The Constitution attributes to parliament several instruments that allow it to control the government (parliamentary scrutiny). Both Houses have the right to information (article 68) and to conduct a parliamentary inquiry (article 70); the Lower House also has the rights of initiative (article 82) and amendment (article 84) in relation to the legislative procedure. The ultimate parliamentary instrument is not mentioned in the Constitution though: the vote of no confidence.

A vote of no confidence in the Lower House ends the term of a minister or the cabinet as a whole; the Senate may also force ministers to step down, for example by rejecting a crucial bill or the relevant chapter of the national budget bill.[14] Nothing of this is written constitutional law; it is customary law. What *is* written is the power of the government to dissolve one or both Houses of Parliament (article 64 of the Constitution). But in practice, this power is not used to solve political conflicts between the government and parliament. It is mainly used to dissolve the Lower House in case of an internal cabinet crisis, in agreement with a majority in the Lower House.[15] At least in theory, this allows the voters to express their opinion on the issue that caused the cabinet crisis.

Crucial elements of the functioning of the Dutch parliamentary system of government are not laid down in written constitutional law: the confidence rule, the motion of censure (or "no confidence"), the consequences thereof, and the meaning of the confidence rule in relation to the Senate. The same is true for the process of cabinet formation. Very little is written: three articles in the Rules of Procedure of the Lower House (articles 11.1 to 11.3). Within a week after general elections, the Lower House debates the outcome; it then appoints an *informateur* (a person who leads negotiations for a possible coalition) or a *formateur* (a person who forms a specific coalition, and usually becomes the new Prime Minister).[16] Tradition dictates that the largest faction in the Lower House takes the initiative in the formation process first. The formation process itself is left completely to the negotiating parties (we will explain more on the formation process below, Sect. 6.6).

The consequences of a lack of written constitutional rules regarding the relation between the government and the Senate became apparent late 2024, when the Senate threatened to reject a budget bill for 2025. This led to some political and legal debate: it was unclear what the consequences of such a decision would be, as there is nothing to be found about it in the Constitution or in other laws.[17] In June 2025,

[13] On coalition agreements, see: Bovend'Eert 1988.

[14] In 1907, the Senate rejected the budget bill for the Ministry of War; this caused a cabinet crisis and eventually, Minister Staal resigned. Oud 1946, pp. 206–208.

[15] Leenknegt 2021a.

[16] After the October 2023 and October 2025 elections, the Lower House appointed a *verkenner* or "scout" in the first phase of the formation process, even though the Rules of Procedure do not mention that as an option.

[17] See https://www.denederlandsegrondwet.nl/id/vmixjn1hcvr8/nieuws/praktische_en_politieke_betekenis_van for an overview of some historical examples, and potential consequences (last visited 17 November 2025). Eventually, the Senate did not reject the bill.

the Council of State published an Opinion on such a scenario. It concluded that the government could then present a new bill immediately, and it advised amendment of the Government Accounts Act 2016 (*Comptabiliteitswet 2016*) to establish this as a written rule.[18]

Why are some crucial rules in relation to the functioning of the Dutch parliamentary system left uncodified in constitutional law? An important part of the explanation for this lies in the historical and political context.

6.5 Some Historical Context

The current monarchy dates back to 1814, but in a sense, it has a much longer constitutional history. The position of the family of Orange-Nassau as political and military leaders dates back to the genesis of the Republic of the United Netherlands, late sixteenth century. For most of its history since 1581, the Netherlands was a confederal republic, and although the members of the Orange dynasty were formally not heads of state but so-called stadtholders (*stadhouders*),[19] the highest executive officers under the sovereignty of the provincial governments, their position and behaviour in the seventeenth and eighteenth century closely resembled that of monarchs.[20]

The last stadtholder, William V of Orange, fled to England during the Batavian Revolution in 1795. After the Batavian-French post-revolutionary republican era (1795–1806), followed by the Kingdom of Holland under Louis Napoleon (1806–1810), and a few years as part of the Napoleonic Empire (1810–1813), the Netherlands became an independent nation again, and a monarchy under the 1814 Constitution. The son of the last stadtholder of the Republic became King William I of the new unitary state of the Netherlands.

Between 1814 and 1848, the King himself actually governed; ministers were his personal advisors, and parliament had limited legislative powers and few instruments to control the government.[21] The constitutional reform of 1848 brought fundamental changes.[22] The introduction of ministerial responsibility limited the political role of the King. The Lower House of Parliament would be elected directly, whereas the Senators were no longer appointed by the King, but indirectly elected by the members of the provincial councils. Parliament acquired more rights, including the right to approve the annual national budget. Essentially, the 1848 reform created the foundations of the Dutch constitutional monarchy and parliamentary democracy.

---

[18] Raad van State 2025.

[19] Originally a term for the local representative of the Spanish-Habsburg Kings, Charles V and Philip II.

[20] Stadtholder William III, who was married to Queen Mary II Stuart, actually *was* King as well—of England.

[21] Oud 1946, pp. 1–2.

[22] On the 1848 revision of the Constitution: Buijs 1883–1888; Leenknegt et al. 2010, pp. 133–158.

The implications of the framework laid down in the 1848 Constitution for the King, the government, and parliament, emerged in the decades that followed. The crucial rule of confidence that is at the heart of the parliamentary system of government was not codified in 1848, but its existence became evident in two political conflicts between government and parliament, in 1866 and 1868. In both conflicts, the Lower House disapproved of the actions of the government; in both cases, the government reacted by dissolving the Lower House, resulting in general elections. In the end, the displeased Lower House used the power of the purse—the annual budget—to force its will upon the government.[23] Since then it is clear that ministers are not dependent on the confidence of the King, but of a majority in the Lower House, and that they must resign when the absence of that confidence becomes apparent. The existence of a rule of confidence was a logical and inevitable complement to the principle of ministerial responsibility. Another consequence was that the King could no longer choose cabinet ministers to his liking; his options were limited by the political composition of the Lower House.

Another characteristic element of the 1848 Constitution was that it declared Acts of Parliament inviolable—the predecessor of the now infamous article 120, which states that the courts cannot assess the constitutionality of Acts of Parliament or treaties.[24] Although this does not seem to bear a direct relation to the functioning of the Dutch parliamentary system, it does emphasise that in 1848, after a period of authoritarian rule by King William I under the 1814 Constitution, and prior to that a republican era characterised by the rule of an economic elite, the directly elected parliament was now trusted with ultimate decision-making power. In the current version of the Constitution this is also visible in the fact that it leaves broad regulatory powers to the legislature, either by explicitly attributing specific tasks, or by being silent on many topics. Parliament and government jointly have a general legislative power that allows them to make laws on any subject—under the assumption that the Constitution and other supreme legal norms are respected.[25]

The constitutional history of the Netherlands since 1848 demonstrates that the Constitution mostly codifies generally accepted rules of constitutional law; it rarely creates completely new ones. It contains very little symbolism or superfluous elements, few details, it attributes many topics to the legislature, and it is silent on many other issues. As a result, the text is relatively brief, sober, and open. It provides a framework of principles, but it allows for political practice to develop over time, depending on specific circumstances.

The fact that the relation of confidence remains unwritten constitutional law provides flexibility in its application. In December 2006 for example, a minister

---

[23] For a description and analysis of both conflicts, see: Oud 1946, pp. 78–91.

[24] On this provision, see Chap. 8 in this volume.

[25] Art. 81 Const. reads: "Acts of Parliament shall be enacted jointly by the Government and the States General." (Taken from the 2023 translation by the Ministry of the Interior and kingdom Relations.) On this topic: Voermans 2021a, p. 839. Regulations concerning affairs of the Kingdom are established by or pursuant to a Kingdom Act of Parliament (art. 14 of the Charter for the Kingdom of the Netherlands). In such cases, the institutions of the Caribbean countries within the Kingdom are involved in the legislative procedure.

in a caretaker government awaiting new elections was sanctioned with a motion of no confidence in the Lower House. A strict application of that rule would have meant that she would have been forced to resign with immediate effect. She did not, however, and the prime minister decided to move her to another ministerial department instead.[26] The Lower House accepted this. This was probably only possible because of the caretaker status of the cabinet, and the fact that her term would therefore end soon anyway.[27] It demonstrates the flexibility in the application of even the most basic rules governing the Dutch parliamentary system. The need for this political flexibility was used to argue that the confidence rule, although crucial for the functioning of our parliamentary system, should not be codified in the Constitution.[28]

As a result, crucial elements of the functioning of the Dutch parliamentary system of government remain unwritten; it is partly based on constitutional convention, or even political practice. This rather fragmented character of the written constitutional framework is intentional: it is closely related to the Dutch consensual style of politics.

6.6 Elections and Cabinet Formation

The Netherlands has a proportional electoral system for its national parliament.[29] It is one of the purest proportional systems in the world; there is no threshold for political parties to enter parliament, other than the number of votes required for a single seat—the quota. As a consequence, both Houses of Parliament are composed of a wide range of political factions. In the elections of October 2025, fifteen political parties won seats in the Lower House, which consists of 150 seats in total. In May 2023, fifteen parties won seats in the Senate (75 seats in total). Due to factions splitting after internal conflicts, there were nineteen groups in the Senate in the fall of 2025.[30]

Political majorities in both houses may differ, at least partly due to the high volatility of voters. In November 2023, the new party *Nieuw Sociaal Contract* (NSC) won twenty seats in the Lower House. In the Senate, elected only a few months before that, NSC had no seats, as it did not even exist at the time. It became part of the new coalition government (the Schoof government) in July 2024. After the elections for the Lower House in October 2025, due to a government crisis, NSC failed to win a single seat.

---

[26] See: Heringa et al. 2018, p. 223; Van den Berg 2006.

[27] Groen 2024.

[28] See: *Kamerstukken II* 1980/81, 16 035, No. 11, pp. 1–3; Kortmann 1987, pp. 174–175.

[29] Art. 53 Const.; provincial and municipal councils are elected on the basis of proportional representation, too: art. 129 Const.

[30] See: https://www.eerstekamer.nl/wie_zit_waar (last accessed 17 November 2025).

Unsurprisingly, the Netherlands have had coalition governments for the last eighty years.[31] Government formation means building compromises, between at least two, but more often three or more political factions. Despite long preparations and careful negotiations, resulting in extensive written coalition agreements, the formation process does not always produce stable and effective coalitions. The gradual fragmentation and polarisation of the political spectrum during recent years have made the process even more difficult.

Many have argued in favour of changes to the electoral system, in order to counter the fragmentation of the Lower House, and to make coalition building easier, resulting—hopefully—in more stable governments.[32] Changes that would require amendment of the Constitution need two parliamentary readings, separated by elections for the Lower House, and a two-thirds majority in the second reading in both Houses.[33] Within the existing constitutional framework of proportional representation, there are still possibilities to amend the electoral system, but so far, none of the initiatives taken in this respect have succeeded. Constitutional scholars—and politicians, for that matter—may agree on the problem, but differ with respect to the most desirable solution.

Some have argued for a time limit on the cabinet formation, or other procedural rules forcing the Lower House to speed things up.[34] Generally though, there is little enthusiasm for such measures, as they would put too much strain on the formation process. Months of talks behind closed doors are often needed, for substantive negotiations but even more to allow time to smooth out the wrinkles between the factions in the Lower House after intense election campaigns. Building intricate political compromises requires discretion and time.

Interestingly, cabinet formation is one of the few political processes in which the King used to have a pivotal role. That role dates back to the first half of the nineteenth century, when the King personally decided about the composition of "his" government. After 1848, the parliamentary majority gradually became the decisive factor. But still, until 2010 the King had an initiating and advisory role in the process of cabinet formation after elections for the Lower House. A few days after the elections, the King would receive the advice from the leaders of all political factions, and would then assign a task to a *formateur* or *informateur*, at his or her own discretion. That person would report to the King about the progress. All this was based on political practice, not binding legal rules.

After the 2012 parliamentary elections, a majority in the Lower House concluded that the formation procedure placed too important a task on the inviolable King,

[31] See the overview of coalition governments since 1945 on: https://www.parlement.com/kabinetten-1945-heden (last accessed on 17 November 2025).

[32] For a brief overview of attempts over the last thirty years, see: Leenknegt 2021b, pp. 675–676.

[33] Art. 137 Const.

[34] See e.g. Voermans 2021b; for a critical view on this topic: Oldeman 2022.

for which no minister could take responsibility.[35] Others simply found the involvement of the King "undemocratic".[36] The Lower House decided to take control of the process itself; the King was to be kept informed, for reasons of decorum. This was laid down in the Rules of Procedure of the Lower House (see Sect. 6.4). No constitutional amendment was needed, nor even an Act of Parliament or the amendment thereof. Recently, some Members of Parliament have argued that the role of the King in the formation process should be restored, as his authority could possibly end the bickering and political amateurism that allegedly plagued recent formation processes.[37]

Once a new government is formed, ministers can start functioning under the assumption that they have the confidence of a majority in the Lower House. This is not expressed explicitly at the start; in the event that the *absence* of the confidence of a political majority becomes apparent, for example through the adoption of a motion of no confidence, or the rejection of a crucial bill, a minister or the cabinet as a whole must resign (depending on the addressee of the motion). This is not "just" political practice or tradition, but unwritten constitutional law, which means that it is a binding legal rule.[38]

6.7 Elements of Identity in the Dutch Parliamentary System

On the basis of the above, we can now attempt to formulate an answer to the question of what constitutional law regarding the King, government and parliament reveals about the constitutional identity of Dutch parliamentary democracy.

Our analysis demonstrates that crucial elements in relation to the role of the monarchy and the government, the process of cabinet formation, as well as the functioning of the Dutch parliamentary system remain uncodified. The Constitution creates an open—and in some respects fragmented—framework, supplemented with unwritten principles and rules, and political practice or traditions. The details and dynamics are left to politics, which in the end means: a majority in parliament. This allows for the flexibility that is needed to build consensus and compromise, and to move along with changing ideas on the exact role of political institutions and the balance between them. The proportional election system is a crucial part of that intricate system, if not the very foundation of it.

---

[35] Kortmann 2016, p. 151.

[36] See: https://nos.nl/artikel/2162268-de-koning-zit-bij-kabinetsformatie-op-de-reservebank (last accessed 17 November 2025).

[37] An example is the motion of Member of Parliament Bikker in August 2025, *Kamerstukken II* 2024/25, 36 760, No. 38; the motion was rejected by a majority in the Lower House. For a critical comment on the topic, see: Bovend'Eert 2025.

[38] Kortmann 2016, pp. 298–300.

Much of this can be characterised as *political* constitutionalism. In crucial moments, or when the exact meaning of the constitutional framework is unclear, the functioning of the Dutch parliamentary system relies on political practice and unwritten rules; the interpretation of those practices and rules, and the decision to change them, is determined by a parliamentary majority. This is also visible in the fact that the Constitution leaves much leeway to the legislature, or: the dynamics between a coalition government, based on a majority in the Lower House, and the parliamentary opposition in both Houses of Parliament. This is further strengthened by the constitutional prohibition of constitutional review of Acts of Parliament by the courts.

The result is that it is sometimes unclear what the way forward is when a political crisis or urgent question arises. Politicians and constitutional scholars may disagree, depending on how they interpret the applicable legal rules and conventions. Dutch constitutional law regarding the King, government, and parliament resembles an incomplete jigsaw puzzle, where only part of the picture is visible; everyone involved may have a different idea of the whole picture, and of the best way to fill in the blanks.

References

Bovend'Eert P P T (1988) Regeerakkoorden en regeringsprograms. Sdu, The Hague

Bovend'Eert P P T (2004) Ministeriële verantwoordelijkheid voor leden van het koninklijk huis. Openbaar Bestuur 14(6/7)2–7

Bovend'Eert P P T (2025) De Koning terug in de kabinetsformatie? De Hofvijver Vol. 15 Elections Edition No. 2. https://www.montesquieu-instituut.nl/id/vmqwe34tdle6/nieuws/de_koning_terug_in_de_kabinetsformatie (last accessed 17 November 2025)

Buijs J T (1883–1888) De Grondwet (3 Volumes). Gouda Quint, Arnhem

Groen L (2024) Constitutionele momenten # 3: Een naderend constitutioneel moment? Over de werking van de vertrouwensregel en hoorzittingen met kandidaat-bewindspersonen. Blog on NederlandRechtsstaat.nl, 28 June 2024. https://www.nederlandrechtsstaat.nl/constitutionele-momenten-3-een-naderend-constitutioneel-moment-over-de-werking-van-de-vertrouwensregel-en-hoorzittingen-met-kandidaat-bewindspersonen/ (last accessed 17 November 2025)

Groeneveld H A (1989) De staatssecretaris in Nederland. Kluwer, Deventer

Heringa A W, Van der Velde J, Verhey L F M, Van der Woude W (2018) Staatsrecht, 13th edn. Wolters Kluwer, Deventer

Janse de Jonge E J (2021a) Artikel 42. In: Hirsch Ballin E M H, Janse de Jonge E J, Leenknegt G (eds) Uitleg van de Grondwet. Boom Juridisch, The Hague, pp. 621–632

Janse de Jonge E J (2021b) Artikel 46. In: Hirsch Ballin E M H, Janse de Jonge E J, Leenknegt G (eds) Uitleg van de Grondwet. Boom Juridisch, The Hague, pp. 647–649

Kortmann C A J M (1987) De Grondwetsherzieningen 1983 en 1987. Kluwer, Deventer

Kortmann C A J M, revised by Bovend'Eert P P T, Broeksteeg J W L, Kortmann C N J, Vermeulen B P (2016) Constitutioneel recht, 7th. edn. Kluwer, Deventer

Leenknegt G (2021a) Artikel 64. In: Hirsch Ballin E M H, Janse de Jonge E J, Leenknegt G (eds) Uitleg van de Grondwet. Boom Juridisch, The Hague, pp. 713–721

Leenknegt G (2021b) Artikel 53. In: Hirsch Ballin E M H, Janse de Jonge E J, Leenknegt G (eds) Uitleg van de Grondwet. Boom Juridisch, The Hague, pp. 673–677

Leenknegt G, Kubben R, Jacobs B (2010) Opstand en eenwording. Een institutionele geschiedenis van het Nederlandse openbaar bestuur. Wolf Legal Publishers, Nijmegen

Oldeman J E (2022) Samen krijgen we de kabinetsformatie onder controle, maar niet met maximumtermijnen. Tijdschrift voor Constitutioneel Recht 13(1):49–57

Oud P J (1946) Honderd Jaren. Hoofdzaken der Nederlandsche staatkundige geschiedenis. Van Gorcum, Assen

Raad van State (2025) Voorlichting over de consequenties van en het handelingsperspectief bij een verworpen begroting, 4 June 2025. https://www.raadvanstate.nl/adviezen/@149498/w06-25-00068-iii/ (last visited 17 November 2025)

Van den Berg J Th J (22 December 2006) Onkunde of onwil? Column on Parlement.com. https://www.parlement.com/column/200612/onkunde-onwil (last accessed 17 November 2025)

Vermeulen B P, Krijnen A P, Roos D A (eds) (2005) De Koning in het Nederlandse staatsrecht. Ars Aequi Libri, Nijmegen

Voermans W J M (2021a) Artikel 81. In: Hirsch Ballin E M H, Janse de Jonge E J, Leenknegt G (eds) Uitleg van de Grondwet. Boom Juridisch, The Hague, pp. 839–845

Voermans W J M (2021b) En dan nu: een assertief parlement. NRC Handelsblad newspaper 20 September 2021

Gert-Jan Leenknegt Ph.D., is Associate Professor of Constitutional Law and Vice Dean of Education at Tilburg Law School, Tilburg University, the Netherlands. He is co-editor of the commentary on the Dutch Constitution on NederlandRechtsstaat.nl; his research focuses on systems of government and regional and local government.

Chapter 7
Decentralisation: About the Constitutional Identity of Provinces and Municipalities

Hansko Broeksteeg

Contents

Abstract Though the Constitution makes no mention of it, the Netherlands is a decentralised unitary state comprised of three layers (central government, provinces and municipalities). A number of elements make up the constitutional identity of this decentralisation. For example, the provinces and municipalities have a uniform organisation, regardless of their location, size and population. The Constitution is not very normative and leaves much to the legislature, such as the procedure for reorganising provinces and municipalities, the manner of cooperation between provinces and municipalities and the financial relationship with the central government. The paired concepts of autonomy and co-governance are certainly part of constitutional identity. Though many of the duties fulfilled by the provinces and municipalities are in the domain of co-governance, the concept of autonomy is essential. This comprises the right of the provinces and municipalities to initiate matters relating to their own affairs. Another aspect of constitutional identity is the headship of the provincial and municipal councils, as representatives of the people. The councils are ultimately responsible for the provincial and municipal administration. Lastly, attention is drawn to administrative supervision, which is undeniably necessary in a decentralised unitary state and therefore an element of the relationship between the central government and the decentralised governments. However, the central

H. Broeksteeg (✉)
Radboud University, Nijmegen, The Netherlands
e-mail: hansko.broeksteeg@ru.nl

G. van der Schyff (ed.), *The Constitutional Identity of The Netherlands*,
https://doi.org/10.1007/978-94-6265-779-3_7

government is very reticent when it comes to such supervision, partly to guarantee the autonomy of the provinces and municipalities.

Keywords Decentralisation · Provinces and municipalities · Constitutional guarantees · Autonomy and co-governance · Headship of the councils · Supervision · Annulment and neglect of duties

7.1 Introduction

The Netherlands is often described as a decentralised unitary state, with three layers of government: the central government, provinces, and municipalities. These three layers are sometimes referred to as Thorbecke's House. It was under his leadership that the Provincial Act (1850) and Municipal Act (1851) were established.[1] These two laws provide for the administrative organisation of provinces and municipalities, which consists of a provincial council (*provinciale staten*), a provincial executive (*gedeputeerde staten*) and a King's Commissioner (*Commissaris van de Koning*) for the provinces and a municipal council (*gemeenteraad*), a municipal executive (the council of mayor and aldermen; *college van burgemeester en wethouders*) and a mayor (*burgemeester*) for the municipalities. While his house is still standing, times have changed, bringing consequences for Thorbecke's House. To what extent are the principles of the mid-nineteenth century still relevant?

In this chapter, I will explore the constitutional identity of Dutch decentralisation today. I will begin with a brief history of the law of decentralised governments (Sect. 7.2). I will then discuss the principles of the Constitution in relation to decentralisation (Sect. 7.3) and a few major constitutional doctrines concerning provinces and municipalities (Sect. 7.4). I will end by drawing a conclusion (Sect. 7.5). Since water boards differ significantly from regular decentralised authorities, I will leave these public bodies out of this chapter.[2]

7.2 A Brief History of Decentralisation

The Constitution of 1848 can be seen as the foundation of the provinces and municipalities in their modern form.[3] As has been said, the Constitution established Thorbecke's House, with its government structure comprising three layers. The Constitution abolished the distinction between city and countryside and provided for a uniform structure for all provinces and municipalities. This meant that vastly different

[1] Broeksteeg 2021, pp. 6–8.

[2] See for further information about the water boards: Broeksteeg 2021, pp. 481–498.

[3] Oppenheim 1928, pp. 36–37; Dölle and Elzinga 2004, p. 18; Broeksteeg 2021, pp. 6–7.

municipalities like Amsterdam and Schiermonnikoog had the same internal structure.[4] Also new was the constitutional provision that the provincial or municipal council, directly elected by the population,[5] formed the head of the provinces and municipalities. This shifted the focus of municipal government from the mayor and aldermen to the municipal council.[6] The Constitution of 1848 granted autonomy to municipalities, but at the same time placed them under administrative supervision—through which the unitary state is expressed. Finally, the Constitution obliged the legislature to establish a Provincial Act and a Municipal Act.

These laws appeared in 1850 and 1851, respectively. As mentioned above, they constituted the provincial and municipal councils, the provincial and municipal executives and the King's Commissioner or mayor. The Provincial and Municipal Acts also provided for a division of powers, which resulted from the constitutional status of the councils as head of the provinces and municipalities. In principle, the councils exercised all powers, unless the law placed these powers with the executives or the commissioner/mayor. The laws of 1850 and 1851 had a long life, with only modest changes to the Provincial and Municipal Acts until 1983. The main legal change concerned the introduction, in 1887, of co-governance (*medebewind*), the counterpart of autonomy. Co-governance means that the decentralised governments may be obliged legally to cooperate in the implementation of central government policy. In the same year, administrative supervision was expanded to include an arrangement for the neglect of legal duties by decentralised governments.

In 1983, the new Constitution made some changes, albeit limited in content. These changes mainly concerned the modernisation, simplification and systematisation of the provisions concerning the decentralised governments, which are now merged in this chapter of the Constitution. Moreover, the constitutional legislature sought to deconstitutionalise, in the sense that the Constitution should only contain those topics that are so important that they belong in the Constitution and can only be changed through a rigorous amendment procedure.[7] The constitutional revision of 1983 was followed by a new Provincial Act and Municipal Act in 1992. These new laws did not aim to make any substantive changes. Instead, they had the same goals as the 1983 revision of the Constitution, such as modernisation and systematisation. The main constitutional changes since 1983 have been the removal from the Constitution of the chairing of the provincial and municipal councils by the commissioner/mayor (in 2008) and of the appointment by the Crown (i.e. the central government) of those same offices (in 2018).

Nevertheless, in 2002 and 2003, some major changes—probably the most significant since 1850/1851—were made to the Provincial and Municipal Acts. These

---

[4] Before 1848, the government structure of the municipalities was a matter for the provinces.

[5] People with census voting rights; the right to vote was not awarded to the whole municipal population.

[6] Dölle and Elzinga 2004, p. 19.

[7] Bovend'Eert et al. 2011, pp. 7–27; Broeksteeg 2021, pp. 8–9.

concerned the dualisation (*dualisering*) of the provincial and municipal governments.[8] As mentioned above, in the former monistic system all powers were vested in the provincial or municipal council. Dualisation means that the provincial and municipal executives are given their own powers. They now have an independent legal position. The members of the executive (*gedeputeerden* and *wethouders*) are no longer members of the provincial and municipal councils and no longer have to be appointed by the councils.

7.3 The Constitution and Decentralisation

The provinces and municipalities are regulated in this chapter of the Constitution. This chapter offers some guarantees and contains some major gaps. I will discuss these aspects below, consecutively,[9] though I will begin by making a comment about its structure.

According to its title, this chapter of the Constitution concerns public bodies (*openbare lichamen*). Provinces and municipalities can therefore be regarded as public bodies. The Constitution does not use the terms decentralisation and decentralised government. Besides the provinces and municipalities, the Constitution mentions the water boards, the Caribbean public bodies, the public bodies for professions and trades, and "other" public bodies. The Constitution makes a distinction between provinces and municipalities, on the one hand, and all other public bodies (including the water boards and Caribbean public bodies), on the other. It regulates the provinces and municipalities in a relatively detailed manner, while it does not do so for the other public bodies. The Constitution mentions the institution and reorganisation of provinces and municipalities, the manner in which they obtain their powers, the main offices of provinces and municipalities, the method for electing the provincial and municipal councils and their regulatory powers, some aspects of the legal position of council members and (the different forms of) administrative supervision. With regard to the other bodies, the Constitution is very brief. It mentions that they can be established and organised by law and that the law provides for their regulatory powers and administrative supervision. It would appear that the provinces and municipalities enjoy a different status from that of the other public bodies. The more detailed constitutional arrangement suggests that the constitutional legislature attaches greater importance to the position of provinces and municipalities.

[8] State Commission 2000.

[9] Bovend'Eert et al. 2011, pp. 35–44; Broeksteeg 2021, pp. 30–35.

7.3.1 Constitutional Guarantees Regarding Decentralisation

Firstly, the Constitution guarantees the existence of some public bodies, especially provinces and municipalities. Although the Constitution does not explicitly say so, this (constitutionally mandatory) existence implies that the Netherlands is a decentralised unitary state. Article 134(1) of the Constitution provides for the institution of new public bodies. This includes regional public bodies, i.e. bodies between the provinces and the municipalities, in which the provinces and municipalities can work together on a voluntary basis. However, these regional bodies must not affect Thorbecke's House. If cooperation were to become mandatory rather than voluntary, this would add a fourth layer of government, which the constitutional legislature has always rejected.[10] The guarantee that there will always be provinces and municipalities is also linked to the fact that the entire Dutch territory is divided into provinces and municipalities. This also follows from article 123 of the Constitution. Where that is not the case, the Constitution accounts for this explicitly, as with the Caribbean public bodies (article 132a of the Constitution).[11] In principle, there is no territory that does not belong to a province or municipality.

Secondly, the Constitution explicitly guarantees the autonomous exercising of provincial and municipal duties (article 124(1) of the Constitution). However, it does not indicate where the boundaries of autonomy lie. Furthermore, the Constitution provides for administrative supervision, which can profoundly influence and limit the exercising of autonomous duties. Though the Constitution guarantees provincial and municipal autonomy, the Constitution has little normative significance. The central government can take on duties that rest with the provinces and municipalities and thus reduce their autonomous scope.

Thirdly, the Constitution guarantees uniform provincial and municipal government. As said above, uniformity was one of the goals of the Constitution of 1848 and of the laws of 1850/1851, and it still is.

7.3.2 Constitutional Gaps Regarding Decentralisation

The Netherlands has a simple constitution, which means that it often does not regulate issues of constitutional law or does so only briefly. I mentioned before that the idea of the decentralised unitary state is not mentioned explicitly in the Constitution. Nor does it establish a mission of decentralisation or a commitment to it. In other words, the Constitution has no normative task for the legislature. The guarantee of basic autonomy in article 124(1) of the Constitution can hardly be seen as such.

---

[10] Broeksteeg 2021, p. 32.

[11] The Caribbean public bodies are: Bonaire, Sint Eustatius (Statia) and Saba, sometimes abbreviated as BES. They are part of the Netherlands, which is one of the four countries (besides Curaçao, Aruba and Sint Maarten) of the Kingdom of the Netherlands. See for further information about the BES: Broeksteeg 2021, pp. 467–479.

With regard to regulatory powers too, the Constitution barely offers any guarantees. Article 127 of the Constitution gives the representative bodies of the provinces and municipalities (the councils) the power to adopt regulations, but what the (hierarchical) status of these regulations is, remains unclear. The financial position of provinces and municipalities also lacks constitutional guarantees. Article 132(6) of the Constitution instructs the formal legislature to regulate the financial relationship between the central government, on the one hand, and the provinces and municipalities, on the other. The Constitution does not provide any substantive rules. Nor does it do so with regard to provincial or municipal taxes. Therefore, formal legislation may (and does) severely limit provincial and municipal financial autonomy.[12] The same goes for the establishment and dissolution of provinces and municipalities; the Constitution does not provide any substantive criteria. In other words, article 123(1) of the Constitution leaves huge scope in terms of policy for the legislature. What is more, the procedure for establishing and dissolving provinces and municipalities is not regulated.

At first glance, the constitutional provision relating to administrative supervision (article 132 of the Constitution) seems to be more extensive. But here too, the constitutional legislature leaves a lot to the formal legislature. This is already evident from article 132(2) of the Constitution: "Supervision of the administrative organs shall be regulated by Act of Parliament." The Constitution does not impose any conditions on preventive supervision, such as approval, other than a formal legal basis. The annulment of decisions made by provinces and municipalities is more limited (article 132(4)); the application of this power (strict or broad) is not regulated. The same applies to the application of the arrangement for non-compliance or neglect of duties. As a result of the summary constitutional arrangement, the legislature has been able to take the liberty of significantly expanding the rules in this regard.

Finally, I note the constitutional provision relating to collaboration between the provinces and the municipalities (article 135 of the Constitution). This merely assumes that an Act of Parliament will regulate this matter; it does not prescribe the forms of collaboration that provinces and municipalities may choose. It only mentions the most far-reaching form, i.e. collaboration within a new public body to be established. The legislature has developed very different policies over the years.[13]

7.4 Some Elements of the Constitutional Identity of Decentralisation

The foregoing presents a number of elements that clarify constitutional identity with regard to the decentralised authorities. The Netherlands is a decentralised unitary state comprising three layers (Thorbecke's House). The provinces and municipalities

[12] See for example the Law on the Financial Relations (*Financiële verhoudingswet*) or the provisions in the Municipal Act concerning the real estate tax (Article 220ff).

[13] Bovend'Eert et al. 2011, pp. 287–310.

have a uniform organisation, regardless of their location, size and population. The Constitution is not very normative and leaves much to the legislature. Some of the elements of the constitutional identity need to be described more extensively because their meaning is not sufficiently clear from the description above. These elements are the concepts of autonomy and co-governance (Sect. 7.4.1), the constitutional position of the provincial and municipal council as the head of those public bodies (Sect. 7.4.2) and administrative supervision (Sect. 7.4.3).

7.4.1 Autonomy and Co-Governance

The concept pairing of autonomy and co-governance is one of the most essential in the law of decentralised governments.[14] It relates to how they obtain their powers. The basis can be found in article 124 of the Constitution. Paragraph 1 concerns autonomy and states: "The powers of provinces and municipalities to regulate and administer their own internal affairs shall be left to their governments." Autonomy means that provinces and municipalities are free to regulate and to administer what they consider necessary in the context of their household (*huishouding*), which means their own internal affairs. They exercise these powers on their own initiative and independently,[15] i.e. without any obligation imposed by another government (mainly the central government). Autonomy also implies the freedom of provinces and municipalities not to regulate or administer a particular matter. In that respect, the constitutional phrase "shall be left to" is relevant. It means that the autonomous regulation and administration of the household is not attributed or delegated to the provinces and municipalities, but rather that it is their own, original competence. The Constitution does not constitute these powers; it merely confirms them.[16]

Nevertheless, regulation and administration in autonomy may also be mandatory. Provincial and municipal autonomy includes the implementation of the Provincial and Municipal Acts. Provinces and municipalities must adopt a budget and annual accounts, establish tax regulations, set up an audit office, and so on. The fact that those laws do not require co-governance follows from article 105(2) of the Provincial Act and article 108(2) of the Municipal Act.

The Constitution does not contain any guarantees against the erosion of provincial or municipal autonomy. It does not provide for a minimum level of autonomy or stipulate that provincial or municipal autonomy must be substantial. The only guarantee the Constitution offers is that there is some autonomy. The expression "shall be left to" means, in that respect, that provinces and municipalities may regulate and administer "new" public interests. The constitutional guarantee therefore implies that

[14] Extensively: Broeksteeg 2021, pp. 48–61.

[15] Van Haaren-Dresens 2018, pp. 153–162.

[16] Bovend'Eert et al. 2011, pp. 59–60.

provinces and municipalities have the freedom to look after public interests as a "first government".[17]

Alongside autonomy there is co-governance. The constitutional basis for this is article 124(2): "Provincial and municipal governments may be required by or pursuant to Acts of Parliament to provide regulation and administration." The term "required" is critical. Co-governance is the obligatory cooperation in the implementation of a formal law. The phrase "by or pursuant to" means that general administrative measures (*algemene maatregelen van bestuur*) may also require co-governance. Provincial regulations may call for co-governance from municipalities. Co-governance thus means that another public body requires cooperation in its policy. Whereas with autonomy the initiative lies with the provinces and municipalities, with co-governance the other government takes the initiative.

Co-governance must have a legal basis in formal legislation. It must concern a specific policy area. This means that general laws, such as the Police Law (*Politiewet*) or the General Administrative Law Act (*Algemene wet bestuursrecht*), do not require co-governance.[18] There are numerous examples of co-governance, for instance with regard to spatial planning and the environment and in the social arena (welfare, participation, youth, etc.).[19]

The distinction between autonomy and co-governance is not always clear. When provinces and municipalities act autonomously, they must also take into account higher regulations, such as the aforementioned General Administrative Law Act or building regulations. It is furthermore somewhat confusing that the Provincial and Municipal Acts impose obligations, but that these must be regarded as autonomous. Sometimes it is also almost irrelevant whether the legislature regulates a matter in the Provincial and Municipal Acts (autonomy) or in a specific regulation (co-governance).

The legal consequences of the distinction are limited. The main consequence concerns the arrangement for the neglect of duties.[20] The arrangement that applies to co-governance differs from that for autonomy. If the provincial or municipal government neglects duties of co-governance, the Provincial Act and Municipal Act prescribe substitution: other public offices, such as the minister or (if it concerns the municipal government) the provincial executive, take the place of the government that has neglected its duties. In the case of a gross neglect of duties (this will generally concern autonomy), the Constitution provides that the legislature will make provisions, whether or not in deviation from constitutional provisions (see article 132(5) of the Constitution). Though the legal consequences may not be very extensive, the distinction is mainly one of principle. Provincial and municipal autonomy is one of the principles that shape the democratic constitutional state.[21] Autonomy is,

---

[17] Bovend'Eert et al. 2011, p. 60.

[18] Van Haaren-Dresens 2018, pp. 176–177.

[19] See for more examples: Broeksteeg 2021, pp. 53, 56–57.

[20] For further consequences, see: Broeksteeg 2021, pp. 57–58.

[21] Dölle and Elzinga 2004, p. 156.

so to speak, a legal principle: the legal recognition of the right of provinces and municipalities to initiate matters relating to their own affairs.

7.4.2 *The Councils as Head of the Local Government*

Article 125(1) of the Constitution provides that the provincial or municipal council is at the head of the provincial or municipal government. There is scarcely any debate about this rule, even though there have been many developments concerning those governments over the last century. On the one hand, the Constitution does not attach any concrete legal consequences to the headship of the councils. On the other hand, the provision makes clear that the councils occupy a central place in provincial and municipal governance.[22] In the 1983 constitutional revision, the headship of the councils was interpreted as meaning that the councils have the final say on the main points of the provincial or municipal policy to be pursued. For that reason, the councils have regulatory authority. Furthermore, they cannot be dissolved prematurely, that is to say before the end of the regular term of office, unless in the case of provincial or municipal reorganisation or of a gross neglect of duties.

Previously, the headship was linked to the monistic administrative structure, in which the councils had all the powers and the executive only had powers derived from the powers of the councils. Upon the dualisation of the provincial and municipal government structure, the question arose as to how dualisation affects the constitutional headship. The government committee that prepared the dualisation reform interpreted headship as meaning that the councils are ultimately responsible for the provincial and municipal administration. This final responsibility gives the councils controlling, regulatory, administrative and budgetary primacy. This does not mean that the executive cannot have its own administrative powers. However, the allocation of administrative powers to the executive must be done with restraint. The councils retain autonomous administrative powers; the executive is always dependent on a specific basis for the allocation of powers. In addition, the loss of some administrative powers was compensated for by the strengthening of controlling, regulatory and budgetary powers. As a result, the councils still have a central role within the provincial and municipal governments.

The term "final responsibility", as used by the legislature with the dualisation reform, means that it has arrived at a different interpretation of article 125(1) of the Constitution. Previously, the meaning was that the councils have all the provincial and municipal powers, whereas nowadays the meaning is that the councils are ultimately responsible for the provincial and municipal administration. Although it remains a vague and not very legal concept that barely defines what the councils' duties are,[23] at the same time it is a generally recognised principle of Dutch decentralisation law.

---

22 Bovend'Eert 2011 et al. 2011, pp. 105–151; Broeksteeg 2021, pp. 65–67.

23 Broeksteeg 2021, p. 67.

7.4.3 Administrative Supervision

In a decentralised unitary state, decentralised governments have the freedom to shape their own policy, but they are subject to administrative supervision. Administrative supervision is a means to prevent the unitary state from disintegrating into provinces and municipalities that operate more or less independently. Just because they are autonomous does not mean that they are independent.[24] Furthermore, administrative supervision can serve as a way to monitor the quality of the provincial and municipal decision-making and to protect the (fundamental) rights and interests of citizens. Administrative supervision ranks alongside judicial supervision.

Given that the autonomy of provinces and municipalities has to be guaranteed, administrative supervision must always be proportionate, which means that it must never go beyond what is necessary. In addition, to prevent far-reaching infringement of provincial and municipal autonomy, administrative supervision must be based on law. As said before, article 132(2) of the Constitution provides little direction, but it does stipulate that administrative supervision is regulated by law. This is a blank assignment.[25] The administrative supervision of provinces and municipalities is provided for not only in the Provincial Act and Municipal Act, but also in the General Administrative Law Act.

In 2012, the system of administrative supervision was revised. The Act on the Revitalisation of Generic Supervision (*Wet revitalisering generiek toezicht*) sought to ensure that specific supervision, often laid down in co-governance laws, was abolished. The generic supervisory instruments of the Municipal Act should be applied more often. Moreover, administrative supervision was seen as the *ultimum remedium* or last resort. The 2012 Act abandons this restraint. It assumes a broader and more proactive application of administrative supervision. This is possible within the confines of the Constitution. It simply gives the legislature a lot of freedom to shape and apply supervision.[26]

One of the main and most far-reaching forms of administrative supervision is the right of the central government to annul provincial and municipal decisions (spontaneous annulment).[27] According to article 132(4) of the Constitution, decisions made by provincial and municipal governments can by annulled by Royal Decree, which means by the central government, on the grounds of a conflict with the law or with the public interest. Conflict with the law means a conflict with any higher written and unwritten rule, including the law, the Constitution and treaty provisions. Conflict with the public interest is more difficult to explain. This involves a weighing of interests, namely the municipal interest versus a higher interest, mostly an interest of the central government. The supervisor, i.e. the central government, makes that decision and determines which interest carries more weight. This is broader than a

[24] Oppenheim 1928, p. 92.

[25] Bovend'Eert et al. 2011, pp. 182–186.

[26] Broeksteeg 2021, pp. 336–337.

[27] Broeksteeg 2021, pp. 342–355.

test for legality; efficiency considerations may also play a role here. Annulment due to a conflict with the public interest can therefore have a political quality.

In practice, however, there is no evidence of less restrained application. Since 2012, there have been two annulments of municipal decisions (and none of provincial decisions). In 2021, the central government annulled a decision by the municipal council of Westland, which refused to include an Islamic primary school in a municipal school plan, contrary to the law.[28] In 2023, it overturned a decision by the municipal council of Utrecht, which, according to the central government, was pursuing an income policy that was contrary to the public interest because such policy is a matter solely for the central government.[29] We can therefore conclude that annulment still is a last resort.[30]

The same applies, more or less, to the arrangement for a neglect of duties.[31] Though the legislature's purpose was to revitalise that arrangement, the practice is different. The first sentence of article 132(5) of the Constitution provides for a co-governance arrangement, though the provision implies little more than that the law provides for further regulation. In the event that the municipal council or executive neglects its duties, the provincial executive will take its place; if the mayor is negligent, the decisions that the mayor should have made will be made by the King's Commissioner—and in some cases by the relevant minister. If one of the provincial offices neglects its duties, the relevant central government minister will perform the neglected duties.

Since 2012, this arrangement has been applied twice. In 2016, the executive of the Province of Groningen took the place of the executive of the Municipality of Delfzijl, which did not want to provide shelter for refugees with temporary asylum residence permits.[32] In 2019, the Education Minister made the decision that the municipal council of Westland should have made but did not want to, which was to include an Islamic primary school in the municipal school plan (see above).[33]

Intervention due to a gross neglect of duties is much rarer. The second sentence of article 132(5) of the Constitution tasks the legislature with enacting an ad hoc law, thus a law for a specific case. In the few examples of a gross neglect of duties, such an act dissolves the council and the executive and dismisses the mayor. A government commissioner is appointed, who takes over the government of the municipality (there has never been a gross neglect of duties by a province) but has to obey the minister's instructions. In the six cases since 1848, this situation has mostly concerned a refusal to perform certain obligations under the Municipal Act.[34] The last time this arrangement was applied to a municipality was in 1951 (Finsterwolde)[35]; in 2018,

[28] Royal Decree of 29 November 2021, *Stcrt.* 2021, 47,964.

[29] Royal Decree of 20 December 2023, *Stcrt.* 2023, 35,354.

[30] Broeksteeg 2021, p. 355.

[31] Broeksteeg 2021, pp. 357–370.

[32] Decision of the executive of the province of Groningen of 21 April 2017.

[33] Royal Decree of 9 July 2020, *Stcrt.* 2020, 39,162.

[34] Broeksteeg 2021, pp. 366–369.

[35] Act of 20 July 1951, *Stb.* 1951, 308.

the legislature intervened in Sint Eustatius, a Caribbean island, which is a public body within the Kingdom of the Netherlands.[36]

The foregoing leads to the conclusion that while administrative supervision is necessary in a decentralised unitary state, the decentralised governments need to have autonomy to fulfil their duties. For that reason, administrative supervision is still applied in a restrained manner, even after the legislature sought to apply supervision more actively. It is a feature of the constitutional identity of decentralisation that while administrative supervision is part of the relationship between the central government and the decentralised governments, the central government observes restraint in its application.

7.5 Conclusion

Though the Constitution makes no mention of it, the Netherlands is a decentralised unitary state. It is essentially comprised of three layers (together called Thorbecke's House): the central government, provinces and municipalities. A number of elements make up the constitutional identity of this decentralisation. In the first place, the provinces and municipalities have a uniform organisation, regardless of their location, size and population. The Constitution is not very normative and leaves much to the legislature, such as the procedure for reorganising provinces and municipalities, the manner of cooperation between provinces and municipalities, and the financial relationship with the central government. The constitutional identity certainly includes the paired concepts of autonomy and co-governance. Though many of the duties fulfilled by the provinces and municipalities are in the domain of co-governance, the concept of autonomy is essential. This is the legal recognition of the right of the provinces and municipalities to initiate matters relating to their own affairs. Another aspect of the constitutional identity is the headship of the provincial and municipal councils, as representatives of the people. The councils are ultimately responsible for the provincial and municipal administration. This bestows on them various powers, including that to issue binding regulations. Lastly, I wish to draw attention to administrative supervision, which is undeniably necessary in a decentralised unitary state and therefore an element of the relationship between the central government and the decentralised governments, but the central government is very reticent when it comes to application, partly to guarantee the autonomy of the provinces and municipalities.

References

Bovend'Eert P P T et al. (2011) Constitutionele normen en decentralisatie. Kluwer, Deventer
Broeksteeg J L W (2021) Gemeenterecht. Wolters Kluwer, Deventer

[36] Act of 7 February 2018, *Stb.* 2018, 26.

Dölle A H M, Elzinga D J (2004) Handboek van het Nederlandse gemeenterecht. Kluwer, Deventer
Oppenheim J (edited by Van der Pot C W) (1928) Het Nederlandsch Gemeenterecht. De erven F Bohn, Haarlem
State Commission (2000) Dualisme en lokale democratie. Samsom, Alphen aan den Rijn
Van Haaren-Dresens B M (2018) Zelfstandigheid in gebondenheid. Wolf Legal Publishers Oisterwijk

Hansko (J. L.W.) Broeksteeg LL.M. Ph.D., is a Professor of Constitutional Law at the Radboud University, Nijmegen, the Netherlands. He specialises in parliamentary law, decentralisation and some fundamental rights, such as the freedom of religion, of assembly and of education. He is a deputy judge at the district court of Utrecht.

Chapter 8
Courts and the Constitution: The Prohibition on Constitutional Review in the Spotlight

Gerhard van der Schyff

Contents

Abstract This contribution considers that the prohibition on constitutional review by the judiciary in article 120 of the Constitution of the Netherlands is part of the country's constitutional identity. According to the provision, the courts may not review the constitutionality of Acts of Parliament and treaties. However, the fact that the provision is part of Dutch constitutional identity does not mean that it cannot be revisited. In assessing the prohibition, consideration is given to the historical development of the provision and its relationship to treaty review by the judiciary under article 94 of the Constitution. Proposals for reforming article 120 are also discussed. It is concluded that the prohibition in article 120 should be amended to allow the courts to review the constitutionality of Acts to improve citizens' legal protection. At the very least, the courts should be able to decide whether Acts comply with the classical rights in the Constitution. Ideally, all courts should be given this power, rather than setting up a constitutional court.

Keywords Constitution of the Netherlands · Constitutional identity · Judicial review · Constitutional review · Treaty review · Constitutional reform

G. van der Schyff (✉)
Tilburg Law School, Tilburg University, Tilburg, The Netherlands
e-mail: G.vdrSchyff@tilburguniversity.edu

G. van der Schyff (ed.), *The Constitutional Identity of The Netherlands*,
https://doi.org/10.1007/978-94-6265-779-3_8

8.1 Constitutional Cornerstone

Article 120 of the Constitution of the Netherlands is arguably a central part of the identity of the country's constitutional order.[1] Few constitutional rules or conventions are so characteristic and formative for the constitutional order as article 120. The provision reads as follows: "The constitutionality of Acts of Parliament and treaties shall not be reviewed by the courts."[2] In prohibiting the courts from checking the constitutionality of Acts of Parliaments and treaties, a strict separation of powers is maintained between the judicial branch on the one hand, and the legislative branch on the other hand.

Without article 120 of the Constitution, the constitutional order's account of itself would be radically different, thereby affirming its status as a cornerstone of its constitutional identity. However, although the provision can be said to form a part of Dutch constitutional identity, it is not uncontroversial. This is especially the case as the provision prevents the courts from reviewing the constitutionality of Acts of Parliament. Among liberal democratic constitutional orders, especially those in the immediate region, the Netherlands occupies a somewhat unique position in this regard. Whereas other legal orders are preoccupied by questions such as the intensity and shape of judicial constitutional review, the Netherlands still discusses the question whether such review should be introduced or not.[3] For instance, in 2024 the cabinet of Prime Minster Schoof, like the Rutte IV cabinet in 2022, expressed its support for amending article 120 to introduce the judicial review of Acts of Parliament.[4] This is in line with the similar recommendation made by the State Commission on the Parliamentary System in its 2018 report.[5]

In view of the importance of article 120 of the Constitution for the legal order and given the debate on amending this provision, this contribution will analyse this aspect of Dutch constitutional identity. The focus will be on reviewing the constitutionality

---

[1] See also Besselink 2022, p. 406.

[2] Unless indicated otherwise, all translations of the Constitution are taken from the English version published by the Ministry of the Interior and Kingdom Relations in 2023.

[3] For an historical overview, see Van Houten 1997, pp. 117–160.

[4] In July 2025, a month after the Schoof cabinet had become a caretaker government due to its political collapse, it released a draft proposal to amend article 120 of the Constitution for internet consultation. For the Explanatory Memorandum accompanying the proposal, see *Wijziging van de Grondwet ter invoering van constitutionele toetsing*, WGK026600. At the time of writing, October 2025, no constitutional amendment bill had been tabled following the consultation. In February 2025, the Schoof cabinet published a policy note on constitutional review (*Contourennota constitutonele toetsing*, Parliamentary Proceedings II 2024–2025, 36 600 VII, No. 129) in which it outlined its views in some detail. Prior to the note, the cabinet outlined its views briefly in the September 2024 government programme (*Regeerakkoord 2024*, attached to Parliamentary Proceedings II 2023–2024, No. 96) and in the May 2024 coalition agreement (*Hoofdlijnenakkoord 2024–2028*). Regarding the Rutte VI cabinet's views, see especially Parliamentary Proceedings II 2021–2022, 35 925 VII, No. 169, pp. 1–2 (*Hoofdlijnenbrief constitutionele toetsing*). See also the views of P Omtzigt as a Member of Parliament: Parliamentary Proceedings II 2022–2023, 36 344, No. 2.

[5] State Commission on the Parliamentary System 2018, p. 158.

of Acts of Parliament as the most controversial aspect of the prohibition, while the review of treaties will be included where relevant. In what follows, attention will be paid to the development and context of the prohibition, its purpose and reach in positive law, its relationship to treaty review under article 94 of the Constitution, the main arguments for amending article 120 and considerations regarding the future of the provision. Although reference will be made to the Schoof cabinet's reform proposals, the intention is to discuss the issue of constitutional review as such, rather than focusing only on the proposals. The reason for this is that the Schoof cabinet fell in 2025, which raises the question of whether a future cabinet will favour a similar course on constitutional review and adopt like-minded proposals.

8.2 Development and Context of Article 120

While liberal revolutions spread across Europe in 1848, the amendments of the Constitution in that year spared the Netherlands from a similar fate. Fearing revolution, king William II appointed a State Commission on the Constitution, chaired by the liberal statesman J R Thorbecke.[6] The result was to establish the current system of cabinet government by making ministers accountable to parliament, called the States General, thereby limiting the king's political power.[7] The reforms were typical of their time by emphasising the importance of legislatures and their laws. As part of the reforms, the prohibition on constitutional review was inserted in the Constitution in 1848, as article 115. In its first incarnation, the provision simply stated that "Acts of Parliament are inviolable."[8] It was only in 1983 that the provision, now contained in article 120, received its current formulation and included the prohibition on reviewing the constitutionality of treaties. The latter prohibition was previously regulated by article 60, a separate provision in the Constitution.

Such was the respect for the will of the electorate in the nineteenth century that neighbouring Belgium did not introduce a similar prohibition in its Constitution, as it was taken for granted that the courts would refrain from reviewing the constitutionality of Acts of Parliament.[9] While the absence of a constitutional prohibition in Belgium later facilitated the introduction of judicial review, the prohibition from 1848 still has an impact in the Netherlands today.[10] As long as article 120 remains in the Constitution, the courts are prohibited from carrying out review. Whereas the Supreme Court's 1803 judgement in *Marbury v. Madison* meant that the United States of America was an exception because it practised constitutional review while other

[6] See Voermans 2023, pp. 65–66; Leenknegt 2008, pp. 13–16.

[7] Leenknegt 2008, pp. 16–17.

[8] See Ellian and Manenschijn 2022, p. 484. Own translation of: "De wetten zijn onschendbaar." After the revision of 1956, the prohibition was contained in article 131(2) of the Constitution. For the historical context, see Besselink 2020, pp. 568–582.

[9] Claes et al. 2021, p. 11.

[10] On constitutional review's development in Belgium, see Claes et al. 2021, pp. 10–12.

countries refrained from doing so, today the Netherlands has become the exception to the norm. Courts reviewing the constitutionality of Acts of Parliament, a trend that began after the First World War and intensified after the Second World War, is now widely regarded as a standard element of constitutionalism.[11]

The exceptional nature of the prohibition on constitutional review in the Netherlands also becomes apparent when compared to the other autonomous countries in the Kingdom. In addition to the Netherlands, the Kingdom is composed of Curaçao, Aruba and Sint Maarten. The legal relationship between the constituent countries is governed by the Charter for the Kingdom of 1954.[12] Each country has a constitution and adopts its own laws, including Acts of Parliament. Apart from the Netherlands, all three of the other countries allow the courts in some way or another to review whether their Acts of Parliament conform to their constitutions.[13] For instance, the Constitutions of Curaçao and Aruba each contain a prohibition on constitutional review, not dissimilar to the one contained in the Dutch Constitution, but provide for an exception to the prohibition.[14] The exception entails that courts in each country are competent to review whether Acts comply with the mostly classical rights in their constitutions. The courts in Sint Maarten have more powers, as they can in principle review whether Acts comply with the country's constitution in its entirety.[15] In addition, the country has a Constitutional Court which can review the constitutionality of Acts that have been ratified but which have not yet entered into force.[16] The ex post review of Acts in concrete cases is therefore a feature of all three countries' constitutional orders, while Sint Maarten also allows the abstract review of Acts in ex ante cases.

8.3 Purpose and Reach of Article 120

In understanding the prohibition in article 120 of the Constitution, it becomes important to consider the purpose and reach of the provision. The purpose of the provision is chiefly to protect the *primacy* of the legislature, by preventing the courts from reviewing the constitutionality of its Acts.[17] In this regard, the legislature is

---

[11] See Tushnet 2018, pp. 50, 53; Tate and Vallinder 1995.

[12] On the Kingdom and its Charter, see Borman 2012, pp. 1–20; Duijf 2023, p. 216.

[13] See Goudappel and De Wit 2015, pp. 286–287.

[14] Articles I.22, VI.4 of the Constitution of Aruba; article 101 of the Constitution of Curaçao. See Duijf 2023, pp. 220–222; Goudappel and De Wit 2015, pp. 289–290.

[15] Article 119 of the Constitution of Sint Maarten. Judicial review is not possible in the event a constitutional provision does not lend itself to such review, according to article 119(1). The latter provision also excludes the constitutional review by the judiciary of the regulations mentioned in article 81 (h)-(j). See Duijf 2023, pp. 218–220; Claes et al. 2021, p. 54; Goudappel and De Wit 2015, pp. 290–292.

[16] Article 127 of the Constitution of Sint Maarten. See Duijf 2023, pp. 218–220; Claes et al. 2021, p. 53; Goudappel and De Wit 2015, pp. 290–292.

[17] See also Van der Schyff 2020, pp. 893–895.

composed of both the government and the States General, according to article 81 of the Constitution.[18] However, the primacy of the legislature in the Netherlands should not be confused with parliamentary sovereignty as it is traditionally understood in the United Kingdom. A V Dicey explained such sovereignty as the right of parliament "to make or unmake any law whatever; and further, that no person or body is recognised by the law of England as having a right to override or set aside the legislation of Parliament".[19] The concept of parliamentary sovereignty in the United Kingdom is closely tied to the fact that the country does not have a written or codified constitution which expresses higher law.[20] Parliament is therefore not bound by such a constitution, or by the Acts passed by previous parliaments. The constitutional law of the Netherlands is different from that in the United Kingdom in this respect. This is because the country does have a written or codified constitution, dating back to 1814 at the earliest.[21] Moreover, the Constitution is of a higher constitutional rank than Acts of Parliament.[22] The procedure to amend the Constitution is explained in article 137 and requires two readings in both chambers of parliament, the second of which needs a two-thirds majority, as well as a general election of the lower house of parliament between readings. According to article 81, Acts of Parliament on the other hand, only require a simple majority in a single reading in both chambers.[23] As a consequence, the Constitution is superior to Acts and cannot be overridden by simple majorities.

On account of the above, the legislature in the Netherlands cannot "make or unmake any law whatever", as the traditional doctrine of parliamentary sovereignty would have it. An Act of Parliament can be unconstitutional for contradicting the Constitution, a situation which is not affected by article 120. The question in the Netherlands though centres on who ultimately decides whether an Act is constitutional or not. Article 120 answers this question in favour of the legislature, given its democratic legitimacy, as opposed to the courts, whose members are appointed by the executive and not elected by the voters.[24] Acts of Parliament are therefore considered to be constitutional once adopted, unless the legislature itself decides otherwise by amending or repealing an Act on constitutional grounds. This applies not only to the content of such Acts, but also to the legislative procedure for their adoption.[25]

---

[18] Unless contradicted by the context, references to the "legislature" (*formele wetgever*) in the text refer to the construct in article 81 of the Constitution and to "parliament" refer to the States General (*Staten-Generaal*).

[19] Dicey 1959/1885, pp. 39–40.

[20] See Barendt 1998, pp. 1–2.

[21] For an historical overview, see Leenknegt 2008, pp. 12–13.

[22] For an outline of the hierarchy of legal regulations, see Burkens et al. 2022, p. 91.

[23] See Burkens et al. 2022, pp. 117–120.

[24] See also Voermans 2023, p. 669; Burkens et al. 2022, p. 207; Boogaard and Uzman 2021, pp. 1150–1151.

[25] See Voermans 2023, pp. 672–677; Burkens et al. 2022, p. 207.

Article 120 does not apply to regulations that are lower in the legal hierarchy than Acts of Parliament, such as regulations made by the government, ministers, provinces or local councils.[26] The constitutionality of such regulations may be reviewed by the courts. This is because the wording of article 120 only refers to Acts and treaties, thereby excluding other regulations from the prohibition. The reach of the prohibition though, has been interpreted widely by the Supreme Court in the 1989 landmark *Harmonisatiewet* case.[27] The significance of article 120 was understood as reflecting the traditional role of the courts in the constitutional system.[28] According to the Court, the effect of the prohibition in article 120 is not only to prevent the review of Acts against the Constitution, but also against the Charter for the Kingdom.[29] In addition, the prohibition applies to unwritten fundamental legal principles, such as legal certainty and proportionality.[30] This means that courts may not review whether an Act is consistent with such principles. Fundamental legal principles are generally excluded because of legal certainty concerns given their unwritten nature.[31] Courts though are willing to apply such fundamental principles, such as proportionality, in the event the strict enforcement of an Act of Parliament would lead to harsh consequences which had not been factored in by the legislature prior to its adoption.[32] This is referred to as the contra legem application of fundamental principles, which means that such principles are applied instead of the Act in question.

In turning to article 120 and treaties, which parliament must approve in accordance with article 91 of the Constitution, similar principles to Acts of Parliament apply. The courts are not to review the constitutionality of such instruments either.[33] This includes the review of article 91(3), which provides that a treaty which conflicts with the Constitution must be approved in both chambers of parliament by a two-thirds majority, thereby justifying the deviation from the Constitution.[34] As should be clear,

---

[26] See Nieuwenhuis et al. 2021, pp. 53–54. These authors also explain that courts should interpret Acts in accordance with the Constitution, but note that the Constitution offers few guiding principles in this regard.

[27] Supreme Court, judgement of 14 April 1989, ECLI:NL:HR:1989:AD5725 (*Harmonisatiewet*), paras 3.2, 3.5.

[28] Ibid., paras 3.5, 4.2.

[29] Ibid., paras 4.1–4.6. The Court interpreted article 49 of the Charter, which allows rules on the binding effect of legislative measures which are inconsistent with, inter alia, the Charter. It held that an Act of Parliament could not be reviewed against the Charter, unless expressly provided for by a Kingdom Act of Parliament (i.e. an Act which applies to the Kingdom). On article 49 of the Charter, see Borman 2012, pp. 175–178.

[30] *Harmonisatiewet* n. 27, para 3.6.

[31] See Van Houten 1997, pp. 174–175. See also *Wijziging van de Grondwet ter invoering van constitutionele toetsing* n. 4, p. 14; *Contourennota constitutionele toetsing* n. 4, pp. 8–9.

[32] See Boogaard and Uzman 2021, p. 1159. See also the views of Advocate General Snijders, Council of State, opinion of 18 May 2022, ECLI:NL:RVS:2022:1441, para 7; Advocates General Widdershoven and Wattel, Council of State, opinion of 7 July 2021ECLI:NL:RVS:2021:1468, para 9.4 ("Widdershoven and Wattel Opinion").

[33] Regarding treaties and article 120, see the full discussion by Boogaard and Uzman 2021, pp. 1160–1161.

[34] On this provision, see Leenknegt 2021, pp. 891–894.

whether this is the case and therefore the special majority is required is a political and not a judicial decision because of article 120.

8.4 Treaty Review by the Courts

A full account of article 120 of the Constitution as part of Dutch constitutional identity requires a discussion of article 94, which could also be said to form part of such identity.[35] The provision states that: "Statutory regulations in force within the Kingdom shall not be applicable if such application is in conflict with provisions of treaties or of resolutions by international institutions that are binding on all persons."[36] A comparison of the two provisions reveals a dichotomy that goes to the core of the Dutch constitutional order. While article 120 forbids the courts from reviewing the constitutionality of Acts of Parliament, in the spirit political constitutionalism, article 94 calls upon them to review the consistency of such Acts with international law, in the spirit of legal constitutionalism.[37] Where such consistency lacks, the provision requires of the courts (and the executive) to apply international law instead of the Act in question.[38] In practice, this mainly relates to classical rights in treaties such as the European Convention on Human Rights (ECHR), as opposed to social rights in treaties such as the European Social Charter (ESC), which are generally regarded as non-self-executing.[39] The application of EU law, it is important to note, is considered to be a matter of EU law and is therefore unaffected by constitutional rules such as article 94.[40]

In the absence of constitutional review, the review of treaties by the courts has become a mainstay of Dutch constitutionalism, particularly with regard to the protection of fundamental rights.[41] The frequency and importance of such review increased after the Second World War with the adoption of more treaties. For instance, the well-known *Urgenda* climate judgement, in which the Supreme Court ordered the state to reduce greenhouse gas emissions more sharply, was based on the rights to life in article 2 ECHR and to private and family life in article 8 ECHR, and not the state's duty in article 21 of the Constitution "to keep the country habitable and to protect and improve the environment".[42] Because of treaty review, it also became untenable to hold that Acts of Parliament were "inviolable", as was the case in the Constitution

[35] See Besselink 2022, p. 406.

[36] The term "statutory regulations" includes all legal regulations in the Kingdom. Compare Besselink 2022, p. 410.

[37] On these two types of constitutionalism and constitutional review, see Ellian and Manenschijn 2022, pp. 489–490, 492–493.

[38] See Burkens et al. 2022, p. 383 (including n. 27).

[39] See further Burkens et al. 2022, p. 386.

[40] Supreme Court, judgement of 2 November 2004, ECLI:NL:HR:2004:AR1797, para 3.6.

[41] See also Heringa 2023, p. 364.

[42] Supreme Court, judgement of 20 December 2019, ECLI:NL:HR:2019:2006 (*Urgenda*), para 8.3.4. This was the case even though an Act of Parliament was not contested as such. Also, the

before 1983, leading to the more precise wording in article 120 that courts may not review their constitutionality.

The dichotomy between treaty review and constitutional review has been the subject of much debate.[43] In particular with regard to the justification for still prohibiting constitutional review on the one hand, when the courts are obliged to conduct treaty review on the other. The question of constitutional review by the courts would have been redundant if there had been no difference with treaty review. However, the Constitution is not simply a carbon copy of treaties, as a comparison between the right to freedom of religion in article 6 of the Constitution and article 9 ECHR shows. Both provisions, although guaranteeing the same right, do so quite differently.[44] This means that the question of constitutional review can be considered in its own right given the difference. Consequently, the discussion turns to explaining and evaluating the reasons and proposals for reforming article 120.

8.5 Democratic Legitimacy and Legal Protection

The democratic credentials of the legislature, as mentioned above, go to the heart of the prohibition on constitutional review by the courts in article 120 of the Constitution. According to this view, both chambers of parliament have been elected by the voters, and should therefore have the final say in deciding whether its Acts are in line with the Constitution.[45] In addition, the government is accountable to parliament whose confidence it must maintain.[46] This also explains why the exemption only applies to Acts of Parliament and not to all regulations, such as provincial and local ordinances. The fact that only Acts are excluded from judicial review emphasises the importance of parliament as the highest democratic decision-making body in the Netherlands. Other decision-makers such as the provinces and local councils are also democratically accountable to voters, but are not as central to the constitutional system as parliament.

Court did not order the state to adopt an Act of Parliament, instead leaving it to the state to choose how to reduce emissions (para 8.2.7.). See generally, Voermans 2023, pp. 616–618.

[43] See Burkens et al. 2022, p. 208; Van der Schyff 2020, pp. 890–892.

[44] For instance, the constitutional right has stricter legality requirements (was the limitation by - or in accordance - with an Act of Parliament?) than the treaty right (does the limitation have a clear basis in domestic law?). On the other hand, the treaty right includes a proportionality test (was the limitation necessary in a democratic society?), while the constitutional right does not. Requiring a proportionality test for the limitation of constitutional rights, as proposed by the Schoof cabinet (*Wijziging van de Grondwet ter invoering van constitutionele toetsing* n. 4, pp. 15, 24) would still leave the difference regarding the legality test. For an in-depth study of the constitutional limitation provisions, see Claes et al. 2024. See also the clear differences between the right to education in article 23 of the Constitution and article 2 of Protocol 1 of the ECHR. On the right in the Constitution, see Chapter 13 in this volume.

[45] The lower chamber is elected directly by voters and the upper chamber indirectly.

[46] See Burkens et al. 2022, pp. 120–121.

While the legislature undoubtedly fulfils a central role when it comes to Dutch democracy, the question can be put whether this justifies barring the courts from reviewing the constitutionality of its Acts. Although the legislature is accorded primacy, it makes less use of this primacy than the existence of a provision such as article 120 would suggest. There has been a so-called legislative "retreat" in practice, also known as the "deparliamentarisation" of legislation.[47] For example, Acts of Parliament are no longer as important for the regulation of society as they used to be, as the importance of secondary or delegated legislation has increased over time. The Environment Act (*Omgevingswet*) of 2016 is a case in point, as it relies heavily on the government's rule-making powers.[48] This is because the Act creates a general legislative framework, which is then fleshed out in four government decrees. Although the legislature, given its primacy, still takes the initiative to make laws, it does not fully exercise its powers and chooses to delegate rule-making authority. This raises the question of why the courts should still be subject to the prohibition on judicial review, given that Acts of Parliament are no longer as central to the legislative process or as exhaustive in terms of their content as they once might have been.

In support of the prohibition in article 120 of the Constitution, the counterargument could be made that its reach should be extended to more regulations, instead of only to Acts of Parliament. In other words, if the object is to protect democratic decision-making from judicial review, the prohibition should factor in that other democratically legitimate organs than the legislature make important rules. For example, the government has indirect democratic legitimacy by being accountable to parliament for the rules it makes. However, extending the prohibition on review, would not be the most appropriate response to the legislature's "retreat". This is because there is an increased need for legal protection across society as such. The legal regulation of society has become increasingly complex, especially given people's expectations of what may be termed the "welfare state".[49] Legal regulations, including but not limited to Acts of Parliament, cannot always foresee all possible situations. This means that there is a clear need for the courts to interpret and apply such regulations to individual cases in order to protect fundamental rights.[50] Otherwise, legal rules would have to be amended to address such cases. However, this might not always be feasible, apart from being a laborious and time-consuming process which might not prevent related problems from still emerging. The legislative process, therefore, is in need of a judicial check.

The need to improve the legal protection of citizens through judicial review was also one of the main reasons for the Schoof and Rutte IV cabinets to come out in

[47] See, generally, Van Gestel 2013.

[48] See, generally, Nijboer 2023.

[49] Parliamentary Proceedings II 2002–2003, 28 331, No. 9, p. 12 (Explanatory Memorandum of the Halsema Proposal). This private member's bill by F Halsema wanted to amend article 120 to allow constitutional review. The bill passed is first reading, but lapsed in 2018 before the second reading could take place.

[50] Ibid., p. 13. See also the view expressed on constitutional review by the chair of the Administrative Jurisdiction Division of the Council of State, expressed in the letter to the relevant minister on 22 April 2022.

favour of reforming article 120 of the Constitution in 2024 and 2022 respectively.[51] While the Rutte III cabinet had expressed doubts about such a reform in 2019, its successors decided to follow the 2018 recommendation of the State Commission on the Parliamentary System to amend the prohibition.[52] The change of view can probably be attributed in part to the Childcare Allowance Case, in which thousands of parents unjustly accused of fraud had to repay social benefits to the state, thereby causing them financial hardship.[53] The issue led, among other things, to an Opinion by the Venice Commission in 2021 which stopped short of calling for article 120 to be amended. Nonetheless, the Commission concluded that "based on a profound analysis, it could be considered whether article 120 of the Constitution should be amended, or whether other mechanisms of constitutional review should be introduced".[54] While it cannot be said that constitutional review by the judiciary would have prevented the harm caused the Childcare Allowance Case, the matter does reinforce the overall argument that extra legal protection is called for. In addressing this need, amending article 120 so that the courts can review the constitutionality of Acts of Parliament can certainly play a role, instead of relying solely on the legislature for this.

8.6 Amending Article 120 of the Constitution

The question turns to what the future should hold for article 120 of the Constitution, having established that calls for its reform can be justified. In this regard, the provision can either be abolished, or amended. Abolishing the provision would mean that the courts can review the consistency of Acts of Parliament and treaties with the Constitution in its entirety. After consideration, the abolition of the provision is not to be preferred to its amendment for two reasons.

Firstly, to date there has been no pressing reason to allow the courts to review the constitutionality of treaties, in addition to Acts of Parliament. This is particularly the case when one considers that the main purpose of such a reform would be to improve the legal protection of citizens against the exercise of legislative power, implying the review of Acts rather than treaties. Also, it remains unclear why treaties should be reviewed by the courts, while article 91(3) of the Constitution already foresees a mechanism for the adoption of treaties which deviate from its provisions

---

[51] *Wijziging van de Grondwet ter invoering van constitutionele toetsing* n. 4, p. 7 (also mentioning the fostering of a constitutional culture on p. 2); *Contourennota constitutionele toetsing* n. 4, p. 1 (including the fostering of a constitutional culture); *Hoofdlijnenbrief constitutionele toetsing* n. 4, pp. 1, 3. For critical thoughts regarding this argument, see Ellian and Manenschijn 2022, pp. 488–489, 495.

[52] Parliamentary Proceedings I 2019–2020, 34 430, T, p. 9.

[53] See Venice Commission, Netherlands. Opinion on the Legal Protection of Citizens, No. 1031/2021, 15–16 October 2021, paras 6–27.

[54] Ibid., para 137.

with a two-thirds majority, as mentioned above.[55] Allowing the courts to review the constitutionality of treaties is not ripe at the moment. Instead of abolishing the prohibition on reviewing both Acts of Parliament and treaties, it would be more sensible to amend it to review Acts only. Whether this should also include bills, will be discussed under the modalities of review.

Secondly, to date there has been no pressing reason to allow the courts to review the Constitution in its entirety. Instead, it makes more sense to exempt constitutional provisions from the prohibition in article 120 that can help improve the legal protection of citizens, given that this is one of the main reasons to introduce judicial review.[56] This would also be in line with most opinions and proposals on the subject that would allow courts to review classical rights at a minimum, given their function of protecting people against the state.[57] The Schoof cabinet, for instance, also came out in support of the review of classical rights as a category.[58] Typically, many provisions in the first chapter of the Constitution are considered to guarantee such rights, while often provisions in other chapters are added to the list.[59] Again, instead of abolishing the prohibition on reviewing the Constitution in its entirety, it would be more sensible to at the least exempt classical rights.

In addition to classical rights, it needs to be considered whether other constitutional provisions can be exempted from the prohibition in improving the legal protection of citizens, in particular the social rights guaranteed in the Constitution's first chapter. Social rights can be defined as requiring positive action by the state, which is sometimes considered too difficult for courts to judge, as opposed to classical rights requiring negative action, which is generally considered straightforward to judge.[60] This distinction is then advanced as a reason why classical rights can be exempted from the prohibition on constitutional review, but social rights cannot.[61]

---

55 The State Commission on the Parliamentary System 2018, p. 156 mentioned that a newly created constitutional court could be allowed to review article 91(3) of the Constitution, without discussing the merits of the idea. The Schoof cabinet, however, was not supportive of allowing the constitutional review of treaties under article 120 of the Constitution, which would also include article 91(3). See *Wijziging van de Grondwet ter invoering van constitutionele toetsing* n. 4, pp. 16–17.

56 See *Wijziging van de Grondwet ter invoering van constitutionele toetsing* n. 4, p. 14 and *Contourennota constitutionele toetsing* n. 4, p. 1 (regarding the Schoof cabinet); *Hoofdlijnenbrief constitutionele toetsing* n. 4, pp. 1, 3 (regarding the Rutte IV cabinet).

57 See State Commission on the Parliamentary System 2018, pp. 158, 260 (referring to "civil and political rights"); Explanatory Memorandum n. 50, pp. 18–19, which refer to "subjective rights", largely corresponding to provisions of the classical right type.

58 *Wijziging van de Grondwet ter invoering van constitutionele toetsing* n. 4, p. 10; *Contourennota constitutionele toetsing* n. 4, p. 5. Regarding the Rutte IV cabinet, see *Hoofdlijnenbrief constitutionele toetsing* n. 4, p. 11.

59 See State Commission on the Parliamentary System 2018, pp. 149–150, adding to the list a provision such as article 114 (prohibiting the imposition of capital punishment). The Schoof cabinet, however, restricted its proposal to classical rights guaranteed in the first chapter of the Constitution, see *Wijziging van de Grondwet ter invoering van constitutionele toetsing* n. 4, p. 10.

60 State Commission on the Parliamentary System 2018, p. 202.

61 Ibid. Compare the views of the Schoof cabinet, see *Wijziging van de Grondwet ter invoering van constitutionele toetsing* n. 4, pp. 12–14.

Although there is something to be said for the distinction in understanding how rights work, it should not be overemphasised. This is because courts increasingly interpret classical rights in a social sense by requiring positive state action. For instance, the European Court of Human Rights in *Verein KlimaSeniorinnen Schweiz v. Switzerland* found that the right to private and family life in article 8 ECHR requires states to act to mitigate the adverse effects of climate change.[62] If courts are capable of judging such complicated cases of positive state action in the context of classical rights, they should in principle also be capable of judging such cases in the context of social rights. Instead of rejecting the constitutional review of such rights altogether, it would be prudent to decide which rights could improve citizens' legal protection by being reviewable.[63] The same could be said of the general provision included in the Constitution in lieu of a preamble, which guarantees "fundamental rights" and "democracy based on the rule of law", as well as the unwritten fundamental principles.[64] The open wording or nature of these guarantees are relevant to consider when deciding whether or not they should be subject to judicial review. In any case, the general provision and fundamental principles may perhaps guide courts in the interpretation and application of the constitutional provisions to be exempted from the prohibition in article 120.

8.7 The Modalities of Constitutional Review

Amending article 120 of the Constitution to allow for judicial review raises questions about the modalities of such review. There seems to be general support to allow only the review of Acts of Parliament and not of bills, as also implied or expressed by the Schoof cabinet and its predecessor cabinet.[65] In other words, a review which is ex post and concrete in nature, as opposed to ex ante and abstract. There is much to be

[62] ECtHR Case No. 53600/20, judgement of 9 April 2024 (*Verein KlimaSeniorinnen Schweiz v. Switzerland*), paras 573–574. The case was similar to the Dutch *Urgenda* judgement n. 43.

[63] See also the views expressed on constitutional review by the chair of the Administrative Jurisdiction Division of the Council of State in the letter of 22 April 2022. And see the discussion by Leijten and Loven 2023, pp. 110–114.

[64] The general provision states that: "The Constitution guarantees fundamental rights and democracy based on the rule of law." The State Commission on the Parliamentary System 2018, p. 150 also recommended reviewing the provision. The Schoof cabinet, however, did not, see *Wijziging van de Grondwet ter invoering van constitutionele toetsing* n. 4, p. 14. Consider also Leijten and Loven 2023, pp. 107–108. As for the fundamental principles, while the Schoof cabinet (*Wijziging van de Grondwet ter invoering van constitutionele toetsing* n. 4, p. 14; *Contourennota constitutionele toetsing* n. 4, pp. 8–9) and the Explanatory Memorandum (n. 50, p. 19) were not in favour of their review in the context of article 120 of the Constitution, the Rutte IV cabinet (*Hoofdlijnenbrief constitutionele toetsing* n. 4, p. 9) adopted a more careful position. On fundamental principles, see Al Khatib and Tingen 2023.

[65] See *Wijziging van de Grondwet ter invoering van constitutionele toetsing* n. 4, p. 16; *Contourennota constitutionele toetsing* n. 4, pp. 4–5; *Hoofdlijnenbrief constitutionele toetsing* n. 4, p. 14. See also the State Commission on the Parliamentary System 2018, p. 149.

said for reviewing only Acts, as this would be the optimal type of review to increase the legal protection of citizens.[66] Also allowing the review of bills would imply a more relative separation of powers than is necessary in achieving that aim. There seems to be no real reason for the courts to also exercise constitutional control over the legislative process as such.

A related modality concerns whether constitutional judgements should be legally binding, also called strong review; or non-binding, also called weak review. Under treaty review, courts refuse to apply laws that are inconsistent with binding international law, which amounts to strong review. Most proposals on constitutional review also favour strong as opposed to weak review, as in the United Kingdom, where courts can only inform parliament that they consider an Act to be incompatible with the guarantees in the Human Rights Act.[67] While weak review may respect the sovereignty of parliament in that country, strong constitutional review in the Netherlands would better meet the wish to improve citizens' legal protection. However, weak review might be a political comprise when it comes to exempting provisions from the prohibition in article 120 of the Constitution, whose review would be more controversial than classical rights.[68]

Although there is agreement that judicial review should be ex post, concrete and strong, opinions differ as to which courts should conduct such review. While the Rutte IV cabinet expressed its support for diffuse review by all courts, as is the case with treaty review, the Schoof cabinet favoured centralised review by a new constitutional court, as did the State Commission on the Parliamentary System.[69] The Schoof cabinet pointed to a new court as a strong guarantor of the country's democracy based on the rule of law.[70] Treaty review, the Commission reasoned in addition, was diffuse in order to ensure maximum compliance with international law, which did not apply to constitutional review.[71] Instead, constitutional review was more political in nature and required legal certainty and unity on national questions, which a new court could ensure.

---

[66] See also *Hoofdlijnenbrief constitutionele toetsing* n. 4, p. 14.

[67] Articles 3(2) and 6 of the United Kingdom Human Rights Act, 1998. For the Schoof cabinet's support and views regarding strong constitutional review, see *Wijziging van de Grondwet ter invoering van constitutionele toetsing* n. 4, pp. 18–20; *Contourennota constitutionele toetsing* n. 4, pp. 15–17.

[68] For instance, given the open wording of the Constitution's general provision, its weak review might be such a compromise. The weak review of social rights might overcome opposition to their judicial review as well. There is debate as to whether weak constitutional review by the courts is possible under article 120, given at least one example of such review by the Supreme Court (*Harmonisatiewet* n. 27, para 3.1) where it applied an Act of Parliament noting that it violated legal certainty. In practice though, courts are reluctant to follow this precedent. On this topic, see Boogaard and Uzman 2021, p. 1152; Van der Schyff 2020, pp. 902–903. See also Widdershoven and Wattel Opinion n. 32, para 9.5. And, drawing inspiration for the Dutch context from weak review under the United Kingdom Human Rights Act, see Nehmelman and Vetzo 2016.

[69] See *Wijziging van de Grondwet ter invoering van constitutionele toetsing* n. 4, p. 17; State Commission on the Parliamentary System 2018, p. 151.

[70] *Contourennota constitutionele toetsing* n. 4, p. 11.

[71] State Commission on the Parliamentary System 2018, p. 151.

Upon balance, there is more to be said though for diffuse constitutional review than centralised review by a new court. Treaty review, illustrated by the *Urgenda* case which required the state to act more in reducing greenhouse gas emissions, can also involve important political questions and so casts doubts on why constitutional review would need a new court with centralised powers.[72] Also, like treaty review, most proposals for constitutional review, including that of the Schoof cabinet and the State Commission, usually favour the review of classical rights only.[73] However, constitutional courts often review a wider set of provisions, raising questions why a special court would be needed for the review of mostly classical rights.[74] As for legal certainty and unity, the Netherlands has four highest courts with could result in each court adopting a different approach regarding constitutional interpretation and application.[75] By contrast, the legal coherency of an important treaty such as the ECHR is ultimately guaranteed by the European Court of Human Rights.[76] However, the question is whether constitutional coherence necessarily requires a constitutional court, especially given the limited mandate envisaged for the new court. Instead of creating yet another highest court, an existing court could be entrusted with constitutional oversight, or the highest courts could coordinate their approach, as they do now in administrative law.[77] On balance, the latter approach is preferable, thereby avoiding possible procedural conflicts between treaty review by all courts and constitutional review based on centralised review by a new constitutional or current highest court.[78]

---

[72] On the judiciary's role in respect of the political domain, see the *Urgenda* judgement n. 43, para 8.

[73] For the views of the Schoof cabinet, see *Wijziging van de Grondwet ter invoering van constitutionele toetsing* n. 4, p. 10; *Contourennota constitutionele toetsing* n. 4, p. 5.

[74] See also Claes et al. 2021, p. 61. It can be remarked that the State Commission on the Parliamentary System 2018, p. 156 noted that extra powers could be given to a new constitutional court (such as deciding administrative disputes between state organs). See Hoogers 2022, pp. 288–290 in this regard. Also, the Schoof cabinet expressed the intention to examine whether a constitutional court could be entrusted with the review of constitutional provisions that do not create (direct) rights and obligations for citizens, including provisions on legislative procedures and decentralisation, see *Contourennota constitutionele toetsing* n. 4, pp. 20–21.

[75] These are the Supreme Court (*Hoge Raad*); Administrative Jurisdiction Division of the Council of State (*Afdeling bestuursrechtspraak van de Raad van State*); Central Appeals Tribunal (*Centrale Raad van Beroep*); Trade and Industry Appeals Tribunal (*College van Beroep voor het bedrijfsleven*).

[76] Article 31(1) ECHR states that the jurisdiction of the ECtHR extends "to all matters concerning the interpretation and application of the Convention and the Protocols".

[77] See Burkens et al. 2022, pp. 173–174 regarding coordination between the highest courts in administrative law by the Commission on Legal Unity (*Commissie rechtseenheid bestuursrecht*). Consider also views of the chair of the Administrative Jurisdiction Division of the Council of State, expressed in the letter of 23 April 2025 regarding the Schoof cabinet's views on constitutional review, as contained in the *Contourennota constitutionele toetsing* n. 4.

[78] See also *Hoofdlijnenbrief constitutionele toetsing* n. 4, pp. 11–13 and the arguments by Schutgens 2023.

8.8 Conclusion

Although the prohibition on constitutional review in article 120 of the Constitution is undoubtedly a part of Dutch constitutional identity, as explained in the introduction, it is not uncontroversial. As the discussion has attempted to show, there are convincing grounds for amending this relic from the nineteenth century to reflect the needs of a modern state and its society, especially regarding the judicial protection of people's rights. Although the proposals to reform the provision may appear modest compared to constitutional review by the judiciary in many other countries, its amendment would be deeply significant for the Netherlands. While an amended article 120 would rightly not mean the end of the legislature's primacy, it would still require a reconceptualisation of the basic relationship between the courts and the legislature. A discussion of article 120 of the Constitution also shows that even if something is part of a country's constitutional identity, it should not be exempt from scrutiny. On the contrary, it could be said that something should be subject to close scrutiny because it is part of that identity.

Acknowledgements Many thanks to Paul Zoontjens and Gert-Jan Leenknegt for their helpful comments on this chapter.

References

Al Khatib A A, Tingen J (2023) Als je het doet, doe het dan goed: een pleidooi voor toetsing van wetten in formele zin aan algemene rechtsbeginselen. Tijdschrift voor constitutioneel recht 14:174–184

Barendt E (1998) An Introduction to Constitutional Law. Oxford University Press, Oxford

Besselink L (2020) Constitutional Adjudication in the Netherlands. In: Von Bogdandy A, Huber P M, Grabenwarter C (eds) The Max Planck Handbooks in European Public Law, Vol. 3. Oxford University Press, Oxford, pp. 565–618

Besselink L (2022) Artikelen 93 en 94: Doorwerking en voorrang internationaal recht. In: Ellian A, Rijpkema B (eds) Een nieuw commentaar op de Grondwet. Boom, Amsterdam, pp. 406–420

Boogaard G, Uzman J (2021) Artikel 120 Toetsingsverbod. In: Hirsch Ballin E M H, Janse de Jonge E J, Leenknegt G (eds) Uitleg van de Grondwet. Boom Juridisch, The Hague, pp. 1149–1161

Borman C (2012) Het Statuut voor het Koninkrijk. Kluwer, Deventer

Burkens M C, Kummeling H R B M, Uzman J, Vermeulen B P, Widdershoven R J G M (2022) Beginselen van de democratische rechtsstaat: Inleiding tot de grondslagen van het Nederlandse staats- en bestuursrecht, 9th edn. Wolters Kluwer, Deventer

Claes M, Heringa A W, Van der Sluis M, Stremler M (2021) Rechtsvergelijkend onderzoek constitutionele toetsing. Maastricht University, Maastricht

Claes M, Imamović S, Sillen J (2024) Constitutionele toetsing en de toekomst van de beperking van de Nederlandse grondrechten. Maastricht University, Maastricht

Dicey A V (1959/1885) An Introduction to the Study of the Law of the Constitution, 10th edn. Macmillan, London

Duijf C M A M (2023) Constitutionele toetsing in de Caribische landen van het Koninkrijk. Tijdschrift voor constitutioneel recht 14:215–228

Ellian A, Manenschijn J (2022) Artikel 120: Toetsingsverbod wetten en verdragen. In: Ellian A, Rijpkema B (eds) Een nieuw commentaar op de Grondwet. Boom, Amsterdam, pp. 406–420
Goudappel F, De Wit J (2015) Constitutionele toetsing in het Koninkrijk in context. Caribisch Juristenblad (4):285–297
Heringa A W (2023) Constitutions Compared: An Introduction to Comparative Constitutional Law, 7th edn. Eleven, The Hague
Hoogers H G (2022) Kroniek van een aangekondigde revolutie: de hoofdlijnenbrief inzake constitutionele toetsing. Tijdschrift voor constitutioneel recht 13:274–294
Leenknegt G (2008) Constitutionalisation of the rechtsstaat principles in the Netherlands, In: Van der Schyff G (ed) Constitutionalism in the Netherlands and South Africa: A Comparative Study. Wolf Legal Publishers, Nijmegen, pp. 9–23
Leenknegt G (2021) Artikel 91 Goedkeuring verdragen. In: Hirsch Ballin E M H, Janse de Jonge E J, Leenknegt G (eds) Uitleg van de Grondwet. Boom Juridisch, The Hague, pp. 883–894
Leijten A E M, Loven C M S (2023) Rechterlijke toetsing aan de grondwettelijke grondrechtenbepalingen: daadwerkelijke meerwaarde verlangt meer dan het afschaffen van het toetsingsverbod. In: Gerards J H, Goossens J, Van Vugt E Y (eds) Constitutionele verandering in Nederland? De grondwetswijzigingen van 2022–2023. Boom Juridisch, The Hague, pp. 95–120
Nehmelman R, Vetzo M (2016) De verklaring van grondwettelijke onverenigbaarheid: Britse inspiratie voor het vastgelopen Nederlandse debat inzake constitutionele toetsing. In: Ortlep R, Groothuijse F, Kiewit J, Nehmelman R (eds) De rechter onder vuur. Wolf Legal Publishers, Oisterwijk, pp. 319–344
Nieuwenhuis A J, Den Heijer M, Hins A W (2021) Hoofdstukken grondrechten, 5th edn. Ars Aequi Libri, Nijmegen
Nijboer A (2023) Omgevingswet in de praktijk. Boom Juridisch, The Hague
Schutgens R J B (2023) Een constitutioneel hof in Nederland? In: Gerards J H, Goossens J, Van Vugt E Y (eds) Constitutionele verandering in Nederland? De grondwetswijzigingen van 2022-2023. Boom Juridisch, The Hague, pp. 121–140
State Commission on the Parliamentary System (2018) Democracy and the Rule of Law in Equilibrium (Official translation of: Lage drempels, hoge dijken: democratie en rechtsstaat in balans). Boom, Amsterdam
Tate C N, Vallinder T (1995) The Global Expansion of Judicial Power. New York University Press, New York
Tushnet M (2018) Advanced Introduction to Comparative Constitutional Law, 2nd edn. Edward Elgar, Cheltenham/UK, Northampton/MA
Van der Schyff G (2020) The Prohibition on Constitutional Review by the Judiciary in the Netherlands in Critical Perspective: The Case and Roadmap for Reform. German Law Journal 21:884--903
Van Gestel R (2013) The "Deparliamentarisation" of Legislation: Framework Laws and the Primacy of the Legislature. Utrecht Law Review 9:106–122
Van Houten M L P (1997) Meer zicht op wetgeving: Rechterlijke toetsing van wetgeving aan de Grondwet en fundamentele rechtsbeginselen. W E J Tjeenk Willink, Zwolle
Voermans W (2023) Onze constitutie. De geschreven en ongeschreven regels van het Nederlandse staatsbestel. Prometheus, Amsterdam

Gerhard van der Schyff is an Associate Professor in the Department of Public Law and Governance at the Law School of Tilburg University, the Netherlands. His research interests cover European and comparative constitutional law, including fundamental rights.

Chapter 9
International and European Union Law: Openness as Identity?

Monica Claes and Joost Sillen

Contents

Abstract Unlike many European legal systems, Dutch constitutional law does not use the concepts of "constitutional identity" or "national identity" as terms of art. The Dutch Constitution lacks an unamendable core; all provisions can be changed or removed, including the 2022 clause obliging protection of fundamental rights and democracy based on the rule of law. Typical for Dutch constitutional law is however its openness to international and EU law. Since 1953, the Constitution has granted international treaties direct effect and primacy, even over constitutional provisions. This openness compensates for the prohibition of constitutional review, making treaties—particularly the European Convention on Human Rights—crucial for protecting fundamental rights. However, this reliance on external legal sources shifts authority from national constitutional standards to international bodies, which lack the democratic legitimacy that the Constitution has and can impose only minimum standards. This openness has defined Dutch constitutional practice. Yet, it is also an unsettling feature of Dutch constitutional law, supporting the rule of law in some contexts but potentially undermining it in others, particularly when international law itself does

M. Claes (✉) · J. Sillen
Maastricht University, Maastricht, The Netherlands
e-mail: monica.claes@maastrichtuniversity.nl

J. Sillen
e-mail: joost.sillen@maastrichtuniversity.nl

G. van der Schyff (ed.), *The Constitutional Identity of The Netherlands*,
https://doi.org/10.1007/978-94-6265-779-3_9

not meet constitutional standards or when international bodies fail to uphold fundamental rights effectively. Accordingly, while its openness to international law is a typical feature of the Dutch legal order, it is not necessarily essential.

Keywords Primacy and direct effect of treaties · The power to conclude treaties · Fundamental rights · Constitutional judicial review

9.1 Introduction

In contrast to many legal systems in Europe, the concepts of "constitutional identity" and "national identity" are not used as terms of art in Dutch constitutional law. The concept is not used to prohibit specific amendments of the constitution, that is, to protect a core of the Constitution.[1] Common wisdom holds that the Dutch Constitution does not contain an unamendable core: the entire Constitution is open to constitutional amendment, and no provision of the Constitution prevents the abolishment of part or even the entire Constitution. Only very recently, in 2022, a general provision was added to the Constitution, preceding the existing articles, which reads that "The Constitution guarantees fundamental rights and democratic based on the rule of law".[2] With this rather cryptic formulation, the drafters intended to impose a duty on the constitutional legislature to protect fundamental rights and democratic rule. The provision is not, however, intended to create rights for individuals, which they could invoke before the courts.[3] At most, it can serve as guidance in the interpretation of the Constitution. But this provision too can be amended.[4] The notion of identity is also not used in the context of European integration: in contrast to many other European Constitutions, the Dutch Constitution does not impose limits or conditions on European integration, whether based on principles shared with other states, or characteristics that are considered reflective of the state's individuality.[5] These features reflect how the Dutch see their constitution. The Constitution is not considered the vehicle to protect the core values of the State of the Netherlands and Dutch society. It has limited legal practical and symbolic relevance in society.[6] It simply is not the

[1] On this notion of identity as immutable core of the Constitution, see e.g. Polzin 2017, pp. 1595–1616; Roznai 2017.

[2] References in English to the Constitution are taken from the 2023 translation by the Ministry of the Interior and Kingdom Relations.

[3] Kamerstukken I 2017/18, 34,516, No. C, p. 2.

[4] Moreover, even if the Dutch Constitution did have an immutable core, that would only enhance its safeguard function to a limited extent, because the entire Constitution is rather sober and is not explicit on the fundamental values underlying it. If furthermore lacks a preamble as well as provisions setting out the fundamental principles of the state, As is the case in many other European Constitutions, such as article 20 of the German Basic Law, or arts. 1–12 of the Italian Constitution.

[5] On these two aspects of "national identity" in the context of European integration, see Reestman 2009.

[6] See e.g. Gerards 2016.

type of constitutional document that contains the most fundamental principles of the Dutch constitutional system, and it is generally not considered to reflect a common sense of belonging.[7]

Although the concepts of "constitutional identity" and "national identity" are thus not used as terms of art in Dutch constitutional law, there are features of the Dutch constitution that are *typical* to it, in the sense that they distinguish the Dutch legal system from most other legal systems. Its openness to international and EU law is undoubtedly one of them. The constitutional provisions on international relations reflect a clear and conscious choice of the State to actively and constructively participate in the development of the international legal order and to open the legal order to international law. The Dutch legal system is not only monist and awards direct effect to provisions of duly ratified and published international treaties,[8] it also grants primacy to such provisions, even over the Constitution.[9] At the same time, the Constitution explicitly precludes courts to review the constitutionality of statutes and treaty provisions (now article 120). The fundamental rights catalogue enshrined in the Dutch Constitution therefore plays only a secondary role in legal practice. The wording of these constitutional rights reflects this: they grant rights to individuals, but impose very few limits on the power of the legislature to restrict them.[10] When the global proliferation of human rights started in the 1980's, the Dutch therefore did not turn to the fundamental rights catalogue in their Constitution, but to international human rights treaties, especially the ECHR. The importance of this treaty for the Dutch legal order can hardly be overestimated. It can be said to function as a "substitute constitution".

But is this openness also *essential*? Does it define the Dutch constitutional system? Or to put it differently, would the Dutch legal system be altered in a fundamental way without the openness to international treaties? Would the Constitution then still be able to perform its functions in a democratic state governed under the rule of law? This chapter aims to reflect on the role and importance of this openness of the Dutch legal system in the Constitution, by conducting two thought experiments, with reference to actual and (more) tentative proposals for constitutional amendment launched in the past two decades, which could dramatically change the functioning of the system. First, what would be the impact for the Dutch Constitution if treaties which necessitate national authorities to deviate from the Constitution could only be concluded after constitutional amendment (Sect. 9.3) and second, what would

[7] Interestingly, the COVID crisis can be seen as an awakening of the Constitution. All of a sudden, national constitutional rights played a leading role in the public debate and political decision making. See e.g. Van Vugt 2024.

[8] The text of the Constitution refers to provisions that are "binding on all persons" in arts. 93 and 94, which comes close to the concept of direct effect. On this issue, see Fleuren 2004.

[9] Article 94 of the Constitution.

[10] Some articles of the Constitution, however, do impose such limits and sometimes absolutely prohibit the legislature from restricting rights. See article 1 (non-discrimination), article 3 (equal eligibility for appointment in public service), article 5 (right to submit petitions), article 7 (freedom of speech), article 17 (right to a fair trial), article 18 (right to legal representation in court and administrative proceedings).

the impact be if the direct effect and primacy of international law would be made conditional (Sect. 9.4)? This chapter starts, however, with a brief sketch of the history and main features of the openness of the Dutch Constitution to international and EU law (Sect. 9.2).

9.2 The Openness of the Dutch Constitution to International and EU Law

The Netherlands has chosen to make it a constitutional obligation on the government, laid down in article 90 of the Constitution, to promote the development of the international legal order. This is reflective of the type of state the Netherlands wants to be: one that complies with its international obligations, pursues good relations with other states and lasting international peace and security, and strives for peaceful settlement of disputes. It characterises the Constitution and the state governed under it in a crucial way, obliging it to be a good "international citizen". In this chapter, however, we do not focus on this constitutional obligation of the government to develop the international legal order, but on the openness of the Dutch legal order towards the international legal order, that is: on the ways in which national law engages with international law.

The provisions on foreign relations in the Constitution, as they currently stand, date back to the constitutional revisions of 1953 and 1956 which were marked by the increasing involvement of parliament in foreign policy and, more importantly for our purposes, the constitutional anchoring of the Dutch openness to international law.[11] These constitutional revisions were deemed necessary in light of the post-war ambition for a far-reaching European integration and were meant to prepare the Constitution for this process and international cooperation more generally. Prior to these revisions the Dutch Constitution did regulate the power to conclude and ratify treaties, but it was silent on (1) the scope of the power to conclude and ratify treaties and (2) their effect in the Dutch legal order. However, constitutional practice and case law shed some light at how these questions were answered and therefore can show what the importance is of the constitutional revisions of 1953 and 1956.

9.2.1 *The Power to Conclude and Ratify Treaties*

Until the constitutional revision of 1953 two schools of thought could be distinguished in the Netherlands on the scope of the power to conclude and ratify treaties.[12] According to the first, government could conclude and Parliament could ratify any

[11] Van Leeuwen 2012.

[12] See Fleuren 2002.

treaty, unless *the constitutional provisions on foreign affairs* provided otherwise.[13] For example, the fact that the Constitution prohibits censorship, did not—according to this line of thought—prohibit government to conclude a treaty that would compel it to apply censorship, as the prohibition to do so is not part of the constitutional provisions on foreign affairs. According to the second, however, government could not conclude such a treaty and Parliament could not ratify it, because national authorities must always comply with all provisions of the Constitution, also when concluding treaties. The constitutional revision of 1953 brought this debate to an end. Article 90 now mandates government to promote the development of the international legal order.[14] Article 91 aims to ensure parliamentary involvement in foreign relations and lays the ground rules for approval of treaties.[15] The same provision also establishes that the Netherlands can become party to any treaty, regardless of whether it would require national officials to diverge from the Constitution. Article 91(3) of the Constitution only prescribes that such a treaty cannot be approved by a simple majority in both Houses of Parliament but requires a two thirds majority.

The same constitutional provision also implies that that the state can confer any legislative, executive and judicial powers on international institutions by or pursuant to a treaty. The Constitution accordingly does not contain any substantive limits to a transfer of competences, nor does it impose conditions on the nature and functioning of such organisations, as is the case for example in the German Basic Law.[16] At least in theory, under the Dutch Constitution all state powers could ultimately be transferred to international organisations and the Dutch state can effectively "evaporate", although such dramatic transfers would likely be considered unacceptable politically. But legally speaking, article 92 of the Constitution expressly declares that such transfers are permissible, provided that the procedure of article 91(3) is observed when applicable. With regard to the conferral of state powers on international institutions which do not necessitate national authorities to deviate from the Constitution, the provision was in line with longstanding constitutional practice. Already in the nineteenth century and the first half of the twentieth century the Netherlands had become a party to treaties establishing international organisations, such as the Central Commission for the Navigation of the Rhine (1816), the Permanent Court of Arbitration (1899) and the United Nations (1945), without prior constitutional amendment.[17]

---

[13] See, e.g., Buys 1883, pp. 203–204.

[14] We refer here to the current numbering of the relevant provisions.

[15] These rules are further fleshed out in the Law on the Approval and Publication of Treaties of 1994 (*Rijkswet goedkeuring en bekendmaking verdragen*).

[16] See article 23 of the German Constitution.

[17] Van Leeuwen 2012, p. 364.

9.2.2 *The Legal Effects of Duly Ratified Treaties*

During the last quarter of the nineteenth century two opposing theories of the nature of treaty law emerged in the Dutch legal debate.[18] According to the more dualist view, treaties were nothing more than contracts between states and carried no effect in the domestic legal order. They could not of themselves confer rights or impose obligations on individuals. In contrast, according to the monist view, a treaty could confer rights or impose obligations on individuals in and by itself (law-making treaties). In 1906, the Supreme Court settled this debate. It sided with the second, monistic conception, and ruled that treaties could as such have legal effects in the national legal order.[19]

That treaties as such could have legal effect in the Dutch legal order, however, raised new questions. How do treaty law and national law relate to each other in the domestic legal order? The courts tried to avoid the issue but were inclined to hold that a later statute could set aside an older treaty.[20] The constitutional revision of 1953 brought clarity also on this point. Article 93 of the Constitution now provides that treaties which are ratified and published become part of "the law of the land", and treaty provisions which lend themselves to judicial application must be enforced by the courts. Under article 94 of the Constitution conflicting provisions of national law—even the Constitution itself[21]—must be set aside.

9.2.3 *EU Law and the Dutch Constitution*

The Netherlands is one of the founding members of the European Union.[22] Yet, while the 1953 amendment was clearly motivated by the prospect of European integration, the European Union remains absent from the text of the Constitution to this day. Perhaps even more remarkable is the fact that the constitutional provisions on the domestic effect and primacy of treaty law contained in articles 93 and 94 of the Constitution are usually considered not to apply to EU law. The direct effect and primacy of EU law are under the dominant view based on the case law of the Court of Justice of the European Union (CJEU), and hence, on the very nature of EU law.[23] The constitutional provisions are not considered relevant for the domestic effect of EU law in the domestic legal order.

In practical terms, it is of little importance whether EU law takes effect based on the reasoning of the CJEU and the very nature of EU law, or a (re-interpretation

---

[18] See Fleuren 2004, p. 98 ff.

[19] HR 25 May 1906, W. 8383. See also, HR 3 March 1919, NJ 1919, 317 (*Grenstractaat Aken*).

[20] See *Grenstractaat Aken*.

[21] HR 18 September 2001, ECLI:NL:HR:2001:AB1471 (*Decembermoorden*), para 4.5.

[22] Slightly anachronistically, for reasons of clarity, we use the name European Union, not that of its predecessors.

[23] HR 2 November 2004, ECLI:NL:HR:2004:AR1797 (*Rusttijden*), para 3.6.

of) constitutional provisions. But it is remarkable that in the one legal system where the constitutional system was perfectly in sync with the case law of the CJEU, it was considered redundant to achieve the result required by that Court. This confirms the pragmatism that characterises the Dutch constitutional system. Where in other member states constitutional actors and commentators have re-interpreted Constitutional provisions and have developed doctrines and theories to accommodate both the claim to supremacy of the Constitution and the request of the CJEU to award primacy to EU law, the Dutch simply hold the Constitution irrelevant in this matter. Because the case law of the CJEU achieves the same result as application of the Dutch Constitution would have done, they do not feel the need for constitutional pedantry.

Furthermore, the Dutch courts have not developed doctrines to protect the national legal order against the EU or restrict the applicability of EU law, contrary to what has happened in most Member States of the European Union.[24] Dutch courts have never formulated *controlimiti* or *Solange*-type reservations, or doctrines on ultra vires or identity review.[25] Nothing in the Constitution seems to require legal protection against EU law (or, for that matter, against other international law).

9.2.4 The Openness of the Dutch Constitution and the Absence of Judicial Constitutional Review

Many explanations have been offered for the openness of the Dutch constitutional system to international treaty law. Some relate to the law itself and legal culture: the pragmatism of the Constitution and its sober constitutional culture, combined with the absence of judicial constitutional review and a constitutional court (which in most states takes the lead in designing a doctrine on the relationship between domestic and international law). Others point to historical, economic and cultural factors: the position of the Netherlands as a small trading country dependent on trade and good international relations with a strong interest in compliance; or the fact that the Netherlands is a high-trust society governed under the rule of law, where government is required to comply with the law, including international law.

---

[24] See e.g. the contributions to the special issue Fromage and De Witte 2021; Calliess and Van der Schyff 2020.

[25] The doctrine of *controlimiti* or constitutional counterlimits to limitations of sovereignty were developed by the Italian Constitutional Court in *Frontini* (judgement 17 of December 1973, No. 183); *Solange* refers to the case law of the German Federal Constitutional Court establishing that "as long as" the EU does not sufficiently protect fundamental rights, the Federal Constitutional Court will offer protection based on the Basic Law, see BVerfGE 37, 271 (1974) (*Solange I*). That same court developed the doctrine of ultra vires review—it will review whether the EU has transgressed the boundaries of its competences, see BVerfGE 89, 155, judgement of 12 October 1993 (*Maastricht*) and BVerfGE 126, 286, judgement of 6 July 2010 (*Honeywell*) and of identity review, see BVerfGE 123, 267, judgement of 30 June 2009 (*Lisbon*).

Furthermore, as we shall see more in detail in Sect. 9.3, there is an intricate link between the openness of the Dutch legal order and the absence of judicial constitutional review. The Dutch have been able to resist the global trend of judicial constitutional review and opt for a system of political constitutionalism in which the legislature is responsible to uphold the Constitution and review the constitutionality of primary legislation *because* it is embedded in a system of international (human rights) treaties complete with compliance mechanisms in the form of international courts, which are given effect domestically and enforced by national courts.

9.3 Proposals to Restrict the Power to Conclude Treaties (that Would Necessitate Deviation from the Constitution)

Article 91(3) of the Constitution stipulates, as already mentioned, that a "treaty containing provisions deviating from the Constitution or necessitating such deviation" requires the approval of two-thirds of the votes cast in each of the two Houses of Parliament. According to government, Parliament and their main adviser, the Council of State such deviation only actually occurs if the treaty deviates from a *specific provision* of the Constitution.[26] Deviating from "the spirit of the Constitution", i.e. principles enshrined in the Constitution, is not enough. Since its inception, article 91(3) has only been applied a total of three times, namely to the Treaty establishing the European Defence Community (1952, parliamentary debates on the approval of this treaty commenced in 1953,[27] after the constitutional revision of that year), the Agreement with Indonesia on Western New Guinea (1962) and the Rome Statute of the International Criminal Court (1998). On three other occasions, namely the Agreement on the Placement of Cruise Weapons (1985), the Maastricht Treaty (1992) and the Lockerbie Treaty (1998) its application was heavily debated but ultimately rejected. These cases suggest that a provision of a treaty deviates from the Constitution or necessitates such deviation if it requires the Kingdom to exercise its jurisdiction in a manner not permitted by the Constitution. In other words, if an act is not permissible under national law without a prior amendment of the Constitution, the Kingdom can only be bound by a treaty that obliges it to do so following the procedure provided by article 91(3) of the Constitution.

Accordingly, few treaties must be approved with special majority, depending on what the Constitution happens to expressly regulate on the matter. A treaty that, for example, adds one of the border provinces to Germany can be concluded without a constitutional revision and does not even have to be approved by a two-thirds majority in both Houses of Parliament, because the Dutch Constitution, for all sorts

---

[26] Handelingen I 1952/53, pp. 480 and 484. See also Kamerstukken II 1983/84, 17,980, A, pp. 2–3; Kamerstukken II 1999/00, 26,800 VI, A; Kamerstukken I 2000/01, 27,484 (R 1699), No. 237c. On this issue, see Fleuren 2002, pp. 66–67.

[27] Kamerstukken II 1952/53, 2911, No. 1 ff.

of practical, legislative reasons, does not define the Dutch national territory.[28] At the turn of the millennium, that observation led to criticism. In 2001, the Senate adopted a motion calling on the government to examine whether a constitutional amendment was necessary.[29] That study—authored by Leonard Besselink—was published a year later.[30] Besselink concluded that the current interpretation of article 91(3) of the Constitution was too restrictive. He argued that the article should also be applied when a treaty deviates from the spirit, purpose or system of the Constitution, if necessary, by explicitly including in the Constitution that "a treaty involving a substantial transfer of power" can only be approved by a two-thirds majority of votes.[31] The government rejected the proposal. It feared that the proposed criterion was "too vague" to function as a criterion for the application of article 91(3) of the Constitution.[32] Partly in response to that rejection, MPs Van der Staaij (SGP) and Herben (LPF) proposed to amend article 91 of the Constitution so that "a treaty amending the treaties on which the European Union is founded", including the amendment of such treaties and "a treaty concerning the accession of new Member States to the European Union" should always be approved by a two-thirds majority in both Houses of Parliament.[33] At the request of the House of Representatives, the State Commission on the Constitution (*Staatscommissie Grondwet*), established in 2009, considered the proposed amendment. It was of the opinion that under the Constitution as it stood, the Kingdom may never be bound—not even with approval of a two-thirds majority in both Houses of Parliament—to a treaty that violates "core principles [of] the constitutional order".[34] At the same time, it noted that conflict with these principles would not readily be established as such principles were not explicitly enshrined in the Constitution as it stood.[35] The *Staatscommissie Grondwet* accordingly advised to incorporate those core principles into the Constitution. Such a provision would not only serve to make explicit that the Netherlands may not enter into such treaty but could also play a role in interpreting article 91(3) of the Constitution less "restrictively". To this end, according to a majority in the *Staatscommissie*, an amendment to article 91(3) should also be considered in order to anchor that extensive interpretation firmly in the Constitution.[36] However, this majority also felt that the proposed constitutional amendment by Van der Staaij (and initially Herben) was less suitable, considering it both too broad, as it would also apply to EU treaties that would have less of an impact on the Netherlands, and too limited, as non-EU treaties could have a significant impact, while such treaties would always fall out of the scope of the

---

[28] See already Buys 1888, p. 1. See also Duynstee 1954, p. 1 (commentary on article 63).

[29] Kamerstukken I 2001/02, 27 484 (R 1669), No. 174.

[30] Besselink 2002.

[31] Ibid., pp. 47–48.

[32] Kamerstukken I 2003/04, 27 484 (R 1669), A, pp. 4–5.

[33] Kamerstukken II 2006/07, 30 874 (R 1818), No. 1 ff.

[34] Staatscommissie Grondwet 2010, p. 116, referring to the 1953 constitutional amendment and an opinion of the Council of State.

[35] Ibid., p. 116.

[36] Ibid., pp. 118–121.

amendment.[37] Upon the approval of the constitutional amendment by the House of Representatives, the Senate asked a new State Commission to reconsider the issue.[38] That State Commission on the Parliamentary System (*Staatscommissie Parlementair Stelsel*) essentially agreed with the conclusions of the *Staatscommissie Grondwet*,[39] and the Senate rejected the constitutional amendment.

The power and procedure to conclude treaties that derogate from the Constitution thus remains unchanged. One element in the debate, however, did result in a constitutional amendment, be it in a watered-down version: a general provision containing some of the core principles of the Constitution was introduced in 2022.[40] The debate on a more extensive use of article 91(3) of the Constitution reveals an increased concern for the core principles of the Constitution which should never be affected, and which should also be protected against certain international treaties. In this respect, the openness of the Dutch legal order does not seem to be essential for the Netherlands to function as a democratic constitutional state. In this sense, it is not part of the essence of the Dutch legal order, but may have to give way to the core principles of the Dutch Constitution, or, put differently, to its identity. On the other hand, the openness of the Dutch legal order and the choice to allow as much as possible for a smooth participation in the international legal order is laid down in the Constitution, and the failed attempt at restricting it, conforms this choice.

9.4 Proposals to Make the Direct Effect and Primacy of International Law Conditional

As mentioned, the openness of the Dutch Constitution to international law is closely connected to that other specificity of the Dutch legal order, the absence of judicial constitutional review of statutes.[41] It can be argued that the Dutch legal system has been able to resist the global surge of judicial constitutional review and constitutional courts *because of* the openness of the Dutch legal order and its embeddedness in a system of international (human rights) treaties complete with compliance mechanisms and international courts. This has allowed the Netherlands to opt for a form of political constitutionalism in which the legislature, which has much stronger democratic credentials than courts, remains responsible to uphold the Constitution and review the constitutionality of legislation. However, in the Dutch system, the courts can step in when the legislature infringes treaty law or EU law. The limits that treaties and EU law impose on the primary legislature are enforceable by courts. In other words, the absence of constitutional review is compensated by the domestic effect of

[37] Ibid., p. 119.

[38] Kamerstukken I 2016/17, 30 874 (R 1818), G.

[39] Staatcommissie Parlementair Stelsel 2018, pp. 336–337.

[40] See e.g. Stremler 2018.

[41] On constitutional review, see Chapter 8 in this volume.

international treaties, mainly human rights treaties, making the judicial constitutional review less urgent, in any case in the context of fundamental rights protection.

Reversely, the absence of judicial constitutional review and of a constitutional court has contributed to the fact that the direct effect and primacy of treaty law are widely accepted and have mostly gone unchallenged. In many other systems, the existence of a constitutional court and other forms of judicial constitutional review make international human rights treaties less crucial in the domestic legal order. The protection of fundamental rights is mostly provided by the Constitution, and treaties play a much more modest role in this respect. Moreover, it is often the constitutional court in its role of ultimate guardian of the Constitution, that develops doctrines restricting the domestic impact of international and European law. The well-known German example may serve to illustrate this point: the *Bundesverfassungsgericht* famously claims jurisdiction to review EU law on grounds of compliance with national constitutional rights, the limits of competences transferred (ultra vires review) and compliance with the core principles of the Constitution (identity review).[42] Dutch courts have not developed such doctrines.

Nevertheless, two proposals have been put forward to make the Dutch legal order less open and to restrict the role of international treaties in the domestic legal order, one by (half of) a State Commission, the other by a private member bill.

In 2010, half of the members of the *Staatscommissie Grondwet* proposed to change the text of Article 94 of the Constitution to restrict the impact of treaty law in the domestic legal order where it would infringe on the core principles of the Constitution. As was already hinted at, the (unanimous) *Staatscommissie* aimed to codify these core principles in a general provision that would read:

> The Netherlands is a democratic state under the rule of law. The State/government respects and guarantees human dignity, fundamental rights and fundamental principles of law. public authority is exercised only by virtue of the constitution or the law.[43]

These members of the *Staatscommissie* emphasised that in their view, the traditional openness of the Dutch Constitution towards the international legal order should be preserved and judicial review in light of treaty provisions maintained. But they proposed to add the caveat that treaty provisions infringing on the core principles of the Constitution would not carry effect in the domestic legal order. In their view, the core principles of the Constitution merit protection not only against national law, but also against treaty law. The proposal of (half of the) *Staatscommissie* thus aimed to preserve judicial review of primary legislation in light of treaty law, while requesting courts also to review compliance of treaty law with the core principles of the Constitution. The proposal, however, was dismissed by the government.[44]

Another proposal to change the relevant provisions had quite the opposite intention: it was not aimed at protecting core principles of the Constitution but was

42 For more examples, see Claes and De Witte 2023; Grabenwarter et al. 2021.

43 Authors' translation. This proposal ultimately led to the introduction of the – watered-down— general provision in 2022.

44 Kamerstukken II 2011/12, 31 570, No. 20, p. 10.

intended to eliminate judicial review in light of treaty law, which was considered vague and beyond the control of the state. In 2012 MP Taverne tabled a proposal to amend articles 93 and 94 of the Constitution to restrict the impact of international treaty law in the domestic legal order.[45] This proposal must be seen in the context of the critique that was gaining traction at the time,[46] of the growing influence of international human rights treaties, especially the ECHR, on the national legal order and the contention that the European Court of Human Rights (ECtHR) had become a political body developing the ECHR too creatively and encroaching on national sovereignty while not paying sufficient attention to the national cultural context.[47] It intended to amend articles 93 and 94 of the Constitution in crucial respects, restricting the power of courts to review primary legislation in light of treaty law and passing the final say over the direct effect of treaty provisions to the primary legislature.[48] To that effect, Taverne proposed to exempt primary legislation from the rule of article 94 of the Constitution and to change the procedural rules to establish direct effect of treaty provisions under article 93. According to the explanatory memorandum to the proposal the intention was not to detract from provisions of international law the state was bound to respect, but to eliminate judicial (treaty) review of primary legislation.[49] The same grounds for excluding judicial constitutional review of primary legislation in article 120 of the Constitution should also exclude judicial review of such legislation in light of treaties.

The proposal thus intended to align the judicial review of primary legislation in light of treaties with constitutional review: in both cases, the final decision should be left to the legislature. This stands in stark contrast to the parallel debate in the United Kingdom, where repeal of the Human Rights Act 1998 was linked to its replacement with a "homegrown" bill of rights.[50] The proposal thus denied the compensatory function of article 94 in the Dutch Constitution, nor did it consider that, at that time, a proposal was pending to review article 120 of the Constitution in the opposite

[45] In Dutch, the full title of the proposal is: *Voorstel van rijkswet van het lid Taverne houdende verklaring dat er grond bestaat een voorstel in overweging te nemen tot verandering in de Grondwet, strekkende tot aanpassing van de procedure voor vaststelling van rechtstreekse werking van een ieder verbindende bepalingen van verdragen en van besluiten van volkenrechtelijke organisaties*, Kamerstukken II 2011/12, 33 359 (R 1986), No. 1 ff.

[46] And is gaining traction again, see the letter of various European governments to the ECtHR, asking it to reverse its case law. On this letter, see e.g. Ní Chinnéide and Sevrin 2025.

[47] See, e.g., at the time Baudet 2010 and Zwart 2011. On the Dutch debate on the role of the ECtHR and allegations of judicial activism, see Gerards and Terlouw 2012; Oomen 2016; Gerards 2017.

[48] EU law would not be affected by the constitutional amendment, as arts. 93 and 94 of the Constitution did not apply here.

[49] Kamerstukken II 2011/12, 33 359 (R 1986), No. 3.

[50] Despite the fact that the Human Rights Act 1998 would be replaced with a UK Bill of Rights, the plans for repeal are heavily debated. The Independent Human Rights Act Review was set up to consider how the Human Rights Act worked in practice and whether any change was needed. It concluded that there was no strong case for significant changes to the Human Rights Act, with the majority of the evidence suggesting that the existing framework worked effectively. Nevertheless, a Bill of Rights Bill was introduced to Parliament in June 2022. Passage of the Bill was halted later that year. For more on this Bill, see Amos 2024.

direction, namely, to allow courts to review the constitutionality of primary legislation under certain conditions.[51]

The Taverne proposal was met with severe criticism of the judiciary (*Nederlandse Vereniging voor Rechtspraak* and *Raad voor de Rechtspraak*) and Council of State, as well as in scholarship.[52] A few years later, at the instigation of the same private member, the Law on the Approval and Publication of Treaties (*Rijkswet goedkeuring en bekendmaking verdragen*) was amended to create a statutory duty of information for the government with respect to treaty provisions that by their content can 'bind anyone'. Taverne withdrew his proposal to amend the Constitution in 2017.[53]

The Taverne proposal was mainly instigated by a concern for the separation of powers between the courts and the legislature. It aimed to restrict the role of courts vis-à-vis the legislature in the context of treaty law, which was considered to be rather vague and open to judicial creativity of international bodies, imposing duties on the state which had never been approved by the state. Respect for fundamental rights or the core principles of the Constitution beyond the separation of the powers were not central to the proposal. On the contrary, they were in fact neglected: the proposal did nothing to compensate for the elimination of judicial review of compliance with treaty provisions, for instance by making the changes conditional on the introduction of judicial constitutional review.

9.5 Conclusion: Openness as Identity

Openness towards international and EU law is a *typical* feature of Dutch constitutional law. However, the Constitution did not always have that characteristic, at least not to the extent it does now. The Dutch legal order was deliberately opened up to international law in 1953 for the state to be able to fully participate in the process of European integration, which developed rapidly after World War II. In particular, the primacy of international treaty provisions over all national law, constitutionally anchored in that year, contributed to this. The 1953 constitutional revision further settled the debate on the extent to which treaties that departed from the Constitution could be approved. It established beyond doubt that this was indeed possible, but that such treaties required the approval of a two-thirds majority in both chambers of Parliament. Furthermore, the constitutional amendment of 1956 confirmed what already applied under existing unwritten law: that treaty provisions can, under some conditions, have direct effect in the Dutch legal order and that international organisations can be assigned regulatory, administrative and judicial powers.

The process of European integration brought not only (what is today) the European Union, but also major human rights treaties, in particular the ECHR. The Convention proved to be of great significance for the Netherlands, especially from

[51] Kamerstukken II 2001/02, 28 331, No. 1 ff.

[52] Fleuren and De Wit 2012; Brölman and Nijman 2012.

[53] Kamerstukken II 2016/17, 33 359 (R1986), No. 9.

the 1980s onwards for at least two reasons. First, the prohibition of constitutional review prevented courts from reviewing statutes against the Constitution and thus against the fundamental rights it contained. Accordingly, litigants seeking to have their fundamental rights protected turned to human rights treaties, which the courts can use as standards for review. Second, Dutch fundamental rights provide little guidance for judicial review. They usually only determine who can restrict a fundamental right, but not what substantive requirements such a restriction must meet. Treaties such as the ECHR do provide such a framework for review and are apt for judicial application. During this period, the openness of Dutch constitutional law became not only a *typical* feature, but also an *essential* characteristic of the Netherlands as a democratic constitutional state for only through treaty review courts can provide legal protection against statutes. Should the ban on constitutional review be repealed, for which there now seems to be a majority in parliament, however, the openness of Dutch constitutional law may no longer be essential for the state to function as a constitutional democracy governed under the rule of law.

The unconditional application of international law in the domestic legal order can accordingly, in many cases, serve to safeguard the democratic rule of law. However, it can also challenge the same core principles underlying the Constitution, the rule of law and fundamental rights, when international or EU law is itself not compatible with the requirements of the democratic rule of law. In such instances, the openness of the Dutch legal order, a typical feature of the Dutch legal order, may prove an obstacle to the core principles of the Dutch Constitution and should not be considered an essential part of it. The openness of the Dutch legal order to international and EU law can also be unsettling, for other reasons. The chosen path—excluding judicial review in light of the Constitution while allowing review against ECHR, treaty law and EU law devalues the Constitution and outsources the protection of fundamental rights to an important extent to external sources and international bodies. This may affect the legitimacy both of the Constitution, whose significance and authority are questioned and of these international bodies, which are considered to interfere in national sensitive issues. More worryingly, the dependence on international law may lead to a minimal protection of fundamental rights, since European subsidiary minimum standards are used as the national level of protection. Moreover, the dependence on international law makes protection of fundamental rights in the Dutch legal order vulnerable to decline, when the international organisations and institutions which are considered to offer protection fail.

References

Amos M (2024) Democratic State, Autocratic Method: The Reform of Human Rights Law in the United Kingdom. International and Comparative Law Quarterly 73(1):1–27

Baudet T (2010) Het Europees Hof voor de Rechten van de Mens vormt een ernstige inbreuk op de democratie. NRC Handelsblad, 13 November 2010

Besselink L F M (2002) De Constitutionele bepalingen over verdragen die van de Grondwet afwijken en de opdracht van bevoegdheid aan internationale organisaties. Annex to: Kamerstukken 2002/03 27 484 (R 1669), No. 289
Brölman K, Nijman J (2012) Rechtstreekse werking verdragen goed voor Nederland. Openbaar Bestuur 22(6):13–15
Buys J T (1883) De Grondwet. Toelichting en kritiek. Deel I. P Gouda Quint, Arnhem
Buys J T (1888) De Grondwet, Toelichting en kritiek. Deel III. P Gouda Quint, Arnhem
Calliess C, Van der Schyff G (eds) (2020) Constitutional Identity in a Europe of Multilevel Constitutionalism. Cambridge University Press, Cambridge
Claes M, De Witte B (2023) The Roles of Constitutional Courts in the European Legal Space. In: Von Bogdandy A, Huber P M, Grabenwarter C (eds) Constitutional Adjudication: Common Themes and Challenges. The Max Planck Handbooks in European Public Law, Vol. IV. Oxford University Press, Oxford, pp. 495–526
Duynstee F J F M (1954) Grondwetsherziening 1953. Kluwer, Deventer
Fleuren J W A (2002) Verdragen die afwijken van de Nederlandse Grondwet. In: Breillat D, Kortmann C A J M, Fleuren J W A (eds) Van de constitutie afwijkende verdragen. Kluwer, Deventer, pp. 43–78
Fleuren J W A (2004) Een ieder verbindende bepalingen van verdragen. Boom Juridisch, The Hague
Fleuren J, De Wit J (2012) Het voorstel-Taverne; schrapping van de rechterlijke bevoegdheid om wetten aan verdragen te toetsen. Nederlands Juristenblad 87(4):2812–2818
Fromage D, De Witte B (eds) National Constitutional Identity Ten Years on: State of Play and Future Perspectives. European Public Law 27(3):411–614
Gerards J H (2016) The Irrelevance of the Netherlands Constitution, and the Impossibility of Changing It. Revue interdisciplinaire d'études juridiques 77(2):207–233
Gerards J (2017) The Netherlands: Political Dynamics, Institutional Robustness. In: Popelier P, Lambrecht S, Lemmens K (eds) Criticism of the European Court of Human Rights—Shifting the Convention System: Counter-dynamics at the National and EU Level. Intersentia, Cambridge, pp. 327–360
Gerards J, Terlouw A (eds) (2012) Amici Curiae. Adviezen aan het Europees Hof voor de Rechten van de Mens. Wolf Legal Publishers, Nijmegen
Grabenwarter C, Huber P M, Knez R, Ziemele I (2021) The Role of the Constitutional Courts in the European Judicial Network. European Public Law 27(1):43–62
Ní Chinnéide H, Sevrin E (2025) Restoring Balance: A Critical Response to the Open Letter on Migration and Human Rights, blogpost StrasbourgObserver, 17 June 2025, available on https://strasbourgobservers.com/2025/06/17/restoring-balance-a-critical-response-to-the-open-letter-on-migration-and-human-rights/
Oomen B (2016) A Serious Case of Strasbourg-bashing? An Evaluation of the Debates on the Legitimacy of the European Court of Human Rights in the Netherlands. The International Journal of Human Rights 20(3):407–425
Polzin M (2017) Constitutional Identity as a Constructed Reality and Restless Soul. German Law Journal 18(7):1595–1616
Reestman J H (2009) The Franco-German Constitutional Divide: Reflections on National and Constitutional Identity. European Constitutional Law Review 5(3):374–390
Roznai Y (2017) Unconstitutional Constitutional Amendments. Oxford University Press, Oxford
Staatscommissie Grondwet (2010) Rapport Staatscommissie Grondwet. Annex to: Kamerstuk II 2010/11, 31 570, No. 17
Staatscommissie Parlementair Stelsel (2018) Lage drempels, hoge dijken. Boom, The Hague
Stremler M (2018) De voorgestelde algemene bepaling als fundamentele constitutionele norm. Tijdschrift voor Constitutioneel Recht 9(3):204–220
Van Leeuwen K (2012) On Democratic Concerns and Legal Traditions: The Dutch 1953 and 1956 Constitutional Reforms "Towards" Europe. Contemporary European History 21(3):357–374
Van Vugt E (2024) Constitutional Idolatry or Irrelevance in Times of Crisis? The Case of the Netherlands. Constitutional Studies 10:29–62

Zwart T (2011) Een steviger opstelling tegenover Europees Hof voor de Rechten van de Mens bevordert de rechtstaat. Nederlands Juristenblad 86(7):343–346

Monica Claes is Professor of European and Comparative Constitutional Law in the Department of European Law at the Faculty of Law of Maastricht University, the Netherlands.

Joost Sillen is Professor of Constitutional Law in the Department of Public Law at the Faculty of Law of Maastricht University, the Netherlands.

Part III
Themes

Chapter 10
State and Religion: A Question of Constitutional Identity?

Adriaan Overbeeke

Contents

Abstract This contribution attempts to sketch a picture of the constitutional entrenchment of state-religion relations in the Netherlands, focusing on the factors that influenced it. Historical elements are important in this regard, especially the religious development in the Low Countries since the sixteenth century as a result of the Reformation; the associated legal regulation of state-religion relations also deserves attention. Noteworthy is that changes in this area in the constitutional text always involved the influence of international developments or international law. From a system of a dominant church, combined with elements of religious tolerance, a hybrid regime developed, including both regulations of far-reaching separation between church and state and intensive state support in some policy areas, especially regarding religious education. Regarding constitutional identity, no specific model for state-religion relations can be derived from this development. It can be observed, however, that the Constitution leaves room for the legislature to determine concrete state-religion relations, with the leeway largely determined by international law.

Keywords Religion and belief · Separation of state and church · State neutrality · Freedom of religion · Constitutional law · International law

A. Overbeeke (✉)
Faculty of Law, VU University Amsterdam, Amsterdam, The Netherlands
e-mail: a.j.overbeeke@vu.nl

G. van der Schyff (ed.), *The Constitutional Identity of The Netherlands*,
https://doi.org/10.1007/978-94-6265-779-3_10

10.1 Introduction

Ever since the developments that led to the formation and independence of the Dutch Republic[1] from the Spanish crown in the sixteenth century in the context of the conflicts generated by the Protestant Reformation, the relations between religion, religious communities and the state, and the legal regulation of those relations, have had constant attention in the internal legal order.[2] This resulted from the fact that the young Dutch Republic did not opt for a regime characterised by a close relationship or even unity between the state and one specific religion. While the Reformed religion was accorded a privileged position, this state of affairs went hand in hand with granting limited living space to other religions and their adherents. Strictly speaking, this phase was about a very modest protection of religious diversity, without freedom and equality being normative in government action at that time. This phase was about tolerating religious difference so that to some extent a coexistence of adherents of diverse religions within the context of the young Republic was made possible.[3] The relationship to religions thus constitutes one of the oldest constitutional themes for the Netherlands.

This reveals nothing about the model for relations between government and religion applicable to the Netherlands, if such a model exists. Does this system in its characteristics tend towards—to use a tripartite division by Brugger[4] as a starting point—a model of "strict separation", "equality" or "nearness" (cooperation)? Or should one speak of a rather hybrid system? (To what extent) is this system anchored in Dutch law: are constitutional norms available, which determine the applicable system? And, finally, is this shaping of state-religion relations an element of constitutional identity? What follows attempts to answer these questions, focusing mainly on elements that have long been at the heart of these relations: the position of institutionalised (mainly Christian) religion, the collective exercise of religion, that which was traditionally referred to as the *church-state* relationship.

While there is something to be said for describing the current relationship as characteristic of the Dutch system, it will be argued here that at the micro level, there is no specific unambiguous state and religion profile but several divergent profiles, depending on the regulated policy domain. The norms laid down in the Constitution with regard to religion, both in the current text and in previous versions, show that the legislature is competent to make (possibly entirely new) choices here, with shifts conceivable (possibly different per policy domain) on the axis from "nearness" to

[1] The Dutch Republic (formally the United Provinces of the Netherlands) was a confederation of provinces that broke away from Spain beginning in 1579. Initially, it included territory belonging to present-day Belgium.

[2] Van Bijsterveld 2019, p. 409.

[3] Mainly in economically important urban centres, where religious diversity was particularly noticeable, see Kennedy 2017, pp. 165–167.

[4] Brugger 2012, pp. 263–281.

"strict separation".[5] A characteristic of the Dutch system is perhaps that—whatever choices are made—it operates within frameworks of international law, a characteristic reinforced in this case by the sober text of the main constitutional provision in this area.

10.2 Religion and Belief in the Current 1983 Constitution

The Dutch Constitution, as revised in 1983, contains in the first paragraph of article 6 only one, very brief, provision with guarantees on the exercise of religion or belief: "Everyone shall have the right to profess freely his religion or belief, either individually or in community with others, without prejudice to his responsibility under the law."[6] A textual similarity to article 9(1) of the European Convention on Human Rights (ECHR)[7] is not coincidental,[8] but in its brevity, the constitutional text even rivals that of the treaty provision. Moreover, Gerards signals a relative unfamiliarity in the Netherlands with constitutional provisions relating to fundamental rights and concludes: "When it comes to fundamental rights, our Constitution is something of a Calimero, outstripped by the ECHR, which is much better known to us, and increasingly also by the EU Fundamental Rights Charter."[9]

Parallel to article 9 ECHR, the Dutch constitutional text has in common that it does not specify the internal relations that (should) apply between the state party on the one hand, and religion and belief on the other.[10] In this respect, article 6 of

[5] The term "legislature" (*formele wetgever*) refers to the government and parliament (States General) jointly enacting Acts of Parliament, according to article 81 of the Constitution.

[6] Article 6 of the Constitution, reads in full: "1. Everyone shall have the right to profess freely his religion or belief, either individually or in community with others, without prejudice to his responsibility under the law.

2. Rules concerning the exercise of this right other than in buildings and enclosed places may be laid down by Act of Parliament for the protection of health, in the interest of traffic and to combat or prevent disorders." (translation Ministry of the Interior and Kingdom Relations).

[7] Article 9(1) ECHR: "Everyone has the right to freedom of thought, conscience and religion; this right includes freedom to change his religion or belief and freedom, either alone or in community with others and in public or private, to manifest his religion or belief, in worship, teaching, practice and observance."

[8] See, e.g. Parliamentary Documents II 1975–1976, 13872, No. 3, p. 28, regarding the introduction of the concept pair "religion or belief".

[9] Gerards 2023, p. 192 (author's translation).

[10] Perhaps with the exception of an element included in article 6(2) of the Constitution regarding the scope for restricting religious practice "other than in buildings and enclosed places". This contains an echo of the procession ban previously included in the Constitution, a ban which touched on Catholic worship.

the Constitution[11] differs from the previous constitutional provisions.[12] The current constitutional text leaves room for both a system more in line with, for example, the French *laïcité* model (strict separation) and systems characterised by cooperativeness (nearness), including direct financial state aid. The Constitution only provides that it is the legislature that has the power to lay down the basic regulations, especially when it comes to allowing restrictions on freedom of religion and belief.

According to Vermeulen and Van Bijsterveld, however, article 6 of the Constitution is a continuation of the regime that existed before the 1983 constitutional amendment, albeit with one important innovation, the introduction of constitutional protection of non-religious belief.[13] This approach, that of continuity, is important when assessing the particularly rigorous text reduction. Prior to the 1983 constitutional revision, religious matters consistently occupied an entire chapter, with a relatively strong focus on the position of religious denominations[14] and the collective practice of religion.[15] This chapter of the Constitution was the product of a process in which elements were able to be found that could be considered "identity-defining" or that at least played a role in developing the framework for the constitutional church-state relationship. This development process itself is worthy of attention, as it shows that international developments and international law commitments in particular are a regular ingredient in changing this relationship.[16]

This evolution has also been characterised as a process of progressively unbundling relations between the Reformed Church (already privileged since the sixteenth century) and the state,[17] which precluded the introduction of an *established church* model.[18] The development of church-state relations is one that, measured against the constitutional texts, since 1815 has coincided with a pragmatic and step-by-step deletion of those portions of the constitutional text that indicate state involvement, steps that were ultimately aimed at enabling the co-existence of various religions. The constitutional text is not the only measure, as it can be observed that, especially in the period between 1815 and 1848, there were significant internal

[11] Article 23 of the Constitution is not included in this analysis. See Chap. 11 in this volume.

[12] Van der Pot 1947, p. 397 observed that even the then existing chapter "does not contain the expression of one particular, deliberate attitude of the State towards the matters of religion and church" (author's translation).

[13] Vermeulen and Van Bijsterveld 2021, p 121; Van Bijsterveld 2019, p. 414.

[14] Until 1983, the constitutional text used the term *kerkgenootschap* (literally "church society"), a designation only appropriate for Christian churches. However, the term, which is still used in lower law, covers the full breadth of the religious palette. Pleading for a more inclusive terminology, see Van der Ploeg 2008, p. 94.

[15] By contrast, the 1983 revision of the Constitution adopted a more individualistic conception of classical fundamental rights. See Hirsch Ballin 2021, p. 34.

[16] Besselink 2023, pp. 381–430.

[17] See e.g. the report published shortly after the 1983 Constitution, Hirsch Ballin 1988, pp. 21–23.

[18] Symbolic of this is the removal already in 1815 (with a view to uniting with the overwhelmingly Catholic Belgian provinces) of the 1814 constitutional provision that required the king to belong to the reformed religion. On pre-1815 religious diversity in the Netherlands, see Van Eijnatten 2010, p. 126.

developments in church-state relations where constitutional rules proved to be of little influence in determining public policy in the Netherlands.

This contribution focuses on the classic constitutional protection of religious practice, now enshrined in article 6 of the Constitution. However, it would be a mistake to overlook the fact that article 23 of the Constitution on education (thoroughly amended in 1917 and left untouched by the last major revision in 1983) is also indicative of constitutional relations in the field of religion, because of its guarantees for religious-based educational initiatives.[19] The coexistence, on the one hand, of a religion-funding regime that (especially since a 1972 constitutional amendment[20]) amounts to a far-reaching financial *separation* between the state and religious communities,[21] and, on the other hand, an article 23 Constitution-based education system that implies far-reaching cooperation and financial state support, suggests that there is no single constitutionally anchored model in the domain of state and religion, but rather a (dynamic) hybrid constellation.[22]

10.3 State and Religion in the Constitution: An Evolution (1814–1983)

10.3.1 Features (and Dynamics) of the Evolving System

Regardless of the textual changes to the Dutch Constitution over time, it can be argued that partly under its influence a state and religion system developed in which some constant factors are recognisable. Firstly, it allows an increasingly diverse religious landscape to be accommodated. Secondly, it gradually bid farewell to the system of the privileged church(es). Thirdly, linked to the last element, it recognises state neutrality,[23] a principle that helps to create a level playing field for the various relevant actors[24] The last two elements are related to the principle of the *institutional*

---

[19] On article 23 of the Constitution, see Chap. 11 in this volume.

[20] Vermeulen and Van Bijsterveld 2021, p. 121.

[21] The state's abstention goes even beyond the French system in the 1905 *laicité* law. See Prélot 2015, pp. 76–77.

[22] Overbeeke 2013, p. 106.

[23] See the deletion already in 1815 (as part of the amalgamation of the Catholic Belgian provinces with the Northern provinces) of a constitutional provision establishing the (protestant) religion of the king. Van den Berg 2023, pp. 47–48.

[24] Strengthened since 1983 by the prohibition of discrimination contained in article 1 of the Constitution, which includes the prohibition of unequal treatment based on religion and philosophy of life. Kortmann 1982, p. 61 noted that this provision enclosed the Constitution's old provisions (arts. 182 and 183) on the equal protection of denominations.

separation of church and state, a principle that is neither formalised in the Constitution nor in other regulations and about which there is no unanimity,[25] but rather uncertainty.[26]

A fairly precise description of this principle in the Dutch context was provided by the government in 2004 in a detailed memorandum on the role of fundamental rights in an increasingly diverse society:

> (...) both the state and churches and other spiritual-based associations function as independent bodies. For religiously based societies, this means, inter alia, that they elect their officers independently and that they (and their members individually or collectively) can freely determine or profess their religion or belief. They determine their spiritual and institutional order as they see fit. The state respects this independence. It may not exercise coercion with regard to administrative organisation. The state must refrain from any interference in the practice of religion or belief, without prejudice to its power and duty to act against those who break the law in doing so. Religious societies should be treated equally by the state. The state may thus not side with any particular religious or philosophical belief. It is, in the words of the ECtHR, a "neutral organiser". On the other hand, the independence of the state vis-à-vis associations is reflected in the fact that the associations and their officials as such have no powers under public law.[27]

Although the three factors mentioned above are visible in this description, it does not evidence a clear choice for a specific state and religion model. Models with forms of state-religion cooperation could fit well into this separation concept.[28] In essence, the constitutional situation does not exclude significant scope for policy change.

The theme of *religion funding* provides a good illustration of the dynamics in this field. After an initial broadening of state support to several Christian and Jewish religious communities,[29] this direct funding was eventually extinguished in the second half of the twentieth century without prior intense political or social conflict,[30] but also without opting for a principled ban on all public funding.[31] Even though the constitutional provisions regarding the funding of religious denominations have been removed, direct state funding is not considered in itself to violate the principle of the separation of church and state.[32] This allows, for example, on the basis *compensatory equal treatment*, that specific newly arriving groups in the country can due to a disadvantaged position still be provided with forms of support that enable their collective

[25] See Van Bijsterveld 2006, pp. 229–237. See, on the historical development, Van Sasse van IJsselt 2015, pp. 26–30.

[26] Overbeeke 2013, pp. 108–109.

[27] Nota Grondrechten in een pluriforme samenleving, see Parliamentary Documents II 2003/04, 29 614, No. 2, p. 7 (author's translation).

[28] See more extensively Vermeulen and Van Bijsterveld 2021, pp. 147–149.

[29] Van Sasse van IJsselt 2015, p. 28.

[30] By comparison, the fierce political struggle in the last quarter of the nineteenth century led to the end of direct state funding of recognised religions in France by the 1905 (Law on the Separation of Churches and State of 9 December 1905, Official Gazette of France, 11 December 1905). See on this developments Peker 2019, pp. 819–827.

[31] On this process, see Van't Hul 2020.

[32] Van Bijsterveld 2009, pp. 269–270.

practice of religion.[33] However, legislation proposed more recently regarding religion funding seems to enable government intervention in an entirely different way. This legislation seeks to bring religious groups' own internal funding streams, particularly if funding is involved from abroad, under stricter government oversight.[34] Or, to choose another domain that overlaps with the education theme, legislation is opted for that would introduce government oversight of all informal education, an activity that goes to the heart of religious education in the bosom of religious communities.[35]

10.3.2 Impact of International Law and International Context

In the development of Dutch relations between state and religion, international law and international developments are of special significance. Since the start of the nineteenth century, the influence of treaty law on the formulation of the constitutional text regarding religion has been undeniable. When the Constitution was adopted in 1815, that influence proved so central that when amending texts concerning religious freedom and church-state relations, it was explicitly suggested that the constitution-maker was bound by the limits set by a treaty (in this case, a protocol[36] concluded by the Great Powers in the context of the Vienna Congress).[37]

International developments also appear to have played an important role in the adoption of a more liberal constitutional revision in 1848, a year which saw many revolutions across Western Europe.[38] As for religion, the amendments to the constitutional texts were dominated by the principle of the separation of church and state, this included complete freedom for everyone to practise their religion, no government interference in church affairs and the abolition of the right of *placet*.[39] The 1848

---

[33] Van der Burg 2009, p. 33. See also the recommendation for granting compensatory aid in the report by Hirsch Ballin 1988, pp. 83–85.

[34] Proposal for an Act of Parliament on the transparency of civil society organisations (*Wet transparantie maatschappelijke organisaties*), Parliamentary Documents II 2020/21, 35 646, No. 2.

[35] Proposal for an Act of Parliament on the supervision of informal education (*Wet toezicht informeel onderwijs*) (not yet tabled in parliament). See Broeksteeg 2023.

[36] London Protocol of 21 June 1814 (between the United Kingdom, the Kingdom of Prussia, the Austrian Empire, and the Russian Empire) awarding the territories of Belgium and The Netherlands to William I of the Netherlands.

[37] See proclamation text of the Constitution of 24 August 1815, *Nederlandsche Staats-Courant* (Dutch State Gazette) of 26 August 1815 (published in Colenbrander 1909, p. 619). Objections to the provisions relating to religion were not taken into account in determining the number of dignitaries who agreed to the constitutional text to be adopted.

[38] Van Bijsterveld 2019, p. 212.

[39] Right of *placet*: the right of state authorities to approve papal or episcopal decisions (decisions of a religious hierarchy) before they may be published.

Constitution also provided guarantees on the issue of the free exercise of religion that allowed in particular the Roman Catholic Church to emerge from its second class position in society.[40]

10.3.3 Limited Role of the Constitution

Early on, it became apparent that the Constitution was not always considered the appropriate level to answer the most pressing questions about state and religion relations. In 1839 a treaty finalised the separation of (mainly Catholic) Belgium from the Netherlands that had occurred in 1830, the treaty also necessitated the Constitution to be amended. When the Constitution was amended in 1840, the religion chapter was left untouched even though (a) the Belgian question was partly the result of disagreements about church-state relations and (b) the Netherlands itself had been embroiled since 1834 in a serious conflict within Protestantism.[41] This intrareligious conflict led to the rupture of the Reformed Church, the privileged church at the time, and obstructive government action which jeopardised the free exercise of religion by the Protestant communities which had separated from the privileged church.

Therefore, the Constitution, especially in the form of article 6, has a relatively limited role and avoids the concrete elaboration of state-religion relations. In these matters, in particular, it is up to the democratically legitimised legislature to make central decisions.[42] It could be argued though that the Constitution determines the space to be left the legislature in making these choices, and that only in exceptional cases does it record fairly precisely what it deems to be the acceptable place for religion in society. In this regard, one could think of article 23 of the Constitution, which in 1917 recorded the outcome of a long political struggle on the legal and financial status of religious schools.[43] However, the more sober the text, as is the case in Article 6 of the Constitution, the more room the Constitution leaves for the concrete system to be changed. What seems to be excluded though is a return to the eighteenth century system of a privileged church. Article 6 of the Constitution, read together with article 1 of the Constitution (on equal treatment), would preclude this.[44]

---

[40] Homan 1966, pp. 407–408; Kennedy 2017, pp. 309–310.

[41] On the *Afscheiding* (Separation) of 1834, see Kennedy 2017, pp. 302–303.

[42] Adams and Van der Schyff 2017, p. 4.

[43] On this struggle, see Chap. 11 in this volume.

[44] Van Bijsterveld and Vermeulen 2021, pp. 145–146.

10.4 Role of the Legislature, Constitutional Review and International Law

10.4.1 Legislation and Constitutional Review

Where state and religious relations are concerned in the Netherlands, the constitutional text in article 6 provides limited guidance. The text's elaboration, and thus also the solution to newly emerging issues in the field, is left to the legislature, with the possible exception of religion and education issues as regulated in article 23 of the Constitution.

It should be borne in mind that since 1917, the electoral system in the Netherlands has been based on proportional representation, as determined in article 53(1) of the Constitution. A noteworthy consequence has been that governments are dependent on coalition building and—by extension—that enacting legislation by a parliamentary majority often requires compromise. This has contributed to the fact that abrupt changes to existing legislative arrangements in the field of state and religion are rare.

Illustrative of the decisive role of the legislature is the Religious Bodies Act of 1853.[45] This Act, only repealed in 1988 (as a result of the adoption of the 1983 Constitution), gave shape to a comprehensive regulation of religious practice following the constitutional amendment of 1848. This law elaborated on the autonomy of denominations, but also included regulations on, for example, the religious ministry of foreigners, houses of worship, religious bell ringing and the public wearing of religious vestments by religious personnel. Whereas the 1848 Constitution was henceforth less burdened by provisions relating to the internal functioning of religious associations, the Act of Parliament partly compensated for this. However, the 1853 law also had a certain pacifying effect after the Roman Catholic Church had taken concrete steps towards its long-desired greater aim of autonomy under the 1848 Constitution, which became visible by the establishment (controversial among a significant proportion of Protestants) of dioceses.[46] It should be noted that the constitutionality of Acts in this area is not reviewed by the courts, given the prohibition on review contained in Article 120 of the Constitution.[47] That this prohibition does not prevent the constitutional review of regulations lower than Acts is of little significance, given the very sober wording of article 6 of the Constitution.[48] Even if the ban on constitutional review were lifted, there would not be much for the courts to review.[49]

---

[45] Act of 10 September 1853 Regulating the Supervision of Various Religious Bodies (*Wet van 10 september 1853 tot regeling van het toezigt op de onderscheidene kerkgenootschappen*). Repealed by Article IV of the Act of 20 April 1988 on Public Demonstrations (*Wet openbare manifestaties*). On the 1853 Act, see Aalders 1998.

[46] This was controversial because it involved restoring a Roman Catholic episcopal hierarchy created by the Holy See, after an absence of 250 years. See also Van Bijsterveld 2019, p. 412.

[47] On article 120 of the Constitution, see Chap. 8 in this volume.

[48] See Groen and Verhey 2020, p. 427.

[49] Hirsch Ballin 2021, p. 29.

10.4.2 *Treaty Law as a Safety Net*

The lack of an unambiguous "model" in the most relevant constitutional provisions for religion and especially for relations between the state and religion, and the prominent position that the legislature has under the Constitution in shaping these relations, leaves room for variation, the limits of which cannot ultimately be found in internal norms. The robust core of state and religion relations in the Netherlands can ultimately be traced back to treaty provisions, in particular article 9 ECHR and article 18 of the International Covenant on Civil and Political Rights (ICCPR). At the same time, the country's courts are competent and obliged to review Acts of Parliament in the area of state and religion against these treaty provisions.[50] Since the turn of the century, the jurisprudence of the European Court of Human Rights (ECtHR) has provided the elements that provide a fairly precise framework for assessing the development of national state and religion arrangements.[51] The core elements of the current regime, as mentioned above, fit perfectly into that assessment framework. The protective significance of treaty law will become apparent should new legislative initiatives "chafe" or even conflict with the ECHR's review framework. While the evolution towards an alternative design of the state and religion relationship is an open question in the Netherlands, it is at the same time bound by international law and highly dependent on the openness of Dutch constitutional law to international law.

10.5 State and Religion Controversies

Since the end of the twentieth century, a change can be observed in views on the position of religion in society in the Netherlands. Religious plurality, previously tolerated and even legitimised based on the separation of church and state principle (in the meaning given to it above in the Dutch context) is viewed as increasingly problematic.[52] This is partly linked to a profound change in the philosophical landscape in the country, both as a result of the continuing secularisation and the increase of religious diversity caused by migration and the integration challenges associated with it.[53]

---

[50] Van Bijsterveld 2019, p. 415.

[51] See Koenig 2015.

[52] Van Sasse van IJsselt 2006, p. 655.

[53] Ibid.; Van Bijsterveld 2020, pp. 408-410. These societal developments were also a main reason for the government's memorandum on the role of fundamental rights in an increasingly diverse society, see Nota Grondrechten in een pluriforme samenleving, see Parliamentary Documents II 2003/04, 29 614, No. 2.

Discussions of the issues arising in this context show that there is no unanimity on the space that religion can be allowed[54] and on the role that the state should play in regulating the increasingly plural landscape. In the debate, views are put forward that, should they be able to count on a parliamentary majority, could, on certain points, lead to a substantial change in the historically established system without immediately affecting the arrangements in the Constitution. An illustration of this, which touches on the freedom of religious organisation, is the debate on demanding more financial transparency from and stopping undesirable foreign funding of religious communities. Underlying this is a politically widely shared unease about potentially threatening external influence on *Islamic* religious communities in the Netherlands.[55] The intention to impose stricter conditions on the admission of clergy from abroad can also be counted in this problem category.[56]

Moreover, it is remarkable, that instruments dating back to a period of greater state intervention (heir to the then "nearness" approach) are being pulled out from under the dust in the twenty-first century precisely because of growing concern about the relationship of the many different religious movements and the state. This concerns the possible re-evaluation of the governmental "departments of religion" (a ministry of religious affairs), a department that was managed by the Minister of Justice since the nineteenth century. A cautious plea for its re-evaluation can be partly justified by *the need for interaction* between government and religion and belief communities.[57] This is a development that fits well with the task attributed to the state by the European Court of Human Rights (ECtHR) as a "neutral and impartial organiser of religion".[58] The limits of a state's choice of a "hands on" approach have been outlined in a now extensive jurisprudence of the ECtHR.

10.6 State and Religion: Part of Constitutional Identity?

The (continuing) development of the relationship between the state and religion is an important issue in the Netherlands. By not prescribing or excluding any model in this regard, the Constitution leaves little doubt about the central role that the legislature has to play in this regard. Although this is an important constitutional theme, variations

---

[54] Reaching agreement or compromise is also more complex because of the highly fragmented political landscape since 2002. This fragmentation is partly caused by very different views on the place of religion (or specific religions) in Dutch society.

[55] Overbeeke 2018; Van Bijsterveld 2020, p. 412, referring to the 2017 Dutch coalition agreement.

[56] See an overview of recent policy intentions offered in Van Bijsterveld 2020, p. 409.

[57] Steenvoorde and Hirsch Ballin 2013, p. 335. See Overbeeke 2021, pp. 210–212 on the apparent need in the Dutch system for direct consultation opportunities between state authorities and religious communities.

[58] European Court of Human Rights, Application No. 44774/98, judgement of 10 November 2005 (*Leyla Şahin v. Turkey*), para 107.

on it are possible. These variations are potentially wide, as there is no specific constellation or model that as such could be said to constitute a component of constitutional identity that requires stronger constitutional protection or entrenchment.

From the discussion above, it can be inferred that the relatively open Dutch state and religion system, without perhaps itself being a delineated part of constitutional identity, is primarily embedded in an international law framework. Looking back at the development of this system, it can be argued that the international law orientation that has characterised the relationship between the state and religion since 1815 has been a firm anchor in changing this system.

References

Aalders W J (1998) De Wet op de Kerkgenootschappen van 10 september 1853. In: Vree J, Schutte G J (eds) Om de toekomst van het protestantse vaderland. Meinema, Zoetermeer, pp. 91–127

Adams M, Van der Schyff G (2017) Constitutional Culture in the Netherlands: A Sober Affair. In: Adams M, Meuwese A, Hirsch Ballin E M H (eds) Constitutionalism and the Rule of Law: Bridging Idealism and Realism. Cambridge University Press, Cambridge, pp. 358–385

Besselink L F M (2023) The Evolution and Gestalt of the Dutch Constitution. In: von Bogdandy A, Huber P M, Ragone S (eds) Constitutional Foundations. The Max Planck Handbooks in European Public Law, Vol. 2. Oxford University Press, Oxford, pp. 381–430

Broeksteeg H (2023) Koranscholen, toezicht en de Grondwet. De Hofvijver 25 January 2023 (available at : https://www.montesquieu-instituut.nl/9394000/1/j9vvllwqvzjxdyx/vm02l2stcazp?pk_campaign=hofv-2301&pk_kwd=vm02l2stcazp)

Brugger W (2012) Separation, Equality, Nearness: Three Church-State Models. International Journal for the Semiotics of Law 25:263–281

Colenbrander H T (1909) Ontstaan der grondwet: Bronnenverzameling, Tweede Deel-1815. Nijhoff, The Hague

Gerards J (2023) 175 Jaar grondrechten in de Grondwet. In: Heringa A W, Kroeze R, Yesilkagit K (eds) De Grondwet van 1848 tot nu. Ontwikkelingsgeschiedenis, cruciale leerstukken en toekomstperspectief. Boom Juridisch, The Hague, pp. 191–208

Groen L, Verhey L F M (2020) De betekenis van grondwettelijke grondrechten voor de wetgever: dode letter of zelfstandig ijkpunt? RegelMaat 35:426–449

Hirsch Ballin E (1988) Overheid, godsdienst en levensovertuiging. Eindrapport van de Commissie van advies inzake de criteria voor steunverlening aan kerkgenootschappen en andere genootschappen op geestelijke grondslag. Ministerie van Binnenlandse Zaken, The Hague

Hirsch Ballin E (2021) Grondrechten. In: Hirsch Ballin E, Janse de Jonge E, Leenknegt G-J (eds) Uitleg van de Grondwet. Boom, The Hague, pp. 29–42

Homan G D (1966) Constitutional Reform in the Netherlands in 1848. The Historian 28:405–425

Kennedy J C (2017) A Concise History of the Netherlands. Cambridge University Press, Cambridge

Koenig M (2015) The Governance of Religious Diversity at the European Court of Human Rights. In: Boulden J, Kymlicka W (eds) International Approaches to Governing Ethnic Diversity. Oxford Academic, Oxford, pp. 51–78

Kortmann C A J M (1982) De vrijheid van godsdienst en levensovertuiging in de nieuwe Grondwet. In: Chappin M J J G et al. (ed) Godsdienstvrijheid. Beschouwingen voor de vergadering van de Rechtskundige afdeling van het Thijmgenootschap op 28 januari 1983 te Tilburg. Kluwer, Deventer, pp. 55–67

Overbeeke A (2013) Introducing a General Burqa Ban in the Netherlands. In: Ferrari A, Pastorelli S (eds) The Burqa Affair Across Europe. Between Public and Private Space. Ashgate, Aldershot, pp. 101–126

Overbeeke A (2018) Het belemmeren van buitenlandse financiering van geloofsgemeenschappen: Een grondrechtengevoelige kwestie. Tijdschrift voor Religie, Recht en Beleid, 29(3):62–79
Overbeeke A J (2021) The State and Religious Groups. The Case of the Low Countries. No Agreements Needed? The Role of Agreements in Belgium and the Netherlands. In: Piciocchi C, Strazzari D, Toniatti R (eds) State and Religion: Agreements, Conventions and Statutes. Università degli Studi di Trento, Trento, pp. 191–219
Peker E (2019) Bringing the State Back in Secularization: The Development of Laïcité in the French Third Republic (1875–1905). Journal for the Scientific Study of Religion 58: 813–832
Prélot P-H (2015) Public Funding of Religions: The Situation in France. In: Messner F (ed) Public Funding of Religions in Europe. Ashgate Publishing, Farnham, pp. 75–82
Steenvoorde R A J, Hirsch Ballin E M H (2013) Een herleving van de departementen van eredienst? In: Van Bijsterveld S C, Steenvoorde R A J (eds) 200 jaar Koninkrijk: Religie, staat en samenleving. Wolf Legal Publishers, Oisterwijk, pp. 325–352
Van Bijsterveld S C (2006) Scheiding van kerk en staat: een klassieke norm in een moderne tijd. In: Van de Donk W B H J, Jonkers A P, Kronjee G J, Plum R J J M (eds) Religie in het publieke domein. Amsterdam University Press, Amsterdam, pp. 227–260
Van Bijsterveld S C (2009) The Financing of Religious Communities in the Netherlands. In: Basdevant-Gaudemet B, Berlingò S (eds) The Financing of Religious Communities in the European Union. Peeters, Leuven, pp. 269–275
Van Bijsterveld S C (2019) State and Church in the Netherlands. In: Robbers G (ed) State and Church in the European Union. Nomos, Baden-Baden, pp. 409–434
Van Bijsterveld S C (2020) Securitisation of Religious Freedom: Religion and the Limits of State Control in The Netherlands. In: Kiviorg M (ed) Securitisation of Religious Freedom: Religion and Limits of State Control. Comares, Granada, pp. 407–420
Van den Berg P (2023) In Search of a Constitutional Identity: The Making of the Constitution of the Kingdom of The Netherlands of 1815. Osaka University Law Review 70:29–65
Van der Burg W (2009) Het ideaal van de neutrale staat. Inclusieve, exclusieve en compenserende visies op godsdienst en cultuur. Boom Juridische Uitgevers, The Hague
Van der Ploeg T J (2008) De overheid en de rechtspersoonlijkheid van kerkgenootschappen. Nederlands Tijdschrift voor Kerk en Recht 79–95
Van der Pot C W (1947) Handboek van het Nederlandsche Staatsrecht, 2nd edn. W E J Tjeenk Willink, Zwolle
Van Eijnatten J (2010) Contested Unity. Church, Nation and Reform in the Netherlands. In: Van Eijnatten J, Yates P (eds) The Dynamics in Religious Reform in Northern Europe 1780–1920. Leuven University Press, Leuven, pp. 123–152
Van Sasse van IJsselt P (2006) Uitoefening van grondrechten als voorwaarde voor integratie in een democratische rechtstaat. NJCM-Bulletin 31:654–663
Van Sasse van IJsselt P (2015) Public Funding of Religious Organisations in the Netherlands. In: Messner F (ed) Public Funding of Religions in Europe. Ashgate Publishing, Farnham, pp. 23–50
Van 't Hul W (2020) Besloten: Politieke onderhandelingen tussen de Nederlandse overheid en religieuze organisaties, 1946–1996. PhD Thesis, Universiteit van Amsterdam
Vermeulen B P, Van Bijsterveld S C (2021) Artikel 6 - Vrijheid van godsdienst en levensovertuiging. In: Hirsch Ballin E, Janse de Jonge E, Leenknegt G-J (eds) Uitleg van de Grondwet. Boom, The Hague, pp. 119–156

Adriaan Overbeeke (B.A., University of Antwerp, Belgium; M.A., Catholic University of Leuven, Belgium; LL.B., LL.M. and Ph.D. in Law, University of Antwerp) is Assistant Professor in the Department of Constitutional and Administrative Law at the VU University Amsterdam, the Netherlands, and Researcher in the Government and Law Program of the Faculty of Law at the University of Antwerp, Belgium. His primary scholarly interests include religious freedom, education rights and minority rights.

Chapter 11
Law and Education: Balancing Between Constitutional Freedoms and Public Principles; Between Plurality and Equality

B. P. Vermeulen and P. J. J. Zoontjens

Contents

Abstract Article 23 of the Constitution constitutes a dual system of private and public schools, both fully funded by government. This dual system guarantees accessibility and neutrality (public schools) and freedom and pluriformity (private schools). When it was established in 1917, article 23 was the culmination of a long historical development, intimately connected with the creation of the Netherlands as a nation state and as a multireligious society. The dominant wave of secularisation and individualisation in the 1960s and 1970s has led to a drastic re-interpretation of article 23's meaning. In defining the current *constitutional identity of education* in its relationship to government, we arrive at four concepts: quality education, pedagogical autonomy, administrative autonomy and government restraint. *Quality education* is in its essence a shared ambition of schools and government. Because of the *pedagogical autonomy* of private and public schools, the state cannot interfere in the substance of the pedagogical process. Both private and public education enjoy the *freedom to organise themselves*. Freedom and autonomy at the level of schools and school organisations are traditionally mirrored by *reluctance on the*

B. P. Vermeulen (✉)
Faculty of Law, Radboud University Nijmegen, Nijmegen, The Netherlands
e-mail: ben.vermeulen@ru.nl

P. J. J. Zoontjens
Tilburg Law School, Tilburg University, Tilburg, The Netherlands

G. van der Schyff (ed.), *The Constitutional Identity of The Netherlands*,
https://doi.org/10.1007/978-94-6265-779-3_11

part of the legislature and the government to intervene in the primary process, or in matters directly preconditional to it. It is our fundamental conviction, however, that an essential core of educational autonomy is a necessary ingredient that has to be kept intact, without which schools, teachers, principals and boards cannot find and maintain the inspiration and idealism in the primary process.

Keywords Freedom of education · Equality and education · Public schools · Private schools · Civic education · Absence of state pedagogy

11.1 Constitutional History

Seventy years ago, Howard Wilson formulated a general thesis that is still undisputed: "The educational system of a country - its structure and status, its policies and procedures - is inevitably an expression of the country's traditions and mores and values."[1] The inherent connection between the one—the educational system—and the other—the country's traditions, mores and values—is evident for those who delve into the history and structure of the Dutch system. This system is fundamentally defined by its basis in the Constitution, which endeavours to conciliate individual and collective freedom with equality and regulation by the state. Some foreign commentators have characterised its legal design as "the most pluralistic educational system in the world"[2] and as one that facilitates "school choice" to a large degree.[3] And indeed, the particularities of the Dutch system are generally seen as created and then maintained by a constitutional view of freedom of education, and its interaction with equality and state intervention. Article 23 of the Constitution (*Grondwet*), the most comprehensive and complex of its provisions, is therefore the starting point of any exploration of what freedom of education, the level of equality and the role of the state in education should be in the Netherlands.[4]

The Dutch education system is intimately connected with the creation of the Netherlands as a nation state.[5] After the successful revolt in the sixteenth century, in response to the attempt of its Spanish king Philip II to eradicate the Reformation, the Netherlands became an independent Republic. This was a defence alliance of seven fairly autonomous provinces, based upon a treaty, the Union of Utrecht of 1579. From then on, the Netherlands became a multi-religious society, where significant dominant groups of Protestants and a Catholic majority had to live together

---

[1] Wilson 1955, p. 135.

[2] Rogers Berner 2012, p. 119.

[3] Patrinos 2009, p. 55.

[4] The English text of article 23 of the Constitution is included at the end of this chapter. The text is taken from the 2023 translation by the Ministry of the Interior and Kingdom Relations. Unless indicated otherwise, all other translations are by the authors.

[5] Literature on this subject is abundant. We mention only a few publications: Idenburg 1964, pp. 11–134; Schelfhout 1976; De Bruin 1985; Boekholt 2002, pp. 3–10; Storimans 2002, pp. 87–101; Hirsch Ballin 2017; Mentink 2021.

peacefully. That required practical tolerance, in part guaranteed by article 13 of the Union of Utrecht, which protected religious freedom in the private sphere of the family. Until the occupation by France in 1795, the political structure of the Netherlands was that of a *con*federation, with limited central governance, and a very large degree of cultural and financial autonomy at the level of the provinces and municipalities. Educational competences with regard to schools, curricula, teaching qualifications, certification, etc. were defined and administered by provinces, municipalities, churches and religious communities, as well as private institutions.

From the era of French rule (1795–1813) onwards, the Netherlands gradually evolved from a fragmented confederacy into a unitary state, with *central* legislative and administrative powers regarding matters of general interest, such as education. The necessity of some kind of central steering and state responsibility was, and has been maintained, ever since the first Dutch Constitution of 1814. An education inspectorate was instituted as early as 1801 and the School Law of 1806 formulated a central curriculum, which played an instrumental role in the creation of the nation state. Its aim was to develop intellectual capacities and useful skills, as well as formation in social and Christian virtues, combining the enlightenment and liberal religion. Every primary school, whether public or private, was required to hold a permit from a provincial or municipal authority. Public schools were subsidised, mostly by municipalities.

The original education project was intended to create an undivided *common school*, inspired by a mild, rational Christianity devoid of partisan doctrines.[6] In the long run that project did not satisfy various orthodox groups that began to demand the freedom to establish their own schools, based on their specific religious beliefs and traditions. The ensuing School Struggle (*schoolstrijd*), starting in the 1830s—linked to the Suffrage Struggle (*kiesrechtstrijd*) since the 1880s—would dominate Dutch politics and society for some 80 years.

The *first phase* of the School Struggle saw the inclusion in the Constitution of the freedom of education in 1848, which protected the right to found one's own schools without local government permission[7] and the freedom to base education on a specific religion or philosophy.[8] This freedom was rather theoretical, however, as private schools were not subsidised by central government. The dominant a contrario interpretation of the provision in the Constitution was that whereas *public* education was the concern (including financial support) of central government private schools were *excluded* from receiving subsidies. And funding by local government was only permitted when the private school continued to accept the non-doctrinal, detached Christianity of the common public school as its philosophical and religious foundation.

[6] See article 140 of the 1814 Constitution: "In order to promote religion, as a permanent support of the state and to expand knowledge, public education [...] is a constant object of government care."

[7] Philipsen 2017, p. 45.

[8] It took nine years to implement this constitutional right in the School Act of 1857, an indication of the depth of the religious-political conflict behind the School Struggle.

The School Struggle gradually transformed into a *second phase*: its objective shifting from formal freedom to equality and thereby to real, substantive freedom. Christian groups started to demand that private schools be subsidised by the state just like public schools. However, the liberal majority in parliament, hostile to doctrinal religion, enacted legislation providing for (more) state funding exclusively for public schools in combination with higher quality standards. Private education—mostly provided in denominational schools—became more expensive as such education had to uphold the same standards. In response Christian groups in parliament (that later became political parties) blocked further extension of the right to vote, unless some kind of government funding of their schools was introduced (the "non possumus" strategy). Some liberal politicians then modified their a contrario interpretation of the constitutional provision that only public education (therefore not: private education) was the subject of the government's continuing concern. From then on, it was agreed that government funding of private education, though not required, was compatible with the Constitution.

The School Act of 1889 provided 30% state subsidy for private schools. In the *third and last phase* of the School Struggle, legislation extending suffrage went hand in hand with a gradual increase in government subsidies for private schools. Eventually, both conflicts were resolved by a pact between the dominant political movements in the Netherlands, laid down in the Constitution in 1917 and further implemented in the Electoral Act (*Kieswet* 1919 and 1922) and the Primary Education Act (*Lager-onderwijswet* 1920). The Christian parties got full government funding for their confessional schools, while the liberals and social democrats obtained the electoral reform they desired in the form of constitutional guarantees for universal suffrage and proportional representation. This *Pacification* marked the legal resolution of the School Struggle, as well as the Suffrage Struggle, the two fundamental political and social conflicts that dominated the second half of the nineteenth century and the beginning of the twentieth century.

The 1917 Pacification was the outcome of a development that started in the second half of the nineteenth century, namely the process of "pillarisation" (*verzuiling*).[9] This development had its sources in the major issues of that century, covering the School Struggle, the Suffrage Struggle and the interlinked Social Question (*sociale kwestie*). Pillarisation denotes the vertical division of society into semi-autonomous groups based on religion (or socialist/liberal laicism) and associated political beliefs. The liberal concept of freedom, the Calvinist notion of sphere sovereignty and the Catholic doctrine of subsidiarity, together with the social-democratic ideal of emancipation of the labour class, merged and provided a strong ideological base for the creation of pillars. These pillars contained political parties, trade unions, media, schools and other collective structures, grounded in their specific views and convictions. Until the 1960s, this model created the conditions for peaceful coexistence, with public life running quite smoothly through frequent and intensive compromises made between the foremen of the different pillar organisations.

---

9 Lijphart 1967.

Ever since then, motivated by strong trends towards secularisation, individualisation and multiculturalism, a continuing process of de-pillarisation has taken place, which has transformed Dutch society making it much more individualistic, pluralist and secular. Most schools have adapted to these trends. The majority of Catholic and Protestant schools became fairly neutral, while remaining Christian in the formal sense and often maintaining some religious remnants and rituals. These schools did not become less popular, partly because of their reputation regarding quality, atmosphere and discipline. Although socialist and liberal political parties are rather critical of the system, there is no strong movement to abolish it either. One main reason is the freedom enjoyed by parents and pupils to choose between a variety of schools, as well as appreciation for the openness created by article 23 of the Constitution, the text of which has been essentially unaltered since the constitutional compromise of 1917.[10]

However, the constitutional text's continuity does not imply that the education system and legislation have never been changed. There have been fundamental changes, in concepts, structures and objectives, sometimes through legislation that was not really compatible with the intention of article 23. Such de facto constitutional changes are legally untouchable, because the legislature (King in Parliament) is the *ultimate interpreter* of the Constitution, as it cannot be overruled by courts due to the prohibition of constitutional judicial review in article 120 of the Constitution.[11]

[10] The only substantive change was the addition of a clause to article 23(4) of the Constitution, allowing for so-called "cooperation schools". A private member's bill to fundamentally change the constitutional provision, giving more equality claims and education rights to "consumers" (pupils, students, parents) was introduced in 2021 (Kamerstukken II 2021/22, 35924, No. 1–3). To date there have been no signs of progress in parliament.

[11] On article 120 of the Constitution, see Chap. 8 in this volume.

11.2 A Dual System: Public and Private Schools, Neutrality and Denomination

One of the characteristics of the era of pillarisation that has survived until now is that the Dutch school system is based on a duality/binarity of two publicly funded sub-systems, namely that between public[12] and non-public—"private"[13]—schools.[14] The differences between the two sub-systems can be described in four characteristics: (1) These two school types fall under different types of law. Public schools are principally part of the public law system, whereas private schools are organisations under civil law. (2) Their legal relationship with government differs. Unlike public schools, private schools enjoy a constitutional protection of their autonomy: the freedom of education. (3) The core of this freedom is the freedom of worldview (*vrijheid van richting*), which allows private schools to define their ideological basis in terms of a specific worldview, often a religion, and to select pupils and teachers on that basis. By contrast, in these matters public schools have to be ideologically neutral and non-exclusive. (4) Finally, public schools are still given some priority, in that they function as schools of last resort. Article 23(4) of the Constitution lays down the principle that in every municipality there must be a sufficient number of public primary schools. This echoes the nineteenth century view of the public school as the common school, the place where every child is welcome: the so-called guarantee function of public education. Evidently, for private schools no such principle is applicable, depending as it does on private initiatives.

As to the legal form of private schools, the education acts stipulate that the school board is "a legal person under civil law whose aim is to provide education without intending to make profit" (i.e. an association or foundation).[15] On the other hand, public schools are part of the public law system and are public organisations. Originally, such schools were an organ or department entirely within the public sphere—an institution of the municipality or other public authority. However, since the 1990s it has become possible for public schools to be set apart from the municipality and be

---

[12] Note that the English translation of the Constitution by the Ministry of the Interior and Kingdom Relations (included at the end of this chapter) uses the term "public-authority school", while we prefer and use the term "public school".

[13] The Dutch dual system is often characterised by the contrast between "public" and "private" schools. However, this terminology is inadequate to the extent that it ignores the fact that both are part of a public education system, governed by law (albeit sometimes differently) and financed from public funds. Furthermore, in the Netherlands the term "private schools" also is used to indicate schools that are not funded from public funds and are regulated by a much more limited legal regime. These types of purely private—that is: commercial—schools are beyond the scope of this contribution. *We nevertheless use the term "private schools" here, however keep in mind that these schools are funded by the state and regulated by extensive legislation.*

[14] The main focus of this contribution is on primary and secondary education, which we refer to as "schools". But the duality of the education system also extends to secondary vocational education and higher education, which are defined as "institutions". Depending on the context, the term "schools" must therefore be understood here in a broad sense, also encompassing "institutions".

[15] See, for instance, article 55 Wet op het primair onderwijs.

governed by a foundation (a legal person under civil law), provided that there still is a dominant public influence (de facto by the municipality) on the composition of the board. This variant—a civil law foundation with various guarantees of public governance—is prominent nowadays, as almost all public schools are governed by a foundation.

A consequence of being a public school is that such schools are primarily subjected to public law regulations, while these regulations hold obligations for private schools only if they are conditional for government funding. Within private schools these obligations therefore apply in principle only to the recipient of the funding, the legal person that acts as the board of the private school. Most of these obligations do not bind the persons within the school as such. The legal obligations of teachers, pupils and parents within private schools depend on the civil law rules applicable within the legal entity (the statutes and/or regulations) and the contractual agreement that the board has concluded with them.[16] This division between public schools regulated by public law, and private schools regulated by civil law, determines the type of legal protection procedure. For instance, if a child is not admitted to a public school, the parents will have to litigate before an administrative court, and before a civil court if the child is refused admission to a private school.

Education provided by public schools must have a *neutral* character, which according to article 23(3) of the Constitution implies that *by* and *in* public education "due respect" must be paid "to everyone's religion or belief". Furthermore, article 23(4) of the Constitution enshrines the principle—subject only to specific exceptions by Act of Parliament—that there must be a sufficient number of public schools in every municipality to provide compulsory education.[17] A third of all 6,500 elementary schools provide public education. According to article 23(2) of the Constitution, individuals and (private law) legal entities (associations, foundations, churches) are free to establish private schools. Such schools are fully funded by government, provided they meet various requirements, the most important being a prognosis that the school will draw a sufficient number of pupils. Private schools are free to provide education in a school climate that is not ideologically neutral. More than two thirds of all elementary schools are private schools and thus located outside the public sphere. These are schools based on a religious worldview, such as Catholic (30%), Protestant (29%) and Islamic (1%) schools, or schools inspired by a specific pedagogical orientation (7.5%).[18]

---

[16] Zoontjens 2023, p. 250.

[17] The fact is that especially in rural areas many municipalities do not have state schools on their territory. The aim of government, however, is to ensure that public education is accessible to everyone.

[18] OCW in Cijfers (2024) for primary and secondary education, to be consulted on https://www.ocwincijfers.nl/.

Denominational schools in particular enjoy the constitutionally guaranteed "freedom of worldview", the freedom to express a fundamental normative orientation in their education, derived from a specific religious affiliation or belief system.[19] The freedom of worldview of private schools comprises the freedom to articulate a specific, even outspoken and fundamental moral and metaphysical vision on mankind, society and the world. Clearly, such an outspoken view cannot be a basis for public schools, which must be neutral. Public education however does not imply an indifferent or even negative perception of worldviews in general, or religions in particular. Its character should be that of *positive neutrality* or *pluralism*: public schools should "contribute to the development of pupils with attention for the religious, philosophical and societal values as exist in Dutch society and with understanding of the variety of those values".[20] This "positive" connotation of neutrality can be considered as a reflection of the multi-religious and pluriform character of Dutch society. Furthermore, it must be stressed that public schools—like private schools—have a fair amount of pedagogical-organisational autonomy, which is reflected for instance in their choice of didactic and pedagogical methods (e.g. public Montessori and Dalton schools).

The legal framing of the Dutch education system as dual or binary must be qualified in the light of ongoing processes, such as the "mingling" of both subsystems. This is in particular due to the weakening of the denominational identity of formally Catholic and Protestant schools in the past decennia due to society's increasing secularisation and individualisation, resulting in many such schools being Christian only in name or on paper (in their statutes, etc.). On the other hand, the link between public schools and (local) government has also been weakened by their "privatisation", being transferred to foundations, albeit with some kind of public governance. Both tendencies find expression in the so-called "cooperation school" (*samenwerkingsschool*), a configuration made possible by an amendment in 2006 to article 23(4) of the Constitution. Cooperation schools are the product of a fusion between a public and a private school and controlled by a foundation. These schools endeavour to provide both public neutral education and denominational private education. Though these schools have been portrayed as rare exceptions to the rule (of dualism), changes to the Education Acts have in fact made them regular variants.[21] A further indication that the dual nature of the system is waning can be found in the mingling (or perhaps blurring?) of public and civil law elements. Although public schools still have a link with local government, their employees are no longer public servants, but are employed on the basis of a civil law contract. And although all institutions for secondary and higher vocational education and some universities are controlled by civil legal entities, legal protection of students (on issues including admission, grades, disciplinary sanctions, etc.) is provided by an administrative court, the Council of State.

---

[19] Standard definition in case law: "it concerns a religion or philosophy regarding the essence of education, influencing alle spheres of life", Koninklijk Besluit (Royal decree) 11 November 1983, Administratieve Beslissingen 1984, 209.

[20] Article 55 Wet op het primair onderwijs.

[21] Noorlander 2011.

11.3 Freedom of Worldview in Practice

The freedom of worldview (*vrijheid van richting*) is a rather abstract principle or concept, from which two other—more specific—freedoms are derived. These are the freedom to establish a school (*vrijheid van oprichting*), and the pedagogical-organisational autonomy within the school (*vrijheid van inrichting*).

Ever since 1920, when the constitutional Pacification was implemented in legislation a private primary or secondary school had to have a worldview (i.e. *richting*, ethos, denomination, philosophy of life) which was "recognisable" in society in order to be eligible for funding. On the basis of a set of criteria developed in practice and case law, various worldviews have been qualified as such by the government, such as Roman Catholic, different Protestant denominations varying from liberal to orthodox, Jewish, Islamic, Hindu, private-neutral, humanist and Steiner schools. The term worldview did not include principles of a pedagogical nature. Schools that called themselves Montessori, Dalton or Jena plan could not, on that basis, appeal to the freedom of establishment. As such, they were not eligible for funding, but were eligible for funding on the basis of a worldview, for instance as a *Catholic* Montessori school. In 2020, the law finally changed and the legal requirement that private schools needed a basis in a specific worldview was removed.[22] New schools with a purely pedagogical, philosophical, social basis or any denominational basis (or none at all), now have an equal chance of being admitted to the system. When applying for a new school, quantitative requirements relating to the expected number of pupils are decisive. The specific worldview (or absence thereof) is no longer relevant for the prognosis.[23] This does not mean that it is very easy to qualify, as the paperwork associated with the application is much more extensive than it used to be and, in particular, the stricter requirements for school plans for civic education (introduced in 2021) are not so easy to fulfil.

Because of a private school's freedom of worldview, the school board can in theory select pupils on the basis of their parents' endorsement of the school's (religious or other) foundation. However, this freedom to select is restricted by three conditions: (1) the worldview must be described in the statutes of the foundation or association that governs the school, (2) the selection may not constitute discrimination, on the basis of race, sex, etc., and, last but not least, (3) the actual selection should not be random but must be consistent with a general pre-established school policy. These criteria, indicated first in the landmark *Maimonides* judgement of the Court of Cassation[24] and later developed in the General Equal Treatment Act of 1994 (*Algemene wet gelijke behandeling*), are so strict in practice that most private schools are unwilling or unable to meet them. Only a small number of schools manage to maintain a consistent school policy to select students to qualify for government funding. These tend to be orthodox Protestant schools, insofar as they are located in areas with a homogeneous following such as in the rural southwest and centre

[22] Wet meer ruimte voor nieuwe scholen, Stb. 2020, 160.

[23] Zoontjens 2023, p. 52.

[24] HR (Court of Cassation) 22 January 1988, AB 1988/96 (*Maimonides*).

of the country, and Jewish and Islamic schools, which tend to be located in urban areas. Their total number can be estimated somewhere between 150 and 300: official figures are lacking. The vast majority of the approximately 4,500 private schools for primary and secondary education in the Netherlands have an open policy, whereby pupils cannot be refused admission and only have to show respect (i.e. no disrespect) for the school's worldview.

Freedom of worldview also implies that the board of a private school may select its staff according to denominational criteria laid down in its statutes and regulations. To prevent discrimination, the criteria in the General Equal Treatment Act are applied even more strictly in such cases than for pupils. In each individual case it is necessary to justify whether the job requirement imposed on an applicant is substantial, legitimate and justified in relation to the school board's worldview. For example, according to the case law of the Netherlands Institute for Human Rights, the dismissal of a crafts teacher at an orthodox Protestant secondary school was considered permissible, because this teacher could no longer agree with the worldview of the school and had resigned from the church affiliated with the school.[25] It implies also that a private school may require that an applicant for the position of teacher must be "church-minded", or that a Catholic school board may require that staff members do not visibly express a conviction other than the Catholic faith. There are also limits though. If a function is filled on a temporary basis, the board has less room to reject an applicant, unless the statutes and a clear policy in practice also require them to endorse the school's worldview. Furthermore, the importance of the function in the light of the realisation of the worldview is relevant: a roster maker probably may not be required to endorse it.[26]

11.4 Islamic Schools

An outline of the constitutional education freedom of private schools would be incomplete without paying attention to the rise of publicly funded Islamic schools in the Netherlands since the 1990s. On the one hand, these schools are the legitimate product of the constitutional right to establish publicly funded private schools; on the other hand, their existence is a pars pro toto source of arguments to call this constitutional freedom into question. At present there are 59 Islamic elementary schools and 2 secondary schools. This is a small number when compared to the group of approximately 900,000 Muslims in the country, or when viewed in relation to the total number of primary schools (some 6,500) and secondary schools (1,450). However, since 2021, as a consequence of the new legislation according to which admission

[25] The case law (which is not binding on the parties) can be found on the institute's website: https://www.mensenrechten.nl/.

[26] Zoontjens 2023, pp. 47–48.

to the subsidised school sector is based primarily on quantitative prognoses,[27] their number has been gradually growing.

Over the years, the issues confronting these schools can be characterised as political, administrative and social. For instance, there have been several incidents of administrative mismanagement. One example concerned the secondary school Ibn Ghaldoun in Rotterdam, where the inspectorate in 2008 found that government funds had been spent unlawfully over a period of four years, used for financing pilgrimages to Mecca. The Minister of Education, Culture and Science then successfully reclaimed an amount of € 1.4 million.[28] Other issues concerned very high salaries, for instance at two elementary schools. It was established that in addition to the two directors of these schools, various other persons were employed as policy officers or paid directors. The minister reclaimed an amount of more than € 900,000[29] and succeeded to ensure that the directors were replaced.[30] These and other cases were widely reported in the media; however—apart of the Haga case discussed below—no financial misconduct of Islamic schools has been reported in recent years. It seems that after 30 years, the Islamic school pillar has adapted rather well to Dutch administrative regulations.

Another source of concern is the tendency of segregation attributed to Islamic schools. Since the turn of the century, Islamic schools have been regarded as sources of cultural separation, where indoctrination, language deprivation, socio-economic disadvantage and poor-quality education were concentrated. This seems to justify the idea in government circles and the media that establishing this type of school should be discouraged.[31] However, all attempts to achieve that until now have failed. The national discussion on integration is now focused on the content of education and teaching materials that can be considered as detrimental to integration and undermining the rule of law. Following reports in September 2019 about "homophobic" teaching materials in Islamic schools, the inspectorate launched investigations. And in 2021, the inspectorate acquired a legal basis for the stricter supervision of civic education in schools.[32]

Related political issues also drew a lot of attention in recent years. One example is illustrative. In 2019, the National Coordinator for Counterterrorism and Security (NCTV) warned the mayor of Amsterdam about the situation at the Haga Lyceum, an Islamic school for secondary education. According to signals from the Dutch Intelligence and Security Service (AIVD), "certain prominent figures within the school

[27] Wet meer ruimte voor nieuwe scholen, Stb. 2020, 160.

[28] Inspectie van het Onderwijs 2013, p. 8.

[29] Rb Den Bosch (District Court Den Bosch) 22 April 2011, ECLI:NL:RBSHE:2011:BQ2321; ABRvS (Administrative Law Division of the Council of State) 8 February 2012, ECLI:NL:RVS:2012:BV3186.

[30] Rb Den Bosch (District Court Den Bosch) 30 January 2008, ECLI:NL:RBSHE:2008:BC3002; Hof Den Bosch (Appeal Court Den Bosch) 22 October 2008, ECLI:NL:GHSHE:2008:BG2138.

[31] See for a more detailed overview Zoontjens 2023, pp. 54–59 from which the following has been derived.

[32] Wet verduidelijking van de burgerschapsopdracht aan scholen in het funderend onderwijs, Stb. 2021, 321.

wanted to dedicate half of the curriculum to the Salafist faith and (they) plan (…) to also bring pupils under their sphere of influence outside regular school hours". Furthermore, there were indications, according to the AIVD, that these persons "in the period 2009–2012 (…) maintained contact with the terrorist group the Caucasus Emirate". This message caused great upheaval inside and outside the political arena. It resonated with already existing criticisms of Islamic schools by populists and liberals. However, the outcome of the allegations proved to be an anti-climax: the main observations were found to lack factual basis. In a public response in 2019, the body supervising the security service seriously questioned the statements about Salafist influences and contacts of persons within the school with a terrorist organisation. In addition, the Minister of Education, who wanted to intervene in the school, was proven wrong in court in various instances.[33]

Recently, the government published detailed plans to combat "informal education" that is harmful to democracy and the rule of law by giving new supervisory and sanctioning powers to the minister of Education.[34] In the government's plans informal education is broadly defined as "an activity or a series of related activities aimed at the systematic and organised transfer of knowledge, skills or attitudes to children aged four to seventeen". This definition includes every mode of teaching beyond formal education, such as in driving schools, football clubs or climbing lessons. The plans are being met with fierce criticism, especially from Christian and Muslim organisations that fear a threat of state influence in their informal Bible and Koran schools respectively.[35]

In our view, the reactions of the government, in particular towards Islamic schools and also towards informal education are "over the top". Since the financial misconduct issues in the period 2008 to 2012 no big scandals concerning school administration or serious anti-integrationist tendencies have come to the fore.[36] Particularly with regard to the Haga Lyceum affair, the ministry went much too far. In 2024, the Hague District Court ruled that the state had unjustifiably created an unproven image that the Haga Lyceum had allowed anti-democratic and anti-integration ideas, which had very negative consequences for the school, and concluded that the state would have to pay damages.[37] And as to the quality of Islamic primary schools with regard to the basic subjects of language and arithmetic/mathematics, research of RTL

---

[33] See for instance, Rb Amsterdam (District Court Amsterdam) 20 January 2020, ECLI:NL:RBAMS:2020:226.

[34] Preliminary draft of the Informal Education Supervision Act (*Voorontwerp van Wet toezicht informeel onderwijs*) 12 November 2024, https://www.internetconsultatie.nl/informeel_onderwijs/b1.

[35] The preliminary draft received 2,855 reactions that were mainly critical and coming from the aforementioned groups in society. See further Van Sasse van IJsselt 2024, pp. 48–66.

[36] Most allegations of financial misconduct against the Haga Lyceum were found to be unsubstantiated. See ABRvS (Administrative Law Division of the Council of State) 19 October 2022, ECLI:NL:RVS:2022:3014.

[37] Rb Den Haag (District Court The Hague) 4 September 2024, ECLI:NL:RBDHA:2024:13925.

News for 5 consecutive years (including 2021[38]) found that their final examination results were the best (when taking into account the socio-economic background of the pupils).

11.5 Positive Neutrality in Public Schools

What positive neutrality in public education, as prescribed in the Education Acts, means in practice is not easy to define. In fact, it is only clear that no emphasis may be placed on a particular religion, as this is prohibited by article 23(3) of the Constitution. But positive neutrality encompasses more. In Dutch education law, there is a principle flowing from the Constitution for private schools, but also valid as an unwritten constitutional principle for public schools, requiring the state not to unduly interfere with pedagogical practices ("absence of state pedagogy").[39] For example, it is perfectly acceptable for a public school to base its methods and educational content on a pedagogical vision that is part of a general and consistently designed idea about humanity and society. With the stricter requirements for civic education in force since 2021, it is obvious that all schools, and so every public school, must also consider the social and moral values in which pupils should be formed in its education and school environment. For example, one cannot simply mention democracy and the rule of law as phenomena. One must also make these concepts a living reality for pupils and students by connecting these concepts to their own aspirations and life plans. In pedagogical and social terms, some kind of education is required that presumes a basic view of humanity and society. The provisions in the education laws presume a pluralistic-cooperative concept of neutrality.[40] Therefore, neutrality in public education does not imply secularism and the absence of any religious aspect or philosophy of life—the classic French model of laicism—but rather its presence by calling attention to the underlying religious and other values within society, as well as the diversity of those values.

A consequence of this model of "positive" neutrality is that there is no general or school-specific ban on wearing religious symbols—for instance head-scarves—for pupils in public schools.[41] That probably is not only the case with regard to pupils and students, but also with regard to teachers.[42] Of course, such a ban may be applied in private schools because of their freedom of education, if the ban fulfils the criteria

---

[38] No more recent figures have been published.

[39] Akkermans 1980, p. 119.

[40] Vermeulen 2007, pp. 10–11.

[41] Kamerstukken II 2003/04, 28689, No. 8–9, p. 545.

[42] CRM (Netherlands Human Rights Institute) 9 February 1999, 99–18. The line is drawn where the teacher expresses his/her religious beliefs too actively and does not exercise the restraint required by the neutral nature of public law education.

of consistency and clarity implied in the General Equal Treatment Act.[43] And in public schools, a ban on wearing a burqa or similar clothing would generally be justified because of the pedagogical freedom and autonomy that a public school and its teachers need to achieve its educational goals.[44] A burqa ban would not be based on a secular view, but would be inspired by didactic and pedagogical motives. Since 2019, the issue of the "burqa ban" has been "resolved" by an Act of Parliament containing a partial prohibition on face-covering clothing, which also applies to schools.[45] But this was in fact a purely symbolic gesture: there is hardly any problem in this area, and so far, no burqa wearer has ever been sanctioned.

A general ban on praying in public schools is also not much of an issue; just as in private education, the school board has discretionary powers in this regard.[46] Furthermore, the choice to hang crucifixes in the classrooms of public schools may not necessarily be in conflict with its neutral character. According to the European Court of Human Rights, this is a matter that falls within the state's margin of appreciation.[47] It is unclear however, whether that would be compatible with the Dutch concept of neutrality. As to the freedom to pray in public schools, the law has not imposed or regulated a ban. Article 50 of the Primary Education Act merely states that "(t)he competent authority shall give pupils the opportunity to receive religious education or philosophical education at the school, during school hours. (…) For pupils who do not follow this education, the competent authority provides for other educational activities at the school".

Teachers in public schools are required to provide education that respects everyone's religious or philosophical beliefs. In other words, they may be expected to have an open attitude and express this attitude towards the various religious and philosophical values. At the same time, this does not exclude the possibility of expressing individual religious beliefs in a certain way, although case law allows for some restrictions. For instance, the refusal to shake hands with colleagues of the other sex because of Islamic religious objections has been qualified as an acceptable reason for dismissal by a multicultural public school.[48]

---

[43] See for instance CRM (Netherlands Human Rights Institute) 19 April 2012, 2012–68; CRM (Netherlands Human Rights Institute) 11 October 2018, 2018-102.

[44] CRM (Netherlands Human Rights Institute) 20 February 2003, 2003–40; CRM (Netherlands Human Rights Institute) 7 July 2015, 2015–17.

[45] Wet gedeeltelijk verbod gezichtsbedekkende kleding, Stb. 2018, 222.

[46] CRM (Netherlands Human Rights Institute) 3 August 2000, 00-51.

[47] ECtHR (Grand Chamber) 18 March 2011, No. 30814/06 (*Lautsi v. Italy*).

[48] CRvB (Administrative Appeal Court) 7 May 2009, ECLI:NL:CRVB:2009:BI2440, AB 2009, 280 (annotated by L C Groen and B P Vermeulen). See also CRM (Netherlands Human Rights Institute) 20 December 2018, 2018-140.

11.6 Towards an Individual (Equal) Right to Education

Earlier we already stressed that although the text of article 23 of the Constitution has not been modified substantially since 1917, its doctrinal and legislative interpretation and its actual application have fundamentally changed. We will discuss two main trends which were unforeseen while this provision was drafted.

Historically, the constitutional architecture of education was based on the primacy of private school boards (foundations and associations) and public administrations: these bodies were the "owners" and "governors" of the school. In public schools the municipality was in charge and boards, consisting of parents and/or local notables, were dominant in private schools. Since the 1990s, that has changed as municipalities transferred their main powers to foundations, while parents and notables largely lost their primary role in private schools. School boards nowadays are composed of professionals—following the logic of merging into larger administrative organisations, which often direct multiple schools.[49] Municipalities as well as parents and local notables have been promoted (or demoted?) to a supervisory role. This professionalisation and scaling up simultaneously created a distance between school boards and their schools. The boards often concentrate on finance, large scale organisational issues and accountability, and leave educational matters primarily to the level of the individual school, including rectors, directors and teaching staff. The freedom of education now primarily lies at this level, although less than before as a freedom that offers protection against the government, but as the necessary room to optimally realise the right to education of pupils and students.

In line with this development, the position of parents has to a certain extent been strengthened in that they have been given participation and complaint rights. Furthermore, this trend is strengthened by a conceptual change[50] from a freedom of school boards to a consumer education right of parents and their children. Since some 25 years there has been a strong movement stressing not so much the freedom of education—which rests with school boards and staff—but the *right to* education. As such, the right to education is not explicitly guaranteed in article 23. But from the outset it was considered by the framers of the Constitution as a corollary of the freedom of education, which allows for a structural diversity of schools and an incentive to compete for pupils, giving parents and pupils freedom of choice. However, this right of choice is regularly ineffective, as schools still have some power to select their pupils. In response, there is a tendency—often referring to the individual rights to education enshrined in human rights treaties—to strengthen this right to choose (for instance by overruling the right of orthodox schools to base their admissions policies on their religious identity)—as well as to claim a parental right to (more) adaptive education.[51]

---

[49] For instance, *Ons Middelbaar Onderwijs* is a Catholic association that directs 33 secondary Catholic, Protestant and non-denominational private schools at 78 locations and has some 60,000 pupils and 7,600 staff.

[50] Onderwijsraad 2021.

[51] Zoontjens 2003.

Furthermore, the claims of individual rights to education often go hand in hand with a strong emphasis on equal opportunities. This combination is predominant in the bill submitted in 2021 by member of parliament De Hoop, which proposes to fundamentally change article 23 of the Constitution.[52] It declares that every child has the right to education, that the law establishes rules to promote equality in education and that government funding will only go to schools that admit pupils on an equal basis. These ideals also find expression in a bill by member of parliament Van Meenen, inspired by article 24 of the UN Convention on the Rights of Persons with Disabilities.[53] This bill specifically addresses the problems of handicapped children with special educational needs, combining equality and adaptivity, formulating an individual right to education, the principle (with some limitations) of a right to be admitted to any school and the obligation of schools to ensure every child an adequate education, tailored to personal needs. The chances of these two bills being passed are not that high. However, they are expressions of fundamental changes in the educational mindset; one of the outcomes being a growth in schools for special education.

The claim to equality also is voiced in terms of equal opportunities concerns, in the sense that it is problematic that children from a privileged background have better chances to succeed in education, work and society in general. One example is the plea to counter segregation tendencies. This is due to the cleavage between so called "black (non-white) schools" and "white schools".[54] However, strict desegregation policies have so far not been implemented and are seldom proposed. Municipalities may have some scope for desegregation policies, but these have mostly taken the form of additional support to "black schools".

Another example concerns the plea for the so-called "comprehensive school" (*middenschool*). So far, at the age of 12, at the end of their primary school period, pupils are mainly selected on the basis of their final test (effectively an examination). This results in a de facto division between pupils going to general education schools and subsequently to college and university (including universities of applied sciences) on the one hand, and to schools for basic vocational education and subsequently schools for secondary education on the other. For more than 50 years, there have been several pleas to postpone this selection by about three years at the level of the comprehensive school. The social-democrat Van Kemenade, minister of education in the mid-1970s and the most outspoken defender of this idea, defined the comprehensive school as a place where the joint pursuit of general and vocational education by an entire year group of pupils, regardless of aptitude, environment, gender or educational achievement, should be made possible.[55] This plan generated a storm of comment from society and led to very heated discussions in parliament, resulting in the discussion about comprehensive schools becoming "completely

[52] Kamerstukken II 2021/22, 35924, No. 1–3.

[53] Kamerstukken II 2022/23, 36257, No. 1–3.

[54] Vermeulen 2000.

[55] Ministerie van Onderwijs en Wetenschappen 1975, p. 46.

polarised", in part due to its ideological-political presentation.[56] The plan was the reason for the Christian-democrats and the liberal party to block the proposal to amend article 23 of the Constitution in the 1970s. And to this day, the topic of a system overhaul in education has remained a political taboo.[57] More recently the Education Council (*Onderwijsraad*) again recommended the introduction of some kind of comprehensive school.[58] But even now it is not obvious whether such an initiative will succeed.

11.7 Civic Education and the Public Task to Integrate and Strengthen Democratic Resilience

Another interesting trend is a growing awareness that schools have a specific integrative function that has to be developed towards strengthening civic attitudes and democratic resilience. Of course, because of its primarily collective perspective, schools are institutions which always try to realise at least some sort of integration of individual pupils into a group, a class or the school itself. A minimum of coherence is required in order to enable a teacher to teach and the pupils to feel at home—and maybe even to be happy. But the underlying values, part of the hidden curriculum, are seldom made explicit. Strict denominational schools have a clear intention to shape good Christians or devout Muslims. Most schools, however, do not specify their driving ideals, unless in vague terms about respect, safety, being nice and tolerant towards each other. What is new however, and what we will elaborate here, is that the state has been trying to include explicit aspects of civic education in the curriculum for about 20 years now, gradually deepening its role and moral aspirations. This is new, because the traditional principles of freedom of education of private schools and the neutrality of public schools do not go well with government's message that they should inspire a certain civic attitude and behaviour in their pupils. The basic intuition, strengthened by the 1917 Pacification, was always not to accept any kind of state pedagogy.

However, times are changing. There is now a belief among politicians and public opinion that schools are the only remaining institutions that the government can, to some extent, control; where children from different backgrounds meet and get to know each other; and where it may be feasible to instil in them some common principles and values. There is a growing awareness that this is not only useful, but even necessary.

A first phase arose from the general observation that the Netherlands has become a diverse, multicultural society, in need of bonding and bridging. In 2006 a first articulation of this notion, probably also inspired by the terrorist attacks on the Twin Towers

[56] Wetenschappelijke Raad voor het Regeringsbeleid 1986, p. 73.

[57] This was confirmed once again in the final report of the parliamentary committee on Educational Innovation Research from 2008, Kamerstukken II 2007/08, 31007, No. 6.

[58] Onderwijsraad 2021.

in 2001, was laid down in the education laws, which focused on integration and understanding between children from various cultural and religious backgrounds.[59] However, the obligations laid on schools were rather limited, because of the potential frictions with the freedom of education and the neutrality principle. In 2011, the Council of State ruled, in accordance with legislative history, that it was sufficient "to do something" with multiculturalism.[60]

Politicians and the education inspectorate began to feel that the existing policy instruments were not sufficient, and began to argue for a strong commitment to fundamental values and concrete school strategies furthering that goal. The Haga Lyceum conflict (discussed above), which began in 2018, motivated a much stricter formulation of education targets and inspired parliament to demand stronger requirements aimed at developing knowledge of and commitment to fundamental values as well as civic skills, in short: good citizenship. These fundamental values were found in the principles of rule of law and democracy, and these skills in essence concerned the capacity to live together in peace and with tolerance, first learned in school and later put into practice in society. The primary and secondary education laws were amended accordingly in 2021.[61]

The norms that express the targets related to good citizenship are inspired by lofty ideals. Nevertheless, they are rather problematic. Civic education as envisaged by the law is not only related to knowledge about the rule of law and democracy and skills conducive of dialogue and cooperation. It is also linked to moral values, which can be interpreted according to one's views on morality and justice, etc. While the citizenship mission is primarily aimed at schools to implement it in education according to their own insights and values, in practice it is also a political yardstick for correcting schools and school boards that are expected to act and teach according to the fundamental values of the rule of law. The current focus of authorities on the corrective aspect of citizenship thus limits the actual space for schools to promote active citizenship as a "free" pedagogical mission.

As such, the citizenship mission laid down in the law relies on concepts of the rule of law and democracy that were originally and essentially developed to restrict and control state power, while they are now used to control and restrict schools, forcing them to teach these concepts to their pupils as interpreted by government. In particular, the equality principle is being promoted as an overarching ideal, principle and moral norm, to be fully applied in individual interactions between pupils and between teachers and pupils, etc. Specifically, the duty of respect, which requires great openness towards other views and lifestyles—and specific minorities—and not merely some kind of minimal tolerance, is seen as a basic obligation inherent in the equality principle and directly applicable to the internal sphere of schools.

[59] Wet houdende verplichting voor scholen om bij te dragen aan de integratie van leerlingen in de Nederlandse samenleving, Stb. 2005, 678.

[60] ABRvS (Administrative Law Division of the Council of State) 30 March 2011, ECLI:NL:RVS:2011:BP9541 (*As Siddieq*).

[61] Wet verduidelijking van de burgerschapsopdracht aan scholen in het funderend onderwijs, Stb. 2021, 320.

11.8 Law, Education and Constitutional Identity

The principles regarding the Dutch public education system reveal a fundamental tension between unity and diversity.[62] This tension is not unique of itself: every community or state organisation anywhere in the world has to deal with it to a certain degree. What perhaps makes the Netherlands a special case is its long history of the *institutionalisation of diversity* within unity, starting with the formation of the confederative Republic in 1588 that was formally the beginning of a state, only later developing into a nation state. The young Republic could rely on rather common notions of individual (religious) freedom, of practical tolerance towards religious minorities, of uniting in diverse denominations and cooperation and consultation in social and commercial contexts. It brought the highs of the Golden Age (seventeenth century) and lows of declining commercial entrepreneurship and political power (eighteenth century) before it evolved, under French rule, into a unitary state.

In the first decades of the nineteenth century, the unitary state appeared to be a merely abstract rational choice, incapable to fully win the hearts of the people. This became clear when the School Struggle broke out and dominated most of the 19th and the beginning of the twentieth century. The aim was for various religious groups in society to demand the freedom to establish their own schools, based on their specific religious beliefs and traditions. It resulted in the constitutional amendment (Pacification) of 1917, by which (groups of) citizens not only were given the right to establish their own schools but also to have them fully funded by the government. Since then, the majority of schools in primary and secondary education have been "private". Initially, these private schools were housed and developed within "pillars", semi-autonomous groups based on religion (or socialist/liberal laicism) and associated political beliefs. Until the 1960s, this model created the conditions for peaceful coexistence. Although Dutch society and the education system nowadays are "de-pillarised" and to a large degree secularised, the "private" school sector with its vast majority of formally Catholic and Protestant schools still shows the outward signs of the past. At a time when discussions about a new conception of freedom of education in our Constitution is flaring up, the "private" school sector has no intention to cast off its old shoes until it has got new ones.

If we try to define the constitutional identity of education in its relationship to government, we arrive at four concepts that are still relevant today: quality education, pedagogical autonomy, administrative autonomy and government restraint.

(1) As to quality, the relationship between government and the education sector is often portrayed as antagonistic. However, at its core these aspirations traditionally have been determined by shared goals of high quality in the primary process, for which coordination, consultation and mutual support take place on many levels.

(2) Because of the constitutional freedom of worldview of private schools and the principle of absence of state pedagogy that applies to both public and private

[62] Idenburg 1964, pp. 68–134.

schools, the state cannot interfere in the substance of the pedagogical process, in the ways teachers teach, test and guide pupils and in the choice of learning material. There still is a large pedagogical autonomy, which is granted to schools—as learning associations—and teachers.

(3) Private education enjoys the freedom to organise itself, partly because of its freedom of worldview and partly because of its private law character (which means that it is institutionally not a part of government). This autonomy is not absolute, but can be limited by compelling public interests and circumstances. Even public school organisations enjoy autonomy to a certain degree, as they have almost all been formed as civil law organisations since the 1990s. Autonomy in this sense implies, unless explicitly regulated or forbidden by law, a certain competence to select or suspend pupils and teachers, and a large freedom to cooperate with other schools or organisations, to conclude contracts, to participate in consultative bodies, etc.

(4) Freedom and autonomy at the level of schools and school organisations are traditionally mirrored by the reluctance on the part of the legislature and government to intervene in the primary process, or in matters directly preconditional to it. This explains why legal educational goals with regard to the content of education are generally formulated in abstract terms and why negative judgements concerning the educational quality by the inspectorate have been subject to strict legal conditions.

The Dutch education system has functioned rather well for more than a century on the basis of these constitutional principles. It is questionable, however, whether it is able to continue to do so on that basis: whether it is fit for the future. According to successive PISA student performance reports, the results of Dutch secondary education in mathematics, physics and in particular reading have been declining since the beginning of the century.[63] The traditional constitutional freedom of schools with regard to norms, values and the content of education is under pressure. Principles of quality, adaptivity and care for special educational needs are becoming dominant. Civic education has become a primary goal, pretending to be able to further social cohesion and tolerance. The supervisory role of the inspectorate has been strengthened.

It is unsurprising that schools, teachers and boards feel overburdened. They have the impression of being instrumentalised for a great variety of desirable goals, formulated by government and other stakeholders, having to make up for deficiencies in society and family. An overall revision of the curricula in primary and secondary education is underway. At the same time, a masterplan for basic skills requires improvements in language, civics, digital literacy and arithmetic/mathematics. And on top of that schools are challenged to integrate AI in their lessons. It is not easy to see what kind of transformations are necessary to be able to meet these challenges. It is our fundamental conviction, however, that an essential core of educational autonomy is a necessary ingredient that must be kept intact, without which schools, teachers,

[63] OECD, Programme for International Student Assessment, Netherlands 2022.

principals and boards cannot find and maintain the inspiration and idealism to tackle them.

Article 23 of the Dutch Constitution (Current Legal Text, Including Date of Each Provision's Inclusion)

(1) [1814] Education shall be the constant concern of the Government.
(2) [1848] All persons shall be free to provide education, without prejudice to the authorities' right of supervision and, with regard to forms of education designated by law, their right to examine the competence and moral integrity of teachers, to be regulated by Act of Parliament.
(3) [1848] Education provided by public authorities shall be regulated by Act of Parliament, paying due respect to everyone's religion or belief.
(4) [1848] The authorities shall ensure that primary education is provided in a sufficient number of public-authority schools in every municipality and in each of the public bodies referred to in article 132a. Deviations from this provision may be permitted under rules to be established by Act of Parliament on condition that there is opportunity to receive the said form of education, whether in a public-authority school or otherwise.
(5) [1917] The standards required of schools financed either in part or in full from public funds shall be regulated by Act of Parliament, with due regard, in the case of private schools, to the freedom to provide education according to religious or other belief.
(6) [1917] The requirements for primary education shall be such that the standards both of private schools fully financed from public funds and of public-authority schools are fully guaranteed. The relevant provisions shall respect in particular the freedom of private schools to choose their teaching aids and to appoint teachers as they see fit.
(7) [1917] Private primary schools that satisfy the conditions laid down by Act of Parliament shall be financed from public funds according to the same standards as public-authority schools. The conditions under which private secondary education and pre-university education shall receive contributions from public funds shall be laid down by Act of Parliament.
(8) [1814] The Government shall submit annual reports on the state of education to the States General.

References

Akkermans P W C (1980) Onderwijs als constitutioneel probleem. Samsom, Alphen aan den Rijn

Boekholt P Th F M (2002) De onderwijswet van 1801 en het begin van de Staatszorg voor het onderwijs in Nederland. In: Boekholt P, Van Crombrugge H, Dodde N L, Tyssens (eds) Tweehonderd jaar onderwijs en de zorg van de staat. Koninklijke Van Gorcum, Assen, pp. 3–10

De Bruin A A (1985) Het ontstaan van de schoolstrijd. Ton Bolland/De Vuurbaak, Barneveld

Hirsch Ballin E M H (2017) De stille revolutie van 1917, dwarsverbindingen in democratisch burgerschap en onderwijs. Querido Fosfor, Amsterdam/Antwerp

Idenburg Ph J (1964) Schets van het Nederlandse schoolwezen, 2nd edn. J.B. Wolters, Groningen

Inspectie van het Onderwijs (2013) Rapport van bevindingen: Onderzoek bestuurlijk handelen islamitische scholengemeenschap Ibn Ghaldoun. Rotterdam

Lijphart A (1967) Verzuiling, pacificatie en kentering in de Nederlandse politiek. J.H. de Bussy, Amsterdam

Mentink D (2021) Artikel 23. Vrijheid van en recht op onderwijs. In: Hirsch Ballin E M H, Janse de Jonge E J, Leenknegt G (eds) Uitleg van de Grondwet. Boom Juridisch, The Hague, pp. 465–545

Ministerie van Onderwijs en Wetenschappen (1975) Contouren van een toekomstig onderwijsbestel; discussienota. The Hague

Noorlander C W (2011) Tertium non datur. De samenwerkingsschool: een onderwijsconstitutioneel gedrocht? Gemeentestem (79)419–430

Onderwijsraad (2021) Later differentiëren, beter differentiëren. Onderwijsraad, The Hague

Patrinos H A (2009) School Choice in The Netherlands. CESifo DICE Report 9(2):55-59

Philipsen S (2017) De vrijheid van schoolstichting. PhD dissertation, Erasmus Universiteit Rotterdam

Rogers Berner A (2012) Funding schools. In: Glenn C L, De Groof J (eds) Balancing Freedom, Autonomy and Accountability in Education, Vol. 1. Wolf Legal Publishers, Nijmegen, pp. 115-129

Schelfhout C E (1976) 175 jaar nationale wetgeving op het lager onderwijs. Pedagogische Studiën 53(4):297-304

Storimans Th A L M (2002) Het karakter van 200 jaar regelgeving inzake de inrichting van het lager onderwijs in Nederland. In: Boekholt P, Van Crombrugge H, Dodde N L, Tyssens (eds) Tweehonderd jaar onderwijs en de zorg van de staat. Koninklijke Van Gorcum, Assen, pp. 87–101

Van Sasse van IJsselt P (2024) Informeel onderwijs onder overheidstoezicht. Tijdschrift voor Religie, Recht en Beleid, Tijdschrift voor Religie en Beleid 15(2):48–66

Vermeulen B P (2000) Witte en zwarte scholen. Over spreidingsbeleid, onderwijsvrijheid en sociale cohesie (inaugural address VU Amsterdam). Elsevier, The Hague

Vermeulen B P (2007) Vrijheid, gelijkheid, burgerschap: over verschuivende fundamenten van het Nederlandse minderhedenrecht en -beleid: immigratie, integratie, onderwijs en religie. Sdu, The Hague

Wetenschappelijke Raad voor het Regeringsbeleid (1986) Basisvorming in het onderwijs, Rapporten aan de Regering, No. 27. Wetenschappelijke Raad voor het Regeringsbeleid, The Hague

Wilson H E (1955) Education and National Culture. Current History 29(169):135-139

Zoontjens P J J (2003) Het beweeglijke recht op onderwijs; op zoek naar ankerpunten in een permanente ontwikkeling (inaugural address Tilburg University). Boom Juridische Uitgevers, The Hague

Zoontjens P J J (2023) Onderwijsrecht. Eenheid in verscheidenheid. Boom Juridische Uitgevers, The Hague

B. P. (Ben) Vermeulen Ph.D., Emeritus Professor in Education Law at the Faculty of Law of the Radboud University Nijmegen and Member of the Council of State, the Netherlands.

P. J. J. (Paul) Zoontjens Ph.D., Emeritus Professor in Education Law at the Law School of Tilburg University, the Netherlands.

Chapter 12
Law and Digitalisation: The Rise of the Algorithmic Administrative State

Jurgen Goossens and Johan Wolswinkel

Contents

Abstract This chapter explores how the core public values and principles of the democratic rule of law (*democratische rechtsstaat*)—seen as an expression of the individuality of the Dutch constitutional order—steer digitalisation and how digitalisation transforms the constitutional order. Several digitalisation-related incidents, most notably the Childcare Allowance Scandal, have affected this constitutional identity, raising awareness and scepticism about the government's use of algorithmic systems. After examining the rise of the "algorithmic administrative state", the contribution analyses the role and evolution of the five core principles of the Dutch democratic rule of law: legality, democracy, fundamental rights, checks and balances and judicial review. Next, the chapter reflects on the "government-citizen-algorithmic system" triangle and argues that Dutch constitutional identity requires the government to take more responsibility and disentangle itself from algorithmic systems. In this respect, the Dutch Constitution turns out to have a tech-agnostic character as it does not explicitly deal with the ongoing digitalisation of society and government. Although the Dutch constitutional order should explicitly recognise the existence of the algorithmic administrative state, we conclude that other tech-agnostic elements

J. Goossens (✉)
Utrecht University School of Law, Utrecht University, Utrecht, The Netherlands
e-mail: j.goossens@uu.nl

C. J. Wolswinkel
Tilburg Law School, Tilburg University, Tilburg, The Netherlands
e-mail: C.J.Wolswinkel@tilburguniversity.edu

G. van der Schyff (ed.), *The Constitutional Identity of The Netherlands*,
https://doi.org/10.1007/978-94-6265-779-3_12

of the Dutch constitutional order, such as existing monitoring institutions and principles of good administration, could serve as essential building blocks to further shape a digital-proof constitutional identity capable of counterbalancing the exercise of authority by the algorithmic administration.

Keywords Constitutional resilience · Algorithmic administrative state · Democratic rule of law · Checks and balances · Legality · Tech-agnostic constitutionalism

12.1 Introduction

This chapter examines the resilience of the Dutch constitutional order in the face of increasing digitalisation in recent decades, thereby focusing on digitalisation within government. The constitutional order has two core functions. Firstly, it enables the functioning of the legal order by constituting institutions and conferring power upon these institutions to exercise public authority. Secondly, it functions as a defence mechanism encompassing both substantive and procedural safeguards to preserve its constitutional identity, understood as the core values and principles of democracy and the rule of law.[1] As a recognition of their interconnected nature, these values and principles are referred to as the "democratic rule of law" (*democratische rechtsstaat*). This contribution explores how the democratic rule of law—seen as an expression of the individuality of the Dutch constitutional order—steers digitalisation on the one hand and how digitalisation transforms the constitutional order on the other hand. In this regard, there is a dynamic, reflexive relationship between constitutional resilience of the democratic rule of law and digital transformations. In this chapter, constitutional resilience is defined as the ability of the constitutional order to unlock the benefits of digitalisation and cope with digital transformations and threats, while safeguarding the core values and principles of the democratic rule of law.[2] An often-invoked benefit of digitalisation is improved efficiency through automatisation. At the same time, it pressurises public values, such as transparency, explainability, accountability and participation, as well as fundamental rights such as human dignity, privacy, non-discrimination, equality of arms and good administration.

Digital transformations impact the constitutional identity of the Netherlands, while at the same time constitutional identity plays a pivotal role in the response to digitalisation. It is important to consider the multilevel context at play here,

[1] Without preservation of the core values and principles of the democratic rule of law the core of the Dutch constitutional order would be fundamentally altered and the constitutional identity of the Netherlands would risk to drastically transform. Constitutional identity is thus understood as the aspects without which a constitutional order will be altered in a fundamental way. See Van der Schyff 2012, p. 578.

[2] Goossens 2023.

particularly given the recent wave of data regulation on the EU level.[3] Moreover, several Dutch "incidents" involving digitalisation, most importantly the Childcare Allowance Scandal in which discriminatory practices were carried out using an algorithmic system,[4] have undoubtedly impacted constitutional identity, raising awareness and scepticism about the use of algorithmic systems by government. The title of the Childcare Allowance Parliamentary Inquiry Committee's report has become part of the collective rule of law consciousness: "Unprecedented Injustice".[5]

In the past decades, the vast expansion of government tasks and complexity in the Dutch social welfare state have led to the rise of an "administrative state". To carry out these expanding tasks, public administration increasingly relies on the use of algorithmic systems. Section 12.2 explains how this gradual transformation has resulted in the rise of an "algorithmic administrative state". In this algorithmic administrative state "street level" bureaucrats are being replaced by "screen level" bureaucrats working in "system level" bureaucracies.[6] Consequently, meaningful human contact is under pressure, as digitalisation transforms the nature of interactions between citizens and government.

Subsequently, Sects. 12.3–12.6 analyse the current and future role and evolution of the five core principles of the democratic rule of law within the Dutch constitutional order vis-à-vis the rise of the algorithmic administrative state: legality, democracy, fundamental rights, checks and balances and judicial review.[7] As of 2022, two of these principles (fundamental rights and democracy) and the rule of law are explicitly mentioned in an unnumbered general provision, preceding the body of the Constitution: "The Constitution guarantees fundamental rights and the democratic rule of law."[8] The five principles serve a regulatory function and are themselves subject to interpretation and transformation when applied in a context of digitalisation. We will pay due attention to this dynamic context for each principle.

After zooming in on these five principles, we zoom out again in Sect. 12.7. In this section, we reflect on the "government-citizen-algorithmic system" triangle, arguing that the current Dutch constitutional identity, as among others influenced by pivotal events such as the Childcare Allowance Scandal, requires government to take up its responsibility more firmly in this triangular relation. We also pay attention to the predominant "tech-agnostic" character of Dutch legislation, paying particular attention to the role of the principles of good administration as a counterweight to the exercise of authority by the algorithmic administration. Potentially in part due to

---

[3] See particularly the recent introduction of the "big five" pieces of EU data legislation (in 2022 the Data Governance Act, the Digital Services Act and the Digital Markets Act, in 2023 the Data Act and in 2024 the Artificial Intelligence Act) and already in 2018, the General Data Protection Regulation.

[4] See Venice Commission 2021.

[5] Childcare Allowance Parliamentary Inquiry Committee 2020. The report is also available in Dutch as "Ongekend onrecht".

[6] Bovens and Zouridis 2002.

[7] Burkens et al. 2022.

[8] Stremler 2023.

the "rigid" and "austere" character of the "old" Dutch Constitution, the main constitutional text does not pay attention to digitalisation, notwithstanding its enormous impact on the nature of the Dutch constitutional order.

The—alleged[9]—rigidity of the Dutch Constitution is due to its amendment procedure consisting of two readings, an intervening election and a two-thirds majority in the second reading.[10] In addition, the Constitution also demonstrates a "sober" constitutional culture "in which major and compelling thoughts about the meaning and value of a Constitution are rare".[11] Hence, it is not surprising that the Dutch constitutional legislature has not (yet) jumped on the train of digitalisation. Nonetheless, there are recent signals that the Constitution can no longer ignore the impact of digitalisation on society and government.[12]

12.2 The Rise of the Algorithmic Administrative State

In the past decades, the vast expansion of government tasks and complexity in the social welfare state has led to the rise of the "administrative state" in many democratic rule of law countries, also in the Netherlands. In the administrative state, the formal legislature delegates extensive rule-making powers, often through framework legislation, and attributes broad administrative powers through open norms to administrative authorities, what some have called "deparliamentarisation" or "retreat of the legislator".[13] One of the main invoked reasons for this evolution is the lack of sufficient expertise in Parliament (known as the States General in the Netherlands) to legislate in the numerous policy areas in which government aims to regulate.[14] As a result, the "primacy of the legislature", a traditional core element of the Dutch constitutional system, has come under pressure (not only in the Netherlands).[15]

Moreover, public administration increasingly relies on digital technologies to deal with the increase and complexity of tasks. As a result, the "algorithmic administrative state" saw the light. In this algorithmic administrative state, effective parliamentary control is increasingly difficult to execute due to the rising level of complexity and

[9] For a study that nuances this rigidity based on an empirical analysis of all constitutional amendments from 1814 to 2023, see Goossens and Haex 2023.

[10] See Chap. 5 in this volume.

[11] Barkhuysen et al. 2009, p. 18. See also Gerards 2016.

[12] The Ministry of the Interior and Kingdom Relations recently invited twelve experts to write a contribution for a collection of essays on "The Constitution and New Technology: Ready for the Future?" (in Dutch: "De Grondwet en nieuwe technologie: klaar voor de toekomst?"), which was sent to the Lower House of the States General (i.e. Parliament). The cabinet presented its views on the topics discussed in the volume in 2025 (https://open.overheid.nl/documenten/689fc295-6bf8-441b-acc0-6ef4aa190f66/file).

[13] See, e.g., Van Gestel 2013.

[14] Lindseth 2010; Hirsch Ballin 2015a, para 4; Hirsch Ballin 2019.

[15] Van Gestel and Vleugel 2013, p. 5. See Sect. 12.3 of this chapter.

opacity[16] when algorithmic systems are used to support or fully automate administrative action. Albeit crucial, the States General is facing tremendous challenges to adequately control public administration, as among others shown in the final report "Update Required: Towards More Parliamentary Grip on Digitisation" ("Update vereist: Naar meer parlementaire grip op digitalisering" of 28 May 2020) of the temporary committee Digital Future of the Lower House of the States General.[17] Moreover, notwithstanding its utmost importance, effective and meaningful judicial review of the algorithmic black box also proves to be a challenge.[18]

Hitherto, public administration mainly uses "rule-based" algorithms where the rule to be applied is programmed in advance ("if x, then y"), often as a simple decision tree. Nonetheless, there is an increase of the use of machine learning ("case-based") algorithms, making it possible to derive the rule to be applied to new cases from a set of data derived from previous cases rather than to program this rule in advance. Casey and Niblett warned for "micro-directive", an extensive set of commands for every conceivable scenario.[19] These micro-directives are not founded on general, predictable legal rules adopted in advance by democratically elected bodies but are generated by algorithms guided by software principles and policy objectives and based on data derived from a dataset built up from previous cases.

In the most extreme case of the use of machine learning algorithmic models, the frequent application of case-based algorithms can even lead to what Casey and Niblett have called "the death of rules and standards." We have not yet arrived at this scenario in the Dutch constitutional system. Nonetheless, it is useful to take this future scenario seriously to create constitutional imaginaries that are fit to cope with such evolutions. Constitutional resilience is not static but constantly evolving. There is something at stake for the Dutch constitutional order and identity. Shiffrin pointed out that due to the marginalisation of the importance of general rules laid down in legislation and policy, we might lose the moral aspect in deliberation and public decision-making.[20] Such an evolution would weaken and threaten the Dutch constitutional culture of deliberation, as most importantly embedded by the principles of legality and democracy (see Sect. 12.3) and checks and balances (see Sect. 12.4).

Along with the rise of the algorithmic administrative state, the nature of the relations and interactions between citizens and government has drastically changed. Meaningful (human) contact has come under severe pressure due to automatisation, whereby citizens and public administration usually interact through digital screens and rigid online application forms. As a response, increasingly attention is paid to "the citizen perspective" rather than a mere focus on the government perspective, to responsive government (action) that considers the needs and degree of self-reliance of

---

16 See Burrell 2016.

17 See https://www.tweedekamer.nl/sites/default/files/atoms/files/eindrapport_tijdelijke_commissie_digitale_toekomst_tweede_kamer_der_staten-generaal.pdf.

18 De Poorter and Goossens 2019. See Sect. 12.6 of this chapter.

19 Casey and Niblett 2017, p. 1402.

20 Shiffrin 2010, pp. 1222 and 1244.

its citizens, and to *perceived* procedural justice.[21] The proof of the pudding, however, is in the eating. Much work is still to be done to transform these aims into a constitutional culture and system that effectively realises citizen-oriented legislation, policies and interactions between citizens and government.

12.3 The Principles of Legality and Democracy

The principle of legality requires that government action is based on an Act of Parliament, or "formal law", and is exercised within the limits of the law.[22] The involvement of the elected States General in establishing this legal basis is intended to ensure that the interests of all Dutch citizens are taken into account in a proportionate manner (articles 50 and 81 of the Constitution).[23] As citizens elect their representatives in Parliament, voters—indirectly—have a say in the norms that determine their legal status. Given the democratic legitimacy of Parliament, a core concept of the Dutch constitutional order is the "primacy of the legislature", as coined by the Committee on Legislative Questions in 1985.[24] Underlying is the idea that the formal legislature itself takes the most important normative decisions, neither the executive nor the judiciary.[25] The two latter branches must derive the legitimacy of their actions from sources other than the electoral process.

Given the rise of the algorithmic administrative state and the "retreat of the legislator", as discussed in Sect. 12.2, however, the "primacy of the legislature" is under severe pressure. In fact, this primacy appears to have become virtually obsolete in many areas.[26] One can assume that balancing (individual) interests is not necessarily of such a political nature that only the democratically legitimised Parliament can carry it out. Nonetheless, this assumption is only valid in the Dutch constitutional order if Parliament is able to effectively and adequately exercise control on extensive delegated law-making by the executive branch and the exercise of broad discretionary powers in the algorithmic administrative state. However, as the exercise of parliamentary oversight on the algorithmic administrative state has become difficult or even impossible,[27] the principles of legality and democracy are weakened. Increasingly, complex algorithmic systems are developed far from (control by) democratic arenas, by software developers in private IT companies. These evolutions necessitate compensating measures, for instance more attention for regulatory

---

[21] See, e.g., Scheltema 2015; The Netherlands Scientific Council for Government Policy 2017; Barkhuysen and Den Ouden 2020; Van den Bos 2023.

[22] Bovend'Eert 2019, p. 155.

[23] Van Vugt 2021.

[24] Committee on Legislative Questions 1985.

[25] Ibid., p. 43.

[26] Goossens and De Poorter 2022, p. 9.

[27] Prins and Wolswinkel 2025.

compliance by design and the establishment of independent supervisory authorities, such as the Dutch Data Protection Authority which supervises the application of privacy legislation.

12.4 Checks and Balances

The separation of powers in the Netherlands is not strict but can be characterised as a system of checks and balances. Most importantly, the division of power between the legislative and executive branch is blurred, not least because the Government is both co-legislator together with the States General (article 81 of the Constitution) as well as the apex of the executive branch. In 2019, in a general reflection on the "the rule of law in balance", the Council of State warned that the essential separation of powers between the legislative and executive branches is "disappearing" in the Dutch administrative state.[28] The "Trias Politica" is gradually turning into a "Duas Politica" in which, according to Brenninkmeijer, "the cabinet and the cabinet majority in Parliament operate in a symbiotic relationship."[29]

The automation of administrative decision-making, the complexity of algorithmic systems, and the hyper-connectivity of people, processes, and data through information networks are expected to continue to grow exponentially. These evolutions will likely increase existing challenges to the checks and balances such as transparency, explainability and accountability in the algorithmic administrative state. As a result, the constitutional balance of power and the (information) position of the three branches of government is increasingly under pressure. Therefore, Prins has argued that the constitutional checks and balances must be rethought.[30] According to Passchier, an imbalance in the Trias Politica has grown due to a lack of information and effective control by Parliament and the judicial branch over the rapid digitisation of public administration and administrative decisions.[31]

Following one of the recommendations of the report "Update Required: Towards More Parliamentary Grip on Digitisation", the Lower House of the States General established a standing parliamentary committee on digital affairs in 2021.[32] In 2024, the Upper House of the States General also set up a standing committee on digitisation. These recent evolutions demonstrate that Parliament aims to get a better grip on the impact of digitisation. Nonetheless, sufficient parliamentary control over the large and multi-headed (algorithmic) administrative state seems increasingly utopian.[33] The "retreat of the legislator", as discussed in Sects. 12.2 and 12.3, puts

[28] Council of State 2020, p. 14.

[29] Brenninkmeijer 2021, p. 12.

[30] Prins 2016, p. 909.

[31] Passchier 2020.

[32] See https://www.tweedekamer.nl/sites/default/files/atoms/files/eindrapport_tijdelijke_commissie_digitale_toekomst_tweede_kamer_der_staten-generaal.pdf.

[33] Van Vugt 2022, pp. 131–132. See also Hirsch Ballin 2015b, pp. 26–27.

pressure on another branch, in this case the judicial branch, to compensate for the imbalance.[34] In an article titled "Good-bye, Montesquieu", Ackerman aptly wrote: "Almost three centuries later, it is past time to rethink Montesquieu's holy trinity. [...] A 'new separation of powers' is emerging."[35] This holds even more true in an era where society and government are increasingly digitalising.

12.5 Fundamental Rights

Fundamental rights form an essential part of the Dutch Constitution, as exemplified by its codification in Chapter 1 and the reference to fundamental rights in the general provision preceding the body of the Constitution. The question whether the catalogue of fundamental rights enshrined in Chapter 1 is sufficient to meet the challenges raised by digitalisation of society and government, has already been addressed since 2000. The advisory committee "Fundamental Rights in a Digital Age", installed by the Dutch government, considered whether the process of digitalisation required modification of the Dutch Constitution. In its considerations, the committee paid ample attention to (i) the "austere" (sober) and (ii) "open" nature of the Dutch Constitution, (iii) its limited mutability, (iv) its codifying character and (v) the prohibition of judicial review of the constitutionality of formal legislation, which led to some restraint in proposals to amend the Constitution.[36] Nonetheless, it argued for the revision of several constitutional provisions, including the right to freedom of expression (article 7), the (general) right to privacy (article 10) and the right to privacy of communications (article 13).

In response, however, there has only been a minor modernisation of article 13 of the Dutch Constitution in 2022. Whereas the 1983 version of that provision protected specific types of communications (in particular a paper letter) and communications technology (telephone, telegraph), this dependence on traditional means of communication implied that its scope of protection in relation to digital information and communications technologies was limited. The new version of article 13 therefore protects the privacy of correspondence and of telecommunications in general (Sect. 12.1 of the article), widening its scope to all types of communications, either analogue or digital, independent of the platform or technology used, while providing a carefully worded limitation clause (Sect. 12.2 of the article).[37]

The choice to phrase the right to privacy of communications in article 13 in a technology-independent way is in line with how other fundamental rights have been phrased in the Constitution. These other types of (general) fundamental rights, including equality rights (non-discrimination), freedom rights (expression, manifestation) and procedural rights (effective remedy, fair trial), are equally important

[34] Council of State 2020, p. 14. See Sect. 12.6 of this chapter.

[35] Ackerman 2017.

[36] Commission Franken 2000, pp. 46–50.

[37] Van Vugt et al. 2023; Jansen 2023.

in the context of digitalisation,[38] even though privacy and information rights seem to dominate the debate on fundamental rights and digitalisation. In this regard, the *SyRI* judgement, which will be discussed below in Sect. 12.6, shows that courts prefer to embrace the technology-independent or rather "tech-agnostic"[39] phrasing of fundamental rights (in that case: article 8 ECHR), as that allows them to avoid any evaluation of unduly restrictive legal provisions applicable to digitalisation, such as whether individual decision-making has been *fully* automated or not or involves the processing of "personal data".[40] Relying on fundamental rights makes it possible for courts to incorporate specific legal provisions (e.g. derived from the General Data Protection Regulation (GDPR)) in their reasoning as a source of inspiration to interpret fundamental rights rather than as stand-alone yardstick to evaluate automated decision-making.

12.6 Judicial Review

Partly given the lack of effective parliamentary control over the algorithmic administrative state, judicial review has played a key role in the Netherlands so far in safeguarding citizens' rights in the context of digitalisation, in particular against algorithmic decision-making. The administration of justice is governed by Chapter 6 of the Constitution. The civil court (judiciary) is responsible for the adjudication of disputes involving rights under civil law.[41] These disputes can also cover disputes with administrative authorities insofar as civil rights are involved, for example where an administrative authority acts unlawfully against citizens. In addition, specific administrative courts are responsible for adjudicating disputes concerning administrative decisions (e.g. licensing, subsidising, sanctioning).[42] In adjudicating those disputes between citizens and administrative authorities, courts have developed general principles of good administration to keep tabs on administrative behaviour, especially in cases where legislation has conferred some or even considerable amount of discretion to administrative authorities involved in decision-making (cf. Section 12.3).

Currently, the number of legislative provisions specifically dealing with the implementation of legislation through digital means such as algorithmic systems, is quite

38 Vetzo et al. 2018.

39 Whereas "technology-independent" might suggest a purposeful drafting of fundamental rights to accommodate any use of technology, characterising these rights as "tech-agnostic" (cf. Oswald 2018) indicates their application, irrespective of any awareness or recognition whether technology is at stake or not.

40 District Court The Hague 5 February 2000, ECLI:NL:RBDHA:2020:1878, para 6.60 (*SyRI*).

41 Article 112(1) of the Constitution.

42 Article 112(2) of the Constitution in conjunction with article 8:1 of the General Administrative Law Act (GALA).

limited.[43] Rather, digitalisation seems to be presumed an inherent part of the implementation of legislation, in particular where large-scale decision-making is involved. Nonetheless, in the absence of legislative provisions specifically dealing with *algorithmic* administration, Dutch courts have relied on the principles of good administration in addressing legal issues of digitalisation. The Advisory Division of the Council of State has even suggested that these principles should be interpreted in a more intensified way to accommodate the specific challenges related to algorithmic administration.[44]

A landmark judgement in this respect is the *AERIUS* judgement of 2017 of the Administrative Jurisdiction Division of the Council of State. In that judgement, the Council of State acknowledged that algorithmic decision-making could generate benefits in terms of coherent and efficient decision-making. However, it also stressed that the use of automated systems entails the risk that the resulting decision-making process is not transparent and verifiable due to a lack of insight into the choices made and the data and assumptions used for the automated system. This perception of a "black box" from the perspective of interested parties might result in inequality of arms, as they cannot check on which basis a certain decision is reached.[45] To solve this asymmetrical information position, the Council of State imposes on the administrative authorities the obligation to make public the choices made and the data and assumptions used (i) completely, (ii) timely, (iii) on their own initiative and (iv) in an appropriate manner so that these choices, data and assumptions are accessible to third parties and can be scrutinised and contested.[46] Although the Council of State refers to the existence of an "unequal legal position" when deriving this contextualised obligation for *algorithmic* decision-making, thereby hinting at the "inequality of arms" that article 6 ECHR aims to avoid, this *AERIUS* obligation can also be considered a corollary of the duty to give reasons or the principle of careful decision-making, which are both general principles of good administration. Anyway, this *AERIUS* obligation is a clear illustration how general principles of good administration can be relied upon when deriving more concrete rules on algorithmic decision-making. However, despite some promising judgements right after the *AERIUS* judgement, this *AERIUS* obligation has rarely been followed in more recent case law.

One of the explanations thereof can be found in the Dutch system of judicial review. Where algorithmic systems are mainly used to support human decision-making (rather than to replace it), citizens need to wait for a final administrative decision before they can contest that decision, including the automated system that has been used in preparation thereof. However, the use of an automated system does not need to result in an administrative decision with legal effect, (e.g. if a fraud detection system detects a certain person for further inspection, but that person is not

[43] Wolswinkel 2023a.

[44] Advisory Division of the Council of State 30 August 2018.

[45] Administrative Jurisdiction Division of the Council of State 17 May 2017, ECLI:NL:RVS:2017:1259, para 12.3.

[46] Administrative Jurisdiction Division of the Council of State 17 May 2017, ECLI:NL:RVS:2017:1259, para 12.4.

sanctioned in the end). It is therefore not surprising that another landmark judgement originated from a *civil* court after a claim that the government was acting unlawfully by deploying the use of the algorithmic system SyRI (*Systeem Risico Indicatie*) to detect various forms of fraud, including social benefits, allowances and taxes fraud.[47] In short, the District Court of The Hague ruled that the legislation pertaining to the application of SyRI (both a specific provision in an Act of Parliament and a related chapter in a governmental decree) was "insufficiently transparent and verifiable." For this reason, the court declared that the legal provisions applicable to (and allowing for) the use of SyRI had no binding effect, because they constituted a breach of article 8 ECHR.

As regards constitutional identity, the following observations are important when analysing the *SyRI* judgement. First, the court relied on a tech-agnostic provision of the ECHR (article 8) rather than on tech-specific provisions in the GDPR. But in its application of the proportionality test, the court took into consideration the fundamental principles underlying the protection of data under EU law (the EU Charter of Fundamental Rights of the EU and the GDPR), specifically the principles of transparency, purpose limitation and data minimisation.[48] Second, the court evaluated the SyRI legislation against a treaty provision (article 8 ECHR) rather than a constitutional provision (e.g. article 10 of the Constitution on privacy), which is an immediate consequence of the exclusion of judicial review of constitutionality of formal legislation.[49] Third, the civil court instead of the administrative court evaluated the use of the algorithmic system. According to the civil court, even though the use of SyRI did not necessarily result in an administrative decision (e.g. a sanction), its use as such did already have a significant effect on the private life of the data subject.[50]

12.7 Reflection

In the 1980s, when digitalisation of government was only in its very infancy, it was with foresight that Hirsch Ballin and Kamphuis coined the term "Trias Automatica".[51] Undoubtedly, as follows from the preceding sections, digitalisation has drastically impacted the checks and balances between the legislative, the executive and the judicial branch. In the same vein, digitalisation has also challenged other core principles of the Dutch constitutional order, such as the generality of rules (legality) and parliamentary involvement in assessing algorithmic rules (democracy). One could argue that government should take up its responsibility to uphold and restore these core principles to the extent possible to counterbalance digitalisation. However, one

---

[47] The *SyRI* judgement has been translated into English, which is quite exceptional for Dutch court decisions. For more detail on the *SyRI* judgement, see Meuwese 2020.

[48] *SyRI* judgement, para 6.7. Most attention is paid to the principle of transparency (para 6.87–6.95).

[49] Article 120 Constitution.

[50] *SyRI* judgement, para 6.59.

[51] Hirsch Ballin and Kamphuis 1985.

could also argue that the Dutch constitutional order might additionally need other principles or mechanisms in an era of digitalisation. We believe there is more than sufficient reason to move beyond the traditional, predominantly government-oriented approach founded in the Trias Politica and consider a triangular relationship between government, citizen and algorithmic system.

Due to the rise of the algorithmic administrative state, the (administrative) state and algorithmic systems have become inextricably linked. However, by adopting a citizen perspective to government, the administrative state as such can be disentangled from the algorithmic system where necessary, for instance to realise meaningful contact. Moreover, algorithmic systems give rise to other branches of "power" than the three traditional ones. The traditional Trias does not hold private tech companies accountable for the development of algorithmic systems. The deployment of algorithmic systems necessitates other checks and balances or "monitoring power" through other (independent) institutions than Parliament and the judiciary, e.g. through the Data Protection Authority, the Court of Auditors or the Ombudsman.[52] Thus, where government should more firmly take up its responsibility in this triangular relation, the question is how this should be done. On the one hand, there can be the explicit recognition that digitalisation is here to stay, and that government has a key role to play. On the other hand, the steering role for government is not necessarily to be found in digital-specific constitutional rules, but at least in a digital-proof constitutional order.

Considering the Dutch constitutional order in particular, digitalisation is almost entirely absent in the Constitution itself. This "tech-agnostic" nature of the Dutch constitutional order does not only characterise the Constitution itself, but also foundational legislation adopted on the basis thereof, such as the General Administrative Law Act (GALA). There is no single reference to algorithmic decision-making, not even in the currently pending legislative proposal to strengthen the protective function of the GALA, although this proposal has been presented in response to—inter alia—the misuse of algorithmic systems in the Childcare Allowance Scandal.[53]

The lack of explicit references to digitalisation in the Dutch constitutional order is not necessarily problematic. One could argue that this absence is in line with both the open and the austere character of the Dutch constitution. What is more, general principles and general institutional mechanisms have proven to be important gatekeepers in keeping tabs on the algorithmic administrative state. Courts have relied on—and even preferred—tech-agnostic fundamental rights (privacy, equality of arms) and general principles of good administration instead of tech-specific guarantees (Sects. 12.5 and 12.6). Moreover, other long-established institutions, such as the Ombudsman, the Court of Auditors and (the Advisory Division of) the Council of State, have taken up the responsibility of seriously scrutinising the development and deployment of algorithmic systems where judicial review in individual cases fails to deliver justice beyond the specific legal case.

---

[52] Meijer 2024.

[53] Wolswinkel 2023b.

Given these constitutional responses to digitalisation, one pressing question is how the Dutch constitutional order should move forward, given its characteristics of openness and austerity. One possibility would be to recognise explicitly the duty of care resting on the government in the context of digitalisation. In that regard, inspired by a similar constitutional provision on the physical environment, Wolswinkel advocated for a new constitutional provision explicating that "it shall be the concern of the authorities to protect and improve the digital environment". Even though such a constitutional right might not be enforceable as such before courts, as it imposes a duty on the state rather than confers a right to the citizen, this double duty regarding digitalisation (protect *and* improve) could steer the interpretation of other fundamental rights and the adoption of legislation specifically dealing with issues of digitalisation.[54]

In addition—seemingly paradoxically—there is a need to further strengthen general (tech-agnostic) principles and institutions in the Dutch constitutional order. For instance, Goossens recently called for the introduction of a new constitutional right of access to and meaningful contact with public administration.[55] He extensively argued that there is an "urgent need" and "constitutional maturity"[56] both for the aspect of "access to" and its further operationalisation in the form of "meaningful contact". Such a constitutional amendment would have added value as there is no enforceable right to a response when citizens exercise their constitutional right to petition (article 5 of the Constitution), which is a notable deficiency of the Dutch constitutional system.[57] The importance of the introduction of an enforceable right to meaningful contact with government has grown in view of the ever-increasing digitisation and prevalence of system-level bureaucracies with screen-level bureaucrats. In a similar vein, Wolswinkel argued for codification of the right to good administration in the Dutch Constitution, as it can function as a core fundamental right from which concrete obligations in the context of digital government can be derived.[58] While such constitutional amendments could support and strengthen supervision on the algorithmic administrative state, either by traditional branches of government or by "new" institutions, they acknowledge more broadly the existing responsibilities of government irrespective of the use of algorithmic systems.

---

[54] Wolswinkel 2024.

[55] Goossens 2024.

[56] On the criteria "urgent need" and "constitutional maturity", see, e.g., Commission Franken 2000, p. 48; Leenknegt 2016.

[57] Van der Schyff 2021 and the references in fn. 35. See extensively Riezebos 1992.

[58] Wolswinkel 2024.

12.8 Concluding Remarks

Constitutional identity and digitalisation seem to represent two different worlds. Constitutional identity, on the one hand, could be seen as static and requires looking backward: what have been determining factors in the historical evolution of the Dutch constitutional order? Digitalisation, on the other hand, is dynamic and necessitates looking forward: how will technological developments determine the future structure of society and government and how will digitalisation impact constitutional resilience? On closer inspection, however, constitutional identity and digitalisation are more intertwined than expected: constitutional identity determines the environment in which digitalisation takes shape within the Dutch constitutional order, whereas digitalisation impacts and challenges core pillars of Dutch constitutional identity.

The rise of the algorithmic administrative state has created interesting reflexive dynamics with what is commonly known as five well-established principles of the Dutch constitutional order. Key pillars such as the principles of legality and democracy and checks and balances have come under pressure, as digitalisation has seemingly strengthened the position of the executive branch vis-à-vis the legislative and, although to a lesser extent, the judicial branch. At the same time, other foundational pillars of Dutch constitutional identity, in particular fundamental rights and judicial review, have turned out to be playing a crucial role in the adoption of digitalisation in society and government. What is more, key ideas underlying the Dutch Constitution, including its open and austere character and the technology-agnostic wording of fundamental rights, explain why digitalisation, although omnipresent in society and government, has not (yet) gained a prominent position in Dutch constitutional rules and mechanisms.

However, as digitalisation is constantly challenging these constitutional foundations, the pressing issue is how constitutional identity can evolve to further accommodate digitalisation of society and government while at the same time offering protection against its negative effects. The answer should not be sought in merely reiterating the "traditional" principles of the Dutch constitutional order without recontextualising them. Instead, digitalisation necessitates to consider other checks and balances mechanisms or institutions than the traditional ones. Paradoxically, rather than new technology-oriented mechanisms and institutions, existing tech-agnostic elements of the Dutch constitutional order prove to be able to serve as essential building blocks to deal with the challenges particularly raised by the algorithmic administrative state. In any case, Dutch constitutional identity requires government to take up its responsibility more firmly in keeping tabs on digitalisation.

References

Ackerman B (2017) Goodbye Montesquieu. In: Rose-Ackerman S, Lindseth P, Emerson B (eds) Comparative Administrative Law. Edward Elgar Publishing, Cheltenham, pp. 38–43

Advisory Division of the Council of State (2018) Ongevraagd advies over de effecten van de digitalisering voor de rechtsstatelijke verhoudingen. Parliamentary documents II 2017/18, 266643, 557

Barkhuysen T, van Emmerik M, Voermans W et al. (2009) De Nederlandse Grondwet geëvalueerd: anker- of verdwijnpunt. Kluwer, Alphen aan den Rijn

Barkhuysen T, den Ouden W (2020) Kroniek over het algemeen bestuursrecht. Over responsief bestuursrecht, integrale geschilbeslechting en vooral… maatwerk. Nederlands Juristenblad (15):1042–1053

Bovend'Eert P (2019) Inleiding constitutioneel recht, 8th edn. Wolters Kluwer, Deventer

Bovens M, Zouridis S (2002) From Street-Level to System-Level Bureaucracies: How Information and Communication Technology Is Transforming Administrative Discretion and Constitutional Control. Public Administration Review 62(2):174–184

Brenninkmeijer A (2021) De grondbeginselen van de rechtsstaat zijn geschonden" als "verschrikkelijk ongeluk". Over de noodzaak van behoorlijk bestuur. Nederlands Juristenblad (1) pp. 6–13

Burkens M, Kummeling H, Uzman J, Vermeulen B, Widdershoven R (2022) Beginselen van de democratische rechtstaat. Inleiding tot de grondslagen van het Nederlandse staats- en bestuursrecht. Wolters Kluwer, Deventer

Burrell J (2016) How the Machine "Thinks": Understanding Opacity in Machine Learning Algorithms. Big Data & Society 1–12

Casey A, Niblett A (2017) The Death of Rules and Standards. Indiana Law Journal (4):1401–1447

Childcare Allowance Parliamentary Inquiry Committee (2020) Report "Unprecedented Injustice" (also available in Dutch as "Ongekend Onrecht"). Parliamentary Documents II 2020/21, 35510, No. 2 www.houseofrepresentatives.nl/sites/default/files/atoms/files/verslag_pok_definitief-en-gb.docx.pdf. Accessed 5 February 2025

Commission Franken (2000) Rapport van de Commissie grondrechten in het digitale tijdperk. The Hague

Commission on Legislative Questions (1985) Orde in de regelgeving. Staatsuitgeverij, 's-Gravenhage

Council of State (2020) Jaarverslag 2019. Evenwicht in de rechtsstaat. Een beschouwing. Council of State, The Hague

De Poorter J, Goossens J (2019) Effectieve rechtsbescherming bij algoritmische besluitvorming in het bestuursrecht. Nederlands Juristenblad (44):3303–3312

Gerards J (2016) The Irrelevance of the Netherlands Constitution, and the Impossibility of Changing It. Revue interdisciplinaire d'études juridiques 77(2):207–233 https://doi.org/10.3917/riej.077.0207. Accessed 5 February 2025

Goossens J (2023) Constitutional Resilience in the Algorithmic Administrative State—From the rule of law to the rule of code and back. The Digital Constitutionalist https://digi-con.org/constitutional-resilience-in-the-algorithmic-administrative-state-from-the-rule-of-law-to-the-rule-of-code-and-back/. Accessed 5 February 2025

Goossens J (2024) Het opvullen van een lacune in de Grondwet—Naar een grondrecht op toegang tot en zinvol contact met het bestuur. In: De Grondwet en nieuwe technologie: klaar voor de toekomst? Twaalf pleidooien voor modernisering van de Grondwet. Ministry of the Interior and Kingdom Relations, The Hague, pp. 85–119

Goossens J, de Poorter J (2022) Rechtsvorming in een hypercomplexe samenleving in het licht van evoluties in de horizontale, verticale, stedelijke en publiek-private dimensies. In: Goossens J, de Poorter G, van der Schyff G, Geldof T, van Oirsouw C (eds) Rechtsvorming in een hypercomplexe samenleving. Bundel n.a.v. de Staatsrechtconferentie 2022 (Tilburg University). Wolf Legal Publishers, Oisterwijk, pp. 7–19

Goossens J, Haex K (2023) De rigide Nederlandse Grondwet? Een empirische analyse van de grondwetswijzigingen 1814–2023. In: Gerards J, Goossens J, van Vugt E (eds) Constitutionele verandering in Nederland? De grondwetswijzigingen van 2022–2023. Boom, The Hague, pp. 15–51. www.boomportaal.nl/boek/9789462128262#1. Accessed 5 February 2025

Hirsch Ballin E (2015a) De constitutie van het bestuursprocesrecht. In: Marseille A, Meuwese A, Michiels F, de Poorter J (eds) Behoorlijk bestuursprocesrecht. Opstellen aangeboden aan prof. mr. B.W.N. de Waard over grondslagen, beginselen en vernieuwingen van het bestuursprocesrecht. Boom Juridisch, The Hague, pp. 19–30

Hirsch Ballin E (2015b) Dynamiek in de bestuursrechtspraak. Over de betekenis van veranderingen in economie, politiek en samenleving voor de bestuursrechtelijke rechtsontwikkeling. In: Hirsch Ballin E, Ortlep R, Tollenaar A (eds) Rechtsontwikkeling door de bestuursrechter. Boom Juridisch, The Hague, pp. 7–58

Hirsch Ballin E (2019) De rol van de wetgever: vijftig jaar verder. In: Keppel A, van Arnhem T (eds) De wetsfiguur: Preadviezen van E.M.H. Hirsch Ballin & M.H.A.F. Lokin (Handelingen Nederlandse Vereniging voor Wetgeving). Wolf Legal Publishers, Tilburg, pp. 13–43

Hirsch Ballin E, Kamphuis J (eds) (1985) Trias Automatica. Automatisering in wetgeving, bestuur en rechtspraak. Kluwer, Deventer

Jansen R (2023) De modernisering van artikel 13 Grondwet. Een techniekonafhankelijke bescherming van het communicatiegeheim. In: Gerards J, Goossens J, van Vugt E (eds) Constitutionele verandering in Nederland? De grondwetswijzigingen van 2022–2023. Boom Juridisch, The Hague, pp. 175–202. www.boomportaal.nl/boek/9789462128262#1. Accessed 5 February 2025

Leenknegt G (2016) The Constitutional Ripeness of Principles in Internet Law in the Netherlands. In: Pollicino O, Romeo G (eds) The Internet and Constitutional Law. The protection of fundamental rights and constitutional adjudication in Europe. Routledge, London

Lindseth P (2010) Power and Legitimacy: Reconciling Europe and the Nation-State. Oxford University Press, New York

Meijer A (2024) Pleidooi voor de invoering van een "monitorende macht". Noodzakelijke aanvulling op huidig stelsel van checks & balances. In: De Grondwet en nieuwe technologie: klaar voor de toekomst? Twaalf pleidooien voor modernisering van de Grondwet. Ministry of the Interior and Kingdom Relations, The Hague, pp. 193–203

Meuwese A (2020) Regulating Algorithmic Decision-making One Case at the Time. A Note on the Dutch "SyRI" Judgment. European Review of Digital Administration & Law 1(1):209–211

Oswald M (2018) Algorithm-assisted Decision-making in the Public Sector: Framing the Issues Using Administrative Law Rules Governing Discretionary Power. Philosophical Transactions of the Royal Society A 376:20170359

Passchier R (2020) Digitalisering en de (dis)balans binnen de trias politica. Ars Aequi (10):916–927

Prins C (2016) Digitale (dis)balans binnen de TRIAS. Nederlands Juristenblad (14):909

Prins C, Wolswinkel J (2025) Digitale uitvoering van wetgeving. Een raamwerk voor parlementair toetsen en controleren. Nederlands Juristenblad (12):878–886

Riezebos C (1992) Recht van petitie. Een rechtsvergelijkend onderzoek naar een juridische mogelijkheid van toegang tot het politieke systeem in Nederland en in de Bondsrepubliek Duitsland (dissertation Rotterdam). W.E.J. Tjeenk Willink, Zwolle

Scheltema M (2015) Bureaucratische rechtsstaat of responsieve rechtsstaat. Nederlands Tijdschrift voor Bestuursrecht (37):287–289

Shiffrin S (2010) Inducing Moral Deliberation. On the Occasional Virtues of Fog. Harvard Law Review 123(5):1214–1246

Stremler M (2023) "De kernbeginselen van onze Grondwet": de algemene bepaling in historisch-constitutioneel perspectief. In: Gerards J, Goossens J, van Vugt E (eds) Constitutionele verandering in Nederland? De grondwetswijzigingen van 2022–2023. Boom, The Hague, pp. 15–51. www.boomportaal.nl/boek/9789462128262#1. Accessed 5 February 2025

The Netherlands Scientific Council for Government Policy (2017) WRR-report No. 97: Weten is nog geen doen. Een realistisch perspectief op redzaamheid. Scientific Council for Government Policy, The Hague

Van den Bos K (2023) Elkaar eerlijk behandelen. Wantrouwen, polarisatie en complotdenken voorzijn. Boom Juridisch, The Hague

Van der Schyff G (2012) The Constitutional Relationship between the European Union and its Member States: The Role of National Identity in Article 4(2) TEU. European Law Review 37:563–584
Van der Schyff G (2021) Artikel 5 Petitierecht. In: Hirsch Ballin E, de Jonge E J, Leenknegt G J (eds) Uitleg van de Grondwet. Boom Juridisch, The Hague www.nederlandrechtsstaat.nl/grondwet/inleiding-bij-hoofdstuk-1-grondrechten/artikel-5-petitierecht/. Accessed 1 April 2025
Van Gestel R (2013) The "Deparliamentarisation" of Legislation: Framework Laws and the Primacy of the Legislature. Utrecht Law Review 9(2):106–122
Van Gestel R, Vleugel A (2013) Herijking van het primaat van de wetgever. De betekenis van kaderwetgeving en delegatie. Publication of the Council of State https://www.raadvanstate.nl/publish/library/13/rapport-kaderwetgeving-vgestel-vleugel.pdf. Accessed 1 April 2025
Van Vugt E (2021) De Staten-Generaal vertegenwoordigen het geheele Nederlandsche volk. Een onderzoek naar de veranderingen in de betekenis van artikel 50 Grondwet tussen 1814 en 1983 (dissertation Tilburg University). Boom Juridisch, The Hague
Van Vugt E (2022) De hypercomplexe samenleving, directe democratie en de Nederlandse Grondwet. In: Goossens J, de Poorter J, van der Schyff G, Geldof T, van Oirsouw C (eds) Rechtsvorming in een hypercomplexe samenleving. Bundel n.a.v. de Staatsrechtconferentie 2022 (Tilburg University). Wolf Legal Publishers, Oisterwijk, pp. 131–168
Van Vugt E, Goossens J, Loven C, Leenknegt G (2023) The Netherlands. In: Albert R, Landau D, Faraguna P, De Rossi Andrade G (eds) The 2022 Global Review of Constitutional Law. EUT Edizioni Università di Trieste, pp. 258–262, available at https://doi.org/10.2139/ssrn.5046787. Accessed 11 April 2025
Venice Commission (2021) Opinion on the Legal Protection of Citizens No. 1031/202118. www.venice.coe.int/webforms/documents/?opinion=1031&year=all. Accessed 5 February 2025
Vetzo M, Gerards J, Nehmelman R (2018) Algoritmes en grondrechten. Boom Juridisch, The Hague
Wolswinkel J (2023a) Normering van geautomatiseerde besluitvorming: Tijd voor wetgeving. In: Aarrass B, Albers C, Ortlep R (eds) Digitalisering in de rechtsverhouding tussen burger en overheid. Wolters Kluwer, Deventer, pp. 63–81
Wolswinkel J (2023b) De grote onbekende in de vergelijking: geautomatiseerde besluitvorming binnen de Wet versterking waarborgfunctie Awb. Computerrecht (6):461–468
Wolswinkel J (2024) Behoorlijk bestuur in een digitale leefomgeving: naar een recht op algoritmische besluitvorming? In: De Grondwet en nieuwe technologie: klaar voor de toekomst? Twaalf pleidooien voor modernisering van de Grondwet. Ministry of the Interior and Kingdom Relations, The Hague, pp. 235–248

Jurgen Goossens LL.M., Ph.D., Professor of Constitutional Law at the Institute of Jurisprudence, Constitutional and Administrative Law, and member of the Montaigne Centre for Rule of Law and Administration of Justice at Utrecht University, the Netherlands.

Johan Wolswinkel LL.M., M.Sc., Ph.D., Professor of Administrative Law at the Department of Public Law and Governance of Tilburg Law School, Tilburg University, the Netherlands, acknowledging the Digital Sciences for Society program of Tilburg University for funding the Icon project "Case-Inclusive Transparency for a Digital and Open Government (CITaDOG)".

Chapter 13
Law and the Environment: Towards a Geo-Constitutional Identity

Floor Fleurke and Han Somsen

Contents

Abstract This chapter posits that Dutch constitutional identity is unduly anthropocentric, and explores the potential of different vectors to transform this identity to one that is symbiotic, relational and caring. First, although article 21 *Gw* concerns the country's habitability and living environment, in view of the prohibition of constitutional judicial review (article 120 *Gw*) this provision is unlikely to evolve beyond its current limited substantive and temporal reach. Second, illustrated by cases such as *Urgenda*, articles 2 and 8 ECHR—which Dutch courts must apply and prioritise (articles 93 and 94 *Gw*)—clearly harbour that transformative potential. Yet, procedural requirements, such high degrees of individualisation of environmental harm, as well as the human/nature dichotomy perpetuated by human rights frameworks, have the effect of continuing to exclude non-humans from constitutional imaginary. Finally, unconstrained by legal or political hindrances, legal scholarship constitutes a significant transformative force. The emergence of rights of nature across the globe is a prime example of the productive interaction between academia, judiciaries

F. Fleurke (✉)
Tilburg Law School, Tilburg University, Tilburg, The Netherlands
e-mail: F.M.Fleurke@tilburguniversity.edu

H. Somsen
Tilburg Law School, Tilburg University, Tilburg, The Netherlands

Lund Law School, Lund University, Lund, Sweden
e-mail: Han.Somsen@tilburguniversity.edu

G. van der Schyff (ed.), *The Constitutional Identity of The Netherlands*,
https://doi.org/10.1007/978-94-6265-779-3_13

and legislatures. A more comprehensive academic ambition is the crafting of geo-constitutional identities, founded on the recognition of the fragility and authority of non-human regulatory agency.

Keywords Right to a healthy environment · Rights of nature · Anthropocene · Geo-constitutional order

13.1 Introduction

Conventional understandings of constitutional identity view it as a fixed, stable concept. Instead, this book seeks to examine constitutional identity as dynamic and fundamentally relational, and considers what happens when constitutional orders are confronted with urgent environmental challenges, such as climate change and biodiversity loss. The term "constitutional identity" as used in this book refers to the unique set of fundamental principles, values, and characteristics directly tied to its legal, political and geographical structure that define a particular constitution and distinguishes it from other constitutions. Lindahl has in this context argued that constitutional identity is not simply about defining who belongs, but about the complex processes of inclusion and exclusion that create political communities. Constitutional identity hence emerges through these boundary-making processes, rather than being a pre-existing, static entity. In this sense constitutional identity is defined in relation to what communities are not—how their sense of self and otherness is constructed—and is always provisional and contested, challenging notions of fixed national or legal identities.

The legal representation of the environment in the Dutch Constitution (*Grondwet:* hereafter *Gw*) reflects a particular relationship between the Dutch and their territory. As a country below sea level, the environment has always been perceived as malleable. Vulnerable to flooding, the country is protected by an impressive flood defence infrastructure, most prominently the Delta Works. Unsurprisingly, article 21 *Gw* therefore focuses on the country's habitability.

As we will show, the practical significance of article 21 *Gw* for Dutch constitutional identity is modest, however. In view of the prohibition to review the validity of Acts of Parliament against constitutional provisions in the constitution, such as article 21 *Gw*, the resulting absence of judicial constitutional dialogue might be presumed to hamper the evolution of such provisions necessary to reflect novel challenges and questions.

Importantly however, articles 93 and 94 *Gw* show that the country's self-understanding is that of an internationally-oriented trading nation. Enthusiastically embracing global collaboration and European integration, Dutch constitutional identity is dynamic rather than static. Indeed, a burgeoning body of international environmental treaties and EU environmental directives constitutes the most relevant applicable environmental law. That comprehensive body of law also is of paramount importance in refining and evolving Dutch constitutional identity in ways conducive to the gradual inclusion of non-human actants hitherto excluded.

Against that background, the first part of this chapter examines case law regarding articles 2 and 8 of the European Convention for the Protection of Human Rights and Fundamental Freedoms (ECHR). It queries how courts addressing pressing environmental challenges including climate change have progressively moulded and refined Dutch constitutional understandings of relationships between inhabitants and their environment. It has long been assumed that, because of the anthropocentric essence of constitutional rights, the latter are unlikely to have a significant role to play in addressing climate change or biodiversity loss. Recently however, the European Court of Human Rights (ECtHR), in the first climate case since the groundbreaking *Urgenda*, cases addressed the obligations flowing from the Paris Agreement interpreted in the light of articles 2 and 8 ECHR. In that case president Spano observed:

> No one can legitimately call into question that we are facing a dire emergency that requires concerted action by all of humanity. For its part, the European Court of Human Rights will play its role within the boundaries of its competences as a court of law forever mindful that Convention guarantees must be effective and real, not illusory.

Subsequent sections of this chapter offer a critical analysis of the limits of these judicial and constitutional approaches in securing respect for so-called planetary boundaries without which human life is predicted to become untenable. That reality was recently passionately echoed in an Opinion of the International Court of Justice (ICJ) on the obligations of states in respect of climate change. The ICJ underscored that "[t]he environment is the foundation for human life, upon which the health and well-being of both present and future generations depend".[1]

The chapter starts by analysing how the environment is conceptualised within the current article 21 of the Dutch Constitution (Sect. 13.2). Subsequently, it provides a concise review of ECtHR's jurisprudence concerning the rights to life (article 2 ECHR) and private life (article 8 ECHR), and their gradual environmental reinterpretation (Sect. 13.3). Section 13.4 explores the judicial response to the climate crisis, demonstrating how Dutch courts and the ECtHR were compelled to develop innovative legal approaches that deviate from established precedents. Despite this evolution towards more environmentally-oriented rights, the analysis reveals a persistent anthropocentric limitation: environmental considerations remain primarily validated through their relevance to human interests, thus presenting an incomplete constitutional identity.

Sections 13.6 and 13.7 delve into these overlooked dimensions, proposing a transformative shift towards a "geo-constitutional order". This paradigmatic approach advocates for an ecological framework where fundamental environmental principles supersede human-constructed legal systems, ensuring compliance with essential ecological boundaries. The chapter ends with concluding remarks.

[1] International Court of Justice, *Advisory Opinion on the Obligations of States in respect of Climate Change* of 23 July 2025, ICJ Rep., para 373.

13.2 The Right to a Healthy Environment in the Dutch Constitution

Crucially for a country mostly situated below sea level, since 1983 article 21 *Gw* guarantees the constitutional right of "the habitability of the country and the protection and improvement of the living environment".[2] Unlike other countries such as neighbouring Germany, the provision was adopted without meaningful debate in parliament.[3]

Article 21 *Gw* contains several key concepts. In its initial proposal, the Cals/ Donner State Commission had referred to "livability". That term, in the government's final proposal, was replaced by "habitability" and "living environment", to signal environmental protection in the broadest sense.[4] Constitutionally, it instructs the state to act so that citizens can live in a country with a high quality of habitability and a good living environment. It is significant in this context that the Constitution explicitly refers to "protection and improvement" of the environment. "Improvement" implies a proactive mandate transcending conventional first-tier preventative obligations to avoid harm.[5] This provision hence establishes a state duty of care, which in turn implies a best-effort obligation for it to pursue pro-active environmental policies. Numerous laws and regulations give shape to this "active" duty of care[6] but, remarkably, the preparatory documents hardly refer to article 21 *Gw*.

The fact that care for the environment is constitutionally embedded hence essentially reflects a declaration of intent of the state to incorporate environmental imperatives into all its policies.[7] To be sure, it was never the intention to create an enforceable right, and only in very exceptional circumstances would a court be in a position to invalidate a decision due to a conflict with article 21 *Gw*. Accordingly, case law on this provision therefore is very scarce and, indeed, in the seminal *Urgenda* cases to be discussed below article 21 *Gw* played no significant role.[8]

Article 21 *Gw* is manifestly anthropocentric: the constitutive elements of the biosphere are not individually specified, and more generally concepts such as "future generations" and "nature" are absent. The notion of "habitability of the country" is inherently inclusive, however, and encompasses water management, sustainable spatial planning, appropriate transport infrastructure, industry, housing, recreation,

---

[2] Authors' translation of the original Dutch text.

[3] Parliamentary Documents II 1975/76, 13 872, No. 3 (MvT/Explanatory Memorandum); Parliamentary Documents II 1980/81, 16 905, No. 3 (MvT/Explanatory Memorandum). See also Gerards 2020.

[4] State Commission Cals/Donner Final Report 3, p. 227.

[5] Verschuuren 1994, pp. 82–83.

[6] E.g. articles 1.6 and 1.7 of the Environment and Planning Act (*Omgevingswet*), which defines a duty of care for the physical living environment for everyone; article 1.3. acknowledges the intrinsic value of Nature.

[7] Van Gestel 2001, pp. 981–1000.

[8] Parliamentary Documents II 1975/76 13,872, No. 3; Parliamentary Documents II 1980/81 16,905, No. 3.

and the preservation of urban and rural beauty, all linked to the fulfillment of human rights.[9] The second core element, "improvement and protection of the living environment", is an inclusive concept that refers to the protection of people and the environment. The term "environment" is etymologically derived from the French spatial notion of "surrounding", with humans at the centre. In 2006, a proposal was submitted to change article 21 *Gw* to include a duty of care towards animals.[10] It becomes clear from the explanatory memorandum that the authors of the proposal were motivated by their intrinsic value, arguing for the inclusion of a "fundamental right of animals". In its advisory opinion on this proposal, the Council of State rejected this idea, arguing that animals cannot be bearers of rights in a legal sense and should be conceived as mere legal objects. In its advice, the Council of State downplays the significance of article 21 *Gw*, assigning the task of adopting appropriate protective rules and securing their effective implementation and enforcement to the legislator.

13.3 Greening Human Rights in the ECHR

Compared to article 21 *Gw*, articles 2 and 8 of the ECHR are much more important in Dutch constitutional practice. This has everything to do with the constitutional prohibition of Article 120 *Gw* for courts to review the legality of legislation against the constitution that is still in place to date despite proposals to change this,[11] whilst, by virtue of articles 93 and 94 *Gw*, the provisions of the ECHR are legally binding on everyone.[12] In environmental cases in particular, these provisions therefore frequently are invoked and interpreted in court, most notably in the *Urgenda* cases to be discussed below.

Unlike the 2009 Charter of Fundamental Rights of the European Union, which in article 37 explicitly recognises the collective right to environmental protection, the ECHR does not contain any reference to the concepts of "environment", "nature", or "future generations". Nevertheless, the Strasbourg Court has developed important case law based on articles 8 and 2 ECHR and, in certain cases, constructed positive obligations to combat and prevent environmental degradation, effectively "greening" those rights.[13] It is important that the ECHR is understood as a "living instrument", thereby becoming an important driver of changes in constitutional identity. This

[9] Parliamentary Documents II 1975/76, No. 3, p. 31. See e.g. ABRvS (Administrative Jurisdiction Division of the Council of State) 27 March 2002, JB 2002, 160 (case note by Heringa).

[10] Parliamentary Documents II 2006/06, 30 900.

[11] See the current plan of Minister to establish a Constitutional Court that would be able to review the legality of legislation against the constitution: https://www.rijksoverheid.nl/onderwerpen/grondwet-en-statuut/nieuws/2025/02/21/grondrechten-van-mensen-beter-beschermd-door-afschaffen-toetsingsverbod (accessed 31 July 2025).

[12] As the Netherlands is bound by the ECHR's jurisdiction (article 32 ECHR), Dutch courts must base their decisions on the ECtHR's interpretation of the provisions.

[13] See e.g. Boyd 2011; Pedersen 2018; Kobylarz and Grant 2022.

teleological plasticity of the ECHR is acknowledged in established case law affirming that "the Convention (...) must be interpreted in the light of present-day conditions".[14] In *Airey v. Ireland,* for example, the ECtHR declared that:

> The mere fact that an interpretation of the Convention may extend into the sphere of social and economic rights should not be a decisive factor against such an interpretation; there is no water-tight division separating that sphere from the field covered by the Convention.[15]

Article 2(1) ECHR concerns the right to life: "Everyone's right to life shall be protected by law." Article 8(1) concerns the right to privacy and family life: "Everyone has the right to respect for his or her private and family life, his or her home and his or her correspondence." A first question is when environmental damage leads to a violation of articles 2 and/or 8 ECHR. As early as 1991, in *Fredin* the ECtHR established that "in today's society, the protection of the environment is an increasingly important consideration".[16] It is now undisputed among the Contracting Parties that environmental issues fall within the scope of the ECHR.[17]

The ECtHR's case-law has concerned, inter alia, pollution, noise, industrial activities, natural disasters and flooding, and most recently of course also climate change. The positive human rights alluded to can engage these human activities as well as natural phenomena, triggering state duties. The scope of these provisions is clearly broad, their engagement merely requiring serious risk to physical safety. The precautionary principle has been a significant force in this case law. For example, in *Tartar* the ECtHR referred to the precautionary principle as enshrined in the Treaty on the Functioning of the European Union. If there is a serious and substantial risk to health but a full causal link cannot be established an obligation to adopt protective measures may still arise.[18]

However, the scope for inclusion of environmental protection under articles 2 and 8 ECHR is not infinite. First, access to the ECtHR is restricted to individuals whose rights are violated by an immediate threat; future generations or non-human actants remain unprotected.[19] Second, articles 2 and 8 ECHR only apply if an environmental issue causes "a real interference with the applicant's private sphere".[20] Therefore, there must be a "direct link between the applicant and the harm suffered as a result of the alleged violation".[21] Factors that may play a role in this determination include, in particular, the geographical proximity of the environmental damage and the duration of exposure to pollution.[22]

---

[14] *Soering v. UK*, No. 1989 439/11 (ECtHR, 1989), p. 102.

[15] *Airey v. Ireland* No. 6289/73 (ECtHR, 1979).

[16] *Fredin v. Sweden (No. 1),* No. 12033/86 (ECtHR, 1991) para 48.

[17] See e.g. *Dubetska and others v. Ukraine*, No. 30499/03 (ECtHR, 2011) p. 95, para 105.

[18] *Tatar v. Romania*, No. 67021/01 (ECtHR, 2009).

[19] *Collectif Melox et Mox v. France*, No. 75218/01(ECtHR, 2006); *Costel Popa v. Romania*, No. 47558/10 (ECtHR, 2016).

[20] *Fadeyeva* v. *Russia*, No. 55723/00 (ECtHR, 2005), pp. 69–70.

[21] *Brudnicka and others v. Poland*, No. 54723/00 (ECtHR, 2005) para 26.

[22] *Cordella v. Italy*, No. 54414/13, 54,264 (ECtHR, 2019) para 100 et seq.

In defining a violation, the ECtHR insists that it must involve a concrete, individualisable threat.[23] For example, in *Cordello v. Italy* the Court ruled that because the applicants did not live in the area designated as at risk the connection between the applicants and the violation was too indirect.[24] Hence, rather than the protection of the environment and biosphere, state-obligations pertain to the protection of residents from significant environmental harm. Article 8 ECHR hence cannot be invoked if the case concerns the destruction of nature per se. The outcome of the *Greek Kyrtatos* case, which concerned the disappearance of a marsh near the plaintiffs' home, is instructive.[25] The applicants claimed that the disappearance of the marsh constituted an unlawful infringement of their right to privacy and family life. The Court ruled otherwise, observing that article 8 ECHR does not establish a general prohibition on habitat destruction. Curiously, the Court suggested that such a violation would arise in the event of felling a forest adjacent to the plaintiffs' home, because in such a case the harm to the plaintiffs' well-being would be more difficult to dispute.

Finally, the ECHR does not recognise an *actio popularis*.[26]

13.4 Extending the Reach of Human Rights: *Urgenda* and *Klimaseniorinnen*

The ECHR was pivotal in the landmark *Urgenda* cases, which have transformed perceptions of constitutional identity. This case was brought by the Dutch NGO Urgenda Foundation and 900 citizens. The essence of their complaint was that Dutch CO2 reduction policy—which would lead only to a 14%–17% reduction by 2020 compared to 1990 levels—constituted a violation of articles 2 and 8 ECHR. In 2019, the Supreme Court upheld the 2018 ruling of the Hague Court of Appeal, mandating the Dutch state to increase emission reductions to 25% below 1990 levels by 2020.[27] It concluded that the state is obliged, pursuant to articles 2 and 8 ECHR, to take appropriate measures to eliminate emissions emanating from Dutch territory.[28]

Regarding article 2 ECHR, it considered that the state is obliged to take appropriate measures if there is a real and immediate risk and the state in question is aware of that risk. According to the Supreme Court, the term "real and immediate risk" must be understood as referring to a risk that is both genuine and imminent. However, the notion of "imminence" implies an actual threat to persons, and may also materialise

---

[23] *Öneryıldız v. Turkey*, No. 48939/99 (ECtHR, 2004) para 93.

[24] *Cordella v. Italy,* 54,414/13, 54,264 (ECtHR, 2019) para 102.

[25] *Kyrtatos v. Greece*, No. 41666/98 (ECtHR, 2013).

[26] *Di Sarno v. Italy*, No. 30765/08 (ECtHR, 2012) para 80.

[27] Hoge Raad (Supreme Court of the Netherlands), 20 December 2019, ECLI:NL:HR:2019:2006 (*Netherlands/Urgenda*); Gerechtshof Den Haag (Court of Appeal of The Hague), 9 October 2018, ECLI:NL (*Netherlands/Urgenda*).

[28] Ibid., para 6.1.

in the longer term.[29] Climate change poses such a real and serious risk, but that risk will materialise in the mediate- or long-term. A characteristic of the greenhouse effect is precisely that its consequences unfold incrementally over decades. For the Netherlands, the associated threat of sea level rise, which will make parts of the country uninhabitable, has a similar risk profile.[30]

Hence, consistent with the precautionary principle, even if a danger will not materialise immediately articles 2 and 8 ECHR require states to take appropriate measures, including preventive measures. According to the Supreme Court the protection of articles 2 and 8 ECHR apply to society as a whole if the threat covers the entire area.[31] The Supreme Court also points out that, according to the ECtHR's case law, international law, scientific information, and generally accepted standards must be taken into account when interpreting the ECHR.

In summary, effective legal protection must be provided against potential violations of the rights and freedoms enshrined in the ECHR. Since the *Urgenda* cases, human rights-based climate litigation in Europe therefore has proliferated with cases brought in states like Ireland, Germany, Norway, Switzerland, France and Belgium.[32]

In 2024, the ECtHR took the opportunity to connect human rights with climate change.[33] *Klimaseniorinnen*, along with *Duarte Agostinho and Others v. Portugal and others*,[34] and *Carême v. France*,[35] for the first time raised the issue of climate change before the ECtHR. Whereas previous case law concerned situations involving specific sources of environmental harm, the characteristics and circumstances defining climate change are significantly different. The ECtHR acknowledged a potentially "irreversible and disastrous" climate risk, which "by its very nature, [is] capable of putting an individual's life at risk".[36] In *Agostinho*, the ECtHR noted that "the problem of climate change is of a truly existential nature for humankind".[37]

The ECtHR concluded that it could not directly transplant previous environmental case law to the context of climate change. Accordingly, while drawing inspiration from the principles set out in that case law, the ECtHR developed a more tailored legal response to climate change. It held that account had to be taken of available

---

[29] Ibid., para 5.2.2.

[30] See in this context also the lawsuit that eight residents of Bonaire and Greenpeace Netherlands initiated against the Dutch state: https://www.greenpeace.org/static/planet4-netherlands-stateless/2024/01/a50849f9-dagvaarding-klimaatzaak-bonaire.pdf.

[31] Ibid., para 5.3.1.

[32] See e.g. High Court of Ireland 2017 No. 793 IESC 49 (*Friends of the Irish Environment v. the Government of Ireland*): Supreme Court of Ireland 2019 IEHC 747 (*Friends of the Irish Environment v. The Government of Ireland*); *Notre Affaire à Tous and Others v. France*, No. 1904967 (Le tribunal administrative, Paris, 2021); *VZW Klimaatzaak v. Koninkrijk België* No. 30/11/23, 2021/AR/1589, 2022/AR/737 and 2022/AR/891 (Brussels Hof van Beroep, 2nd chamber, 2023).

[33] *Verein KlimaSeniorinnen Schweiz and Others v. Switzerland* No.53600/20 (ECtHR, 2024), paras 121–272.

[34] *Duarte Agostinho and Others v. Portugal and 32 Others* No. 39371/20 (ECtHR, 2024).

[35] *Carême v. France* No. 7189/21 (ECtHR, 2024).

[36] *KlimaSeniorinnen*, paras 478–511.

[37] *Duarte Agostinho and Others v. Portugal and 32 Others*, para 194.

and constantly developing scientific evidence of the necessity of combating climate change and addressing its adverse effects, including the grave risk of their inevitability and irreversibility.[38]

In *Klimaseniorinnen* the applicants consisted of an association established under Swiss law to promote and implement effective climate protection for its members, more than 2,000 women (the majority of whom are over the age of 70), and four women suffering health problems exacerbated during heatwaves, significantly affecting their lives, living conditions and health. Relying on articles 2 and 8 ECHR, they alleged failures by Swiss authorities to introduce suitable legislation or adopt appropriate measures to realise the targets for combating climate change in line with its international commitments.

As regards this specific climate context, the ECtHR noted that while state obligations arising from the Convention extended to individuals currently alive, it was clear that future generations were likely to face increasingly severe consequences of present failures to combat climate change. In addition, future generations had no opportunity to participate in current relevant decision-making processes. The ECtHR therefore held inter-generational burden-sharing to be particularly important.

The Court also acknowledged that the issue of causation was particularly challenging, as the causal link between acts or omissions of one state and the (risk of) harm was more "tenuous and indirect" than is the case with local sources of pollution.[39] Furthermore, from a human rights perspective, the essence of the relevant climate duties related to the reduction of risks of harm for humans: issues of individual victim status or the specific nature of state obligations therefore could not be determined on the basis of a *strict conditio sine qua non* review.[40]

In view of the special features of climate change, the exclusion of *actio popularis* under the Convention, and the need to ensure effective protection of Convention rights, applicants needed to show to be personally and directly affected by failures to act. In that regard, the majority judgement accepted a new admissibility test for individual applicants by requiring that the applicants experienced "a high intensity of exposure (…) to the adverse effects of climate change" and "a pressing need … [for] individual protection".[41]

Regarding the merits, the ruling is consistent with outcomes in domestic climate litigation, including *Urgenda.* In particular, the Court confirmed the duty of contracting states to take measures to mitigate existing potentially irreversible future effects of climate change. That obligation flowed from correlations between climate change and the practical and effective enjoyment of Convention rights. Full respect for those rights required states to undertake measures to reduce their greenhouse gas (GHG) emission levels, with a view to realising net neutrality within, in principle, the next three decades.[42] There existed a margin of appreciation, but states needed to

---

[38] *KlimaSeniorinnen*, paras 434, 461, 482.

[39] Ibid.

[40] Ibid.

[41] Ibid., paras 487–488, 527.

[42] Ibid., para 538.

"act in good time" and in an appropriate and consistent manner when devising and implementing relevant legislation and measures.[43] The key factor for determining whether state responsibility is engaged, the majority judgement held, was whether "reasonable measures which the domestic authorities failed to take could have had a real prospect of altering the outcome or mitigating the harm".[44]

More specifically, this required an assessment of the exercise by state authorities of their due diligence duties to take into account "all competing interests". For climate change, the majority judgement held, due to the "nature and gravity" of the threats arising, a "reduced margin of appreciation" for states was justified.[45]

This implies, for example, a duty to specify a timeline for realising carbon neutrality as well as the overall remaining carbon budget for that time frame, or another equivalent method of quantification of future GHG emissions. Those targets obviously must comply with national and global climate-change mitigation commitments, and GHG reduction targets must be updated with due diligence based on best available evidence. The ECtHR also emphasised the importance of procedural safeguards for the purpose of determining whether a state had operated within its margin of appreciation.[46]

Concluding, the ECtHR found that there had been some critical lacunae in the Swiss regulatory framework, including a failure to quantify national GHG emissions limitations, through a carbon budget or otherwise, meaning that the authorities had failed to act in good time and in an appropriate and consistent manner. Accordingly, Switzerland had exceeded its margin of appreciation and failed to comply with its positive obligations under article 8 ECHR.

Understandably, the judgement has been heralded as groundbreaking. Indeed, it acknowledges, in the interpretation of articles 2 and 8 ECHR, that minimum environmental quality standards are a precondition for the fulfilment of human rights to life and health.[47] At the same time, the human-centred nature of these rulings, as well as a strict victim-based procedural requirement, continue to limit their use in addressing environmental issues which, paradoxically, in turn perpetuates threats to the integrity of the natural infrastructure that preconditions the enjoyment of any human right.[48]

---

[43] Ibid., para 550.

[44] Ibid., para 444.

[45] Ibid., para 543.

[46] Ibid., para 553.

[47] See e.g. Shelton 2002.

[48] Peetersmann 2024.

13.5 Rights of Nature and Constitutional Identity

The fact that the constitutional representation of the environment by the ECtHR continues to be constructed anthropocentrically raises the question how non-humans can come to form part of Dutch constitutional identity.[49]

A growing number of constitutional and environmental law scholars indeed challenge the existing framework and demand a reimagination of constitutional identities,[50] questioning whether current constitutions are fit for purpose to engage the existential ecological challenges that mark our times.[51] Often, such calls are accompanied by a plea for the recognition of rights of nature. Many constitutions around the globe, ranging from New Zealand, India, Colombia to Spain, have constitutionally embedded the intrinsic value and certain rights for forests, mountains, rivers, or nature in its entirety.[52]

This novel constitutional imagery is informed by a paradigm of harmonious pluralism, committing to "a new form of public coexistence, in diversity and in harmony with nature".[53] Obviously, this raises a host of important legal questions: which rights to recognise and for which non-human beneficiaries; how to resolve clashes with competing rights and interests? However, in a Dutch constitutional context, marked by the prohibition of constitutional review alluded to earlier, a rights of nature approach, apart from being symbolically significant, offers escapes from legally entrenched harmful anthropocentric path-dependencies, opening avenues leading to a relational constitutional imaginary enjoying strong scientific and normative support.

There are thus at least three important arguments in favour of including nature as part of Dutch constitutional identity.[54] First, constitutional identity is attached to territory, and "habitability" hence implies protection of a territory's constitutive elements (water, air, soil, species, etc.). Second and related, even if we conceive of a constitution as inherently human-centred, overwhelming scientific evidence suggests that the direct and indirect value of wildlife and ecosystems to humans is immeasurable.[55]

For the planet to remain "habitable" (i.e. to offer "a safe operating space for humanity") chemical, biological and physical planetary thresholds must be respected and where necessary restored.[56] Alarmingly, all the evidence suggests that humanity is quickly transgressing those boundaries due to a focus on the short term and

[49] Grant 2015.

[50] Bosselmann 1995; Grear 2015, p. 225.

[51] Vanhala 2022, p. 101.

[52] This debate started with the seminal article by Stone 1972, p. 497. See also Chapron et al. 2019, p. 1392; Kaufman 2021; Den Outer 2023.

[53] See for example, as a first mover the 2008 Constitution of Ecuador, Preamble and article 71.

[54] Trouwborst 2024, pp. 74–118; Dirzo et al. 2014, p. 401; Kolbert 2015.

[55] IPBES (2022): Summary for policymakers of the methodological assessment of the diverse values and IPBES (Secretariat, Bonn, Germany) https://doi.org/10.5281/zenodo.6522392.

[56] Rockström et al. 2009, p. 472.

subservience to economic growth.[57] A rights-based approach, the Report concludes, including rights to a healthy environment and rights of nature, holds great potential to drive these necessary systemic transformations.[58]

Expanding constitutional identity to include nature's constitutive elements, however, by itself is insufficient to take heed of what Trouwborst refers to as "the bigger picture".[59] Thus, a third justification for including Nature as part of our constitutional identity resides in what the drafters of the Biodiversity Convention referred to as "the intrinsic value" of nature and biodiversity.[60]

As early as 1975, the United Nations General Assembly started the drafting process for the World Charter for Nature to pursue a more eco-centric paradigm, which was adopted in 1982.[61] The Charter espouses a relational approach to environmental protection, putting species on a more equal footing. In this spirit, the preamble proclaims that "[m]ankind is a part of Nature" and explicitly provides that "[e]very form of life is unique, warranting respect regardless of its worth to man, and to accord other organisms such recognition, man must be guided by a moral code of action".[62]

To be sure, since adoption of the Charter scientific evidence (accelerated by AI) has mounted confirming the sentience and intelligence of non-human species, laying bare their unique ways of being and experiencing the world.[63] It now appears that even plants are conscious in different ways, and communicate, cooperate, recall past events and plan futures.[64] These insights should give fresh impetus and new meaning to pleas for ecosystems with all their components to be given the space and security to thrive to their fullest extent.[65] If we take seriously the principle of good governance of adherence to the best scientific evidence, we are inclined to conclude that our current human-centred constitutional identity no longer is tenable.[66]

Arguably, intimations of a more proper relational identity are observable in recent Dutch political, judicial and academic practice. Perhaps the most prominent sign is the ongoing debate to grant legal rights to the Dutch part of the Wadden Sea, recognised as a UNESCO site.[67] In 2019, the council of the municipality of Noardeast-Fryslân adopted a resolution advocating the establishment of an independent Wadden Sea Management Authority, so that the Wadden Sea would be recognised as a legal entity, comparable to an independent public authority (e.g. a water board), or a

---

[57] Bridle 2022.

[58] Ibid.

[59] Trouwborst 2024, p. 94.

[60] CBD, Preamble.

[61] UNGA World Charter for Nature (1982) A/RES/37/7; Wood 1985.

[62] Ibid., Preamble.

[63] Safina 2016.

[64] Calvo and Lawrence 2022; Van Laarhoven and Claerhoudt 2024, p. 286.

[65] See e.g. CJEU C-629/23, 12 June 2025, ECLI:EU:C:2025:429 (*Eesti Suurkiskjad*).

[66] Trouwborst 2024, p. 90.

[67] Lambooy et al. 2023, p. 104; Lambooy et al. 2022, p. 70.

company.[68] This has been followed by a motion by two parliamentarians requesting the government to grant legal rights to the Dutch part of the Wadden Sea,[69] triggering a negative response from the Minister.[70] Likewise, there are numerous recent examples at decentralised levels, including motions to grant rights to the Waal and Dommel rivers.[71]

13.6 Towards a Geo-Constitutional Identity

In 2009, a group of Swedish scientists established that out of a total of nine planetary boundaries three had been exceeded, and only 25 years later this number had risen to six.[72] At present, animal and plant species are going extinct over a thousand times faster than can be explained by natural extinction rates, and climate change is occurring visibly and dramatically.[73] It is near impossible precisely to quantify human suffering directly resulting from systemic ecological collapse, but according to reports from organisations like the World Health Organisation (WHO) approximately 9 million people die each year worldwide due to environmental pollution.

It is not too much of a stretch that such suffering exposes law not merely as ineffective in preventing and redressing harm, but also as a driver of such harm. The answer to the quintessentially constitutional question about the factual hierarchy between law (the primary instrument of human regulatory ambition) and the self-regulatory agency of Nature is clear and unambiguous. Thus, the inevitable consequence of law failing to respect nature's self-regulatory agency is that humanity, and in its wake law, perishes. The reverse, on the other hand, does not hold: non-human agency will continue to regulate planetary conditions even in the absence of (human) life.

Despite the growing momentum of the kind of legal initiatives explored above, arguably these fall short of driving fundamental constitutional change respecting this factual hierarchy. A formidable challenge posed by deeper constitutional recalibrations resides in securing continued respect for the rule of law, which simultaneously is the root of the destructive notion that law trumps nature's self-regulating powers, but at the same time must remain the beating heart of any constitution. Related, although establishing hierarchies is a crucial constitutional function, the notion that humans are an intrinsic part of nature rather than superior to it may appear fundamentally at odds with the hierarchical paradigms on which constitutions are premised.

[68] Motion of 11 July 2019 of the council of the municipality of Noardeast-Fryslân.

[69] Parliamentary Documents II 2021/22, 29,684, No. 227 (motion by MPs Wassenberg and Van Raan). See also the debate reported in Parliamentary Documents II 2022/23, 29,684, No. 243, p. 5.

[70] Parliamentary Documents II 2022/23, 29,684, No. 232, p. 6.

[71] See for an overview: website St. Rechten voor de natuur, available at https://www.rechtenvandenatuur.org/initiatieven/motie-rechten-voor-de-natuur-in-nijmegen#:~:text=Op%2024%20april%202024%20diende%20Partij%20voor,en%20dat%20haar%20belangen%20vertegenwoordigd%20moeten%20worden (accessed 31 July 2025).

[72] Persson et al. 2022, pp. 1510–1521.

[73] Kolbert 2015.

These and other conundrums therefore severely complicate constitutional reform aimed at safeguarding simultaneous respect for human and non-human regulatory agency. How can a constitutional identity evolve from anthropocentrically parasitic to a symbiotically, relational and caring?[74] The Global Biodiversity Framework (GBF), adopted in Montreal in 2022, refers to this ambition as "a world of living in harmony with nature".[75]

In that vein, a research agenda has been proposed aimed at constitutional reform in support of what has been coined a "geo-constitutional legal order", grounded in respect for the regulatory authority of planetary (self) regulatory processes, cycles and phenomena, operationalised by a limited number of geo-constitutional principles.[76] The premise driving this agenda is that ecological and climate catastrophes are consequences of law's past and present failures to recognise the regulatory authority of natural systems, which unlike law should command universal rather than local respect.

The core of this newly imagined constitutional framework therefore is a *Grundnorm* establishing the rebuttable presumption that the regulatory agency of nature trumps that of humans (exercised by way of law, markets, technologies, etc.).[77]

That *Grundnorm* should feature in the Constitution itself, essentially in the same way as respect for the authority of international and EU law is enshrined in articles 93 and 94 *Gw*. That technique addresses the rule of law dilemma alluded to above: the constitution claims the final word, thereby respecting the rule of law and the autonomy of the national legal order. Articles 93 and 94 *Gw* demonstrate that law may pledge allegiance to an alternative regulatory order, thereby sovereignly choosing hierarchically to relegate itself to something external to it. It does not take too much imagination to build upon this example, and promote constitutional respect for the universal self-regulatory authority of nature from which, after all, all human ambitions are derived.

Existing conflict of law principles (in the abstract sense of the term) provide guidance how to cope with clashes of regulatory authorities inevitably arising in geo-constitutional legal orders. In the context of EU law, principles of autonomy, loyalty, primacy, preemption and fundamental rights play that role. Hence, when natural and legal regulatory ambitions clash, the *principle of primacy*, derived directly from the *Grundnorm*, should normally resolve the conflict in nature's favour. A second geo-constitutional *principle of preemption* protects nature's regulatory powers in spheres where it has yet to exercise these. By way of illustration, the mere fact that a certain species has not yet established itself in a certain suitable habitat would not necessarily absolve a state from protecting that habitat with a view to accommodating the species in the future. In a geo-constitutional context, third, *fundamental rights* perform two functions. Substantively they protect the integrity of ecological

[74] See, for example, Kotzé 2016; Donaldson and Kymlicka 2011; Matthews 2021; Nussbaum 2006; Serres 1990.

[75] CBD COP Decision 15/4, 2022, para 10.

[76] Somsen 2023, p. 33; Somsen 2025, Chap. 16.

[77] Chapron et al. 2017, p. 1.

core values (derived from planetary boundaries) against what would otherwise be democratically legitimised incursions and through their direct enforceability, instrumentally, they mobilise citizens as agents representing nature's interest and rights. Inspiration can be derived from the *Van Gend & Loos* case:

> The vigilance of individuals concerned to protect their rights amounts to an effective supervision in addition to the supervision entrusted by Articles 169 and 170 to the diligence of the Commission and of the Member States. It follows from the foregoing considerations that, according to the spirit, the general scheme and the wording of the Treaty, Article 12 must be interpreted as producing direct effects and creating individual rights which national courts must protect.[78]

Protection of a "safe operating space for humanity" demands uncompromising unconditionality: associated rights normally should take the form of directly enforceable prohibitions and injunctions. While not all fundamental rights lend themselves to be directly enforced, unambiguously unconditionally formulated and quantitatively expressed ecological limit values and quality standards normally are.

Finally, *the principle of loyalty* in a geo-constitutional setting legally calibrates a constitutional identity revolving around symbiotic harmonious relations with nature, underpinned by an ethics of care. The principle of loyalty at its core obliges elements of a larger system individually and collectively to exercise their agency in ways serving the integrity and well-being of that system. Enforceable prohibitions and positive obligations flow from the principle of loyalty. For example, as an archetypical principle of inclusion, loyalty supports arguments for *actio popularis*, rights of nature, and the empowerment of future generations.

13.7 Concluding Remarks

Departing from the simple argument that constitutional identity is defined as much by what a constitution excludes as by what it includes, we have addressed the question if and how "nature" is included and excluded by Dutch constitutional practice.

The logical starting point for that enquiry was article 21 *Gw*, as it establishes a state duty of care to secure the country's habitability and living environment. There is compelling evidence that the ensuing obligation is broad, encompassing a wide range of environmental concerns. However, those concerns are nonetheless understood as arising in function of human rights and interests, meaning that article 21 *Gw* does not establish a state duty to protect the environment per se. Moreover, as a result of the prohibition of constitutional review, article 21 *Gw* has not been exposed to significant judicial forces allowing it to evolve in any meaningful way.

A potentially powerful force driving constitutional identity change, in contrast, is constituted by articles 2 and 8 ECHR, which by virtue of articles 93 and 94 *Gw* Dutch courts must apply and prioritise in cases of conflict. The landmark *Urgenda* cases, assisted by recent teleological ECtHR case law ensuring the vitality and continued

[78] CJEU 26/62, 5 February 1963, ECLI:EU:C:1963:1 (*Van Gend & Loos*), p. 13.

relevance of the ECHR in times of existential climate change threats, are concrete evidence of that dynamic.

However, the scope for inclusion of non-humans in our constitutional imaginary offered by these two provisions is far from infinite. Even after recent landmark cases such as *Klimaseniorinnen*, the intrinsically human-centred and predominantly individualistic DNA of human rights continues to hamper the emergence of a relational systemic constitutional identity, i.e. one in which human and non-humans are entangled in networks of mutual care.

We have emphatically argued that precisely such a deep constitutional identity transformation is what is needed because, in the words of the ICJ, "[t]he right to a clean, healthy and sustainable environment results from the *interdependence* between human rights and the protection of the environment".[79] That interdependence being factual rather than normative, there should be no place for constitutional imaginaries that perpetuate and legitimise human/nature dichotomies that threaten the future and very survival of a polity.

Regardless of their practical impact, initiatives to endow nature with legal personhood and rights we therefore welcome, first and foremost because they are symbolically powerful vectors signalling commitments to profound constitutional identity change. Academic calls for geo-constitutional transformations, even though they are unlikely to yield immediate results, likewise may help overcome deeply entrenched ideas that law is incapable of empowering non-humans. Courts, as we have shown, are not insensitive to these societal forces, and in fact play crucial roles in carrying such ambitions forward.

There are hence signs that in concert these various different actors and actants—human and non-human, local and global, private and public—are crafting a new constitutional identity, mirroring the fragile nature/human entanglements that form our existence. Supported by an ethics of mutual care, that new relational identity may help direct private action and public policy towards more hopeful futures. Finally, we can think of few better ways to conclude than reciting the recent words of the ICJ:

> [environmental problems pose an] existential problem of planetary proportions that imperils all forms of life and the very health of our planet. International law, whose authority has been invoked by the General Assembly, has an important but ultimately limited role in resolving this problem. A complete solution to this daunting, and self-inflicted, problem requires the contribution of all fields of human knowledge, whether law, science, economics or any other. Above all, a lasting and satisfactory solution requires human will and wisdom—at the individual, social and political levels—to change our habits, comforts and current way of life in order to secure a future for ourselves and those who are yet to come.[80]

[79] International Court of Justice, *Advisory Opinion on the Obligations of States in respect of Climate Change* of 23 July 2025, ICJ Rep. 2025, para 393.

[80] Ibid., para 456.

References

Bosselmann K (1995) When Two Worlds Collide: Society and Ecology. RSVP Publishing Company Limited, Auckland

Boyd D R (2011) The Environmental Rights Revolution: A Global Study of Constitutions, Human Rights, and the Environment. UBC Press, Vancouver

Bridle J (2022) Ways of Being—Animals, Plants, Machines: The Search for a Planetary Intelligence. Penguin, London

Calvo P, Lawrence N (2022) Planta Sapiens: Unmasking Plant Intelligence. Little Brown, London

Chapron G et al. (2017) Bolster Legal Boundaries to Stay Within Planetary Boundaries. Nature Ecology & Evolution 1(3): Article Number 0086

Chapron G et al. (2019) A Rights Revolution for Nature. Science 363(6434):1392–1393

Den Outer J (2023) Rechten voor de Natuur. Lemniscaat, Rotterdam

Dirzo R et al. (2014) Defaunation in the Anthropocene. Science 345(6195):401–406

Donaldson S, Kymlicka W (2011) Zoopolis: A Political Theory of Animal Rights. Oxford University Press, Oxford

Fleurke F, Somsen H, Lindahl H, Petersmann M-C, Leach M, Paiement P (2024) Constitutionalizing in the Anthropocene. Journal of Human Rights and the Environment 15(1):4–22

Gerards J (2020) Het recht op milieubescherming. In: Gerards J et al. (eds) Grondrechten, de nationale, Europese en internationale dimensie. Ars Aequi Libris, Nijmegen, pp. 463–475

Grant E (2015) International Human Rights Courts and Environmental Human Rights: Re-Imagining Adjudicative Paradigms. Journal of Human Rights and the Environment 6(2):156–176

Grear A (2015) Deconstructing Anthropos: A Critical Legal Reflection on "Anthropocentric" Law and Anthropocene Humanity. Law Critique 26:225–249

Kaufman C M (2021) Rights of Nature: Institutions, Law, and Policy for Sustainable Development. In: Sowers J et al. (eds) The Oxford Handbook of Comparative Environmental Politics. Oxford University Press. Oxford, pp. 499–517

Knox J H, Pejan H (eds) (2018) The Human Right to a Healthy Environment. Cambridge University Press, Cambridge

Kobylarz N, Grant E (2022) Human Rights and the Planet: The Future of Environmental Human Rights in the European Court of Human Rights Vol. 3. Edward Elgar Publishing, Cheltenham

Kolbert E (2015) The Sixth Extinction: An Unnatural History. Bloomsbury, Dublin

Kotzé L (2016) Global Environmental Constitutionalism in the Anthropocene. Bloomsbury Publishing, London

Lambooy T, van Soest T, Breemer I (2022) Granting Rights of Nature to the Wadden Sea? Waddenacademie, Leeuwarden

Lambooy T, Jeurissen R, Mackor R (2023) Het verlenen van rechten aan natuurentiteiten onderzocht vanuit een juridischmaatschappelijk en ethisch perspectief. Justitiële verkenningen 49(4):99–113

Lindahl H K (2016) Constituent Power and the Constitution. In: Dyzenhaus D, Thorburn M (eds) Philosophical Foundations of Constitutional Law. Oxford University Press, Oxford, pp. 141–160

Lindahl H (2019) A-Legality, Representation, Constituent Power. Etica & politica: rivista di filosofia 21(3):417–501

Matthews D (2021) Earthbound: The Aesthetics of Sovereignty in the Anthropocene. Edinburgh University Press, Edinburgh

Nussbaum M (2006) Frontiers of Justice: Disability, Nationality, Species Membership. Harvard University Press, Cambridge/MA

Pedersen O (2018) The European Court of Human Rights and International Environmental Law. In: Knox J H, Pejan H (eds) The Human Right to a Healthy Environment. Cambridge, Cambridge University Press, Cambridge, pp. 86–96

Persson L et al. (2022) Outside the Safe Operating Space of the Planetary Boundary for Novel Entities. ACS Environmental Science & Technology 56(3):1510–1521

Petersmann M (2021) Response-abilities of Care in More-than-Human Worlds. Journal of Human Rights and the Environment 12:101–124

Petersmann M (2024) Entangled Harms: A Reparative Approach to Climate Justice. LSE Legal Studies Working Paper No. 19/2024

Rockström J et al. (2009) A Safe Operating Space for Humanity. Nature 461:472–475

Safina C (2016) Beyond Words: What Animals Think and Feel. Picador, NYC

Serres M (1990) Le contrat naturel. François Bourin, Paris

Shelton S (2002) Human Rights and the Environment: Jurisprudence of Human Rights Bodies. Background Paper presented during the Joint UNEP-OHCHR Expert Seminar on Human Rights and the Environment, Geneva (14–16 January 2002)

Somsen J (2023) De Geo-Constitutionele Rechtsstaat: Een Hervormingsagenda. Tijdschrift voor Omgevingsrecht (2–3):33–45

Somsen J (2025) Technologies in Environmental Governance: Two Scenarios (Chapter 16). In: Brownsword R, DiMatteo L A (eds) The Cambridge Handbook of the Governance of Technology. Cambridge University Press, Cambridge

Stone C D (1972) Should Trees Have Standing? Toward Legal Rights for Natural Objects. Southern California Law Review 45(2):450–501

Trouwborst A (2024) The Serengeti Rules and the Untold Value of Fellow Earthlings: Wildlife Law in an Era of Ecological Emergency, Eye-opening Science, and Maturing Morality. Journal of International Wildlife Law and Policy 27(2):74–118

Van Gestel R (2001) Het Grondrecht op een schoon leefmilieu: alibi tot terughoudendheid of prikkel tot actie? NJCM-Bulletin 26(8):981–1000

Vanhala L (2022) Environmental Legal Mobilization. Annual Review of Law and Social Science 18(1):101–117

Van Laarhoven J, Claerhoudt R (2024) A New Leaf: Is It Time To De-Objectify Plants in Private Law? Transnational Environmental Law 13(2):286–311

Verschuuren J M (1994) De zorg van de overheid en het recht van de burger. Milieu en Recht (3):2–83

Wood Jr H W (1985) The United Nations World Charter for Nature: The Developing Nations' Initiative to Establish Protections for the Environment. Ecology Law Quarterly 12(4):977–996

Floor Fleurke is Associate Professor of European Environmental Law at Tilburg Law School, Tilburg University, the Netherlands.

Han Somsen is Professor of European Law at Tilburg Law School, Tilburg University, the Netherlands and Professor of Environmental Law at Lund Law School, Lund University, Sweden.